The Meiji Restoration

Also by Alistair D. Swale

THE POLITICAL THOUGHT OF MORI ARINORI:
A Study in Meiji Conservatism

The Meiji Restoration

Monarchism, Mass Communication and Conservative Revolution

Alistair D. Swale
Senior Lecturer, University of Waikato, New Zealand

First published 2009 by
PALGRAVE MACMILLAN

Palgrave Macmillan in the UK is an imprint of Macmillan Publishers Limited, registered in England, company number 785998, of Houndmills, Basingstoke, Hampshire RG21 6XS.

Palgrave Macmillan in the US is a division of St Martin's Press LLC, 175 Fifth Avenue, New York, NY 10010.

Palgrave Macmillan is the global academic imprint of the above companies and has companies and representatives throughout the world.

Palgrave® and Macmillan® are registered trademarks in the United States, the United Kingdom, Europe and other countries.

ISBN-13: 978-0-230-59386-2   hardback

This book is printed on paper suitable for recycling and made from fully managed and sustained forest sources. Logging, pulping and manufacturing processes are expected to conform to the environmental regulations of the country of origin.

A catalogue record for this book is available from the British Library.

A catalog record for this book is available from the Library of Congress.

10 9 8 7 6 5 4 3 2 1
18 17 16 15 14 13 12 11 10 09

Printed and bound in Great Britain by
CPI Antony Rowe, Chippenham and Eastbourne

For Yurika, Alexander and Sascha

And With Deepest Gratitude to my Parents

Contents

Foreword and Acknowledgments

One concern that has informed the framing of this work relates to the matter of introducing the scholarship of some of the leading commentators on Meiji history in Japanese academia. It goes without saying that non-Japanese scholars already working with primary sources in Japanese will not be greatly surprised at some of the academics quoted here. But for those whose acquaintance with Japanese history has come primarily from English sources, it would be appropriate to highlight some of the leading figures of the contemporary scene, especially since in the last 20 years Japanese historical scholarship on the Meiji period has been prolific.

Some scholars, such as Maruyama Masao and Banno Junji, are justifiably to the fore in the field of English language studies of Japanese history. Yet there are others who have made an exceptional contribution to our understanding of the era but are surprisingly little known outside Japan. Without intending to present an exhaustively representative list, I would highlight the work of Asukai Masamichi, Yamamuro Shinichi, Nakanome Toru, Yamashita Shigekazu and Itō Yukio as having made scholarly contributions that are indispensable to a thorough appreciation of the complexity of the Meiji period; yet most of these scholars remain untranslated and are rarely referenced by non-Japanese readers. This book has in part, therefore, the indirect objective of making the important contribution of such scholars known to a wider, non-Japanese-reading, public.

The aforementioned prolific output of Japanese historiography on the Meiji period over the last 20 years has stemmed from a variety of factors. Perhaps one of the most important ones is that from the late 1980s, Japanese scholarship gradually emerged from a polarized arrangement of "establishment" against anti-establishment (predominantly left-wing) intellectuals, each with fundamentally divergent ideological agendas, to become more genuinely diverse in terms of methodology and intellectual preoccupations. This has also engendered a liberation of sorts from Western academic preoccupations and the development of perspectives that are at once rich and resonant.

This recent trend is particularly significant in relation to the Meiji Restoration. While the Restoration can be regarded as a historical event of significance to world history on a par with other major social transformations such as the French Revolution or the Russian Revolution, it has always required a different set of conceptual tools to make sense of it. Some Japanese scholars have been prepared to set to one side preoccupations with the spread of Western Enlightenment thought and universal progress to engage with their own history on more specific terms. This is not a project born out of indifference to Western scholarship – indeed it is always rather inspiring to see how far Japanese scholars routinely develop an extremely thorough acquaintance with the Western canon in almost any given discipline. Nevertheless their response to Western scholarship has often been ambivalent, and not without good academic reason in certain cases.

In an epoch where a notion of "democratizing" the Middle East has emerged as a twenty-first century correlate to the nineteenth-century notion of "bringing civilization" to the "despotic Orient", this recent turn in Japanese intellectual outlook perhaps has a broader significance. Given that historically Japan has already exhibited a dynamic of engagement with the West that has entailed an ambivalent attitude of partial acceptance and partial rejection, it should not surprise us that this is the position that Japan has ultimately returned to once a level of (economic) superpower status was gained and overt external interference terminated. I have argued that the intellectual developments following on from the Meiji Restoration were, in certain regards, fundamentally questioning the premises of the "Enlightenment", and I believe that we are again at a point of "renegotiation"; we can no longer take it as a given that Japan has embraced Western political values without qualification.

Consequently, the issues that emerged in the wake of the Restoration remain relevant today. The onus is on the West to make good on any assertions of moral authority; and if we care about retrieving the potency of the legacy of the Western Enlightenment in the twenty-first century, we need to be clear about the genuine scope of its appeal, as well as the degree to which it continues to require clarification and a fundamental justification beyond terms that are largely couched in the notion that they are "self-evident".

Moreover, it is also clear that assumptions of a liberal or democratic impetus behind popular political upheavals need to be questioned. The modern social transformations that we broadly describe as "revolutions" do come in various shapes and forms after all, and some of them occur without the consent of the masses. Idealized characterizations of the popular movements underlying the French Revolution or the American Revolution seem to persist; however, it is also needful to countenance the possibility that they were in fact exceptions, and problematic in terms of their popular representativeness in any case. The totalitarian revolutions of the twentieth century, in Russia and in China, as well as those of the Fascist regimes in both Germany and Italy in the 1930s, exemplify scenarios that are no less possible in the present even with knowledge of the past.

Overall, then, it is hoped that this work provides a more nuanced understanding of the Meiji Restoration in particular, as well as mass political transformations in general. Our need to understand political change in the era of mass communication remains as important as ever, and there is a great deal to be gained from reflection on some of the major historical instances of mass mobilization and social transformation.

Naturally, the views expressed in this foreword and in this book are mine alone but I would like to acknowledge the contributions of various persons and institutions for their assistance during the time that this book was being written. I would particularly like to thank my colleagues in the Law Faculty at Kyôto University who provided an intellectually stimulating environment and the resources to complete this manuscript. I would especially like to acknowledge the debt I owe to Emeritus Professor Kimura Masaaki, Professor Ono Noriaki and Professor Itō Yukio. I am also grateful for the support of my colleagues at the University of Waikato, particularly Dr James Beattie for his extremely constructive comments and criticism.

I would also like to acknowledge the assistance of the library staff at Kyôto University, the Institute for Research in the Humanities and the International Research Centre for Japanese Studies. Special acknowledgment should also be given to the National Diet Library which gave permission for the reproduction of the title page illustration.

1
Introduction

There would hardly seem to be any necessity to write a new history of the Meiji Restoration given the sheer volume of research that already exists on the era in question. My justification for attempting to write a new history is the conviction that there is a need for a critical revision of certain preconceptions that remain deeply entrenched in the current historiography. This is not to denigrate the work done to date—the primary aim is to reassert the significance of particular aspects of Japan's political history that have, for a variety of reasons, come to fall outside the purview of mainstream commentary.

Certainly the characterization of the Restoration has undergone a number of subtle revisions and changes over the last 30 years. A great deal of the impetus for this revision has been drawn from persistent dissatisfaction with the use of the term given that it does not convey the essence of the original Japanese, *Ishin*, constructed as it is out of the two Chinese characters for "continuity" and "renewal" (維新). Nevertheless the term "Restoration" has been the long-standing staple by virtue of the fact that, if nothing else, the events that unfolded from that date onward were ostensibly undertaken within the political framework of a restored monarchy.

Even so, many have chaffed at the term pointing out, with considerable justification, that the reforms that followed the Restoration were so radical and transformational that "Restoration" simply does not do the event justice. The other aspect that has made it difficult to label it has been the rather perplexing phenomenon of a society-wide reform carried out—ostensibly at least—by the former ruling class elite, the *samurai*. The changes brought about were indeed "revolutionary" but not in a form that has a parallel in the Western European experience of revolutions.

1

Consequently, there has been a considerable amount of controversy surrounding how one ought to term the "revolution" that occurred in the wake of the January-the-third coup d'état of 1868. The adoption of the term "transformation" in place of *Ishin* or Restoration in the excellent collection of essays edited by Jansen and Rozman[1] was possibly one of the better instances of a thorough attempt to accommodate those concerns. On another tack, some have rejected "Restoration" for the term Revolution, preferring to emphasize the drastic changes wrought upon Japanese society and the hitherto unprecedented degree of popular agitation. In this connection, Huber's book on the revolutionary origins of the Restoration is a prime example, and Wilson's discussion of popular developments, including the "Ee ja nai ka" fad of spontaneous festivals immediately preceding the fall of the Bakufu, merit special attention[2].

Along side the milestone publication of Jansen and Rozman in 1986, which still remains one of the best general introductions to the Meiji period to date, there is another important collection of essays produced at around the same time by Nagai Michio and Miguel Urrutia, *Meiji Ishin: Restoration and Revolution*, which contains the contributions of a veritable "who's who" of Meiji history specialists from both Japan and the US.[3] The essays of the individual contributors are unfortunately brief but content-wise they offer alternative perspectives on key themes. More recently, there has been the excellent overview of the Edo and Meiji periods by Andrew Gordon, which provides one of the more carefully nuanced accounts of Japan's modern political development.[4]

Together, these works constitute a thorough overview of the various facets of the period in question, and those wishing to have a standard text should refer to these works in the first instance—indeed the aim of this book is very much to provide a complementary viewpoint rather than produce an entire replacement. Even so, it should be remarked that some of the key texts remain collections of the work of disparate authors and therefore do not always hold together as seamlessly integrated narratives. Others are reworked versions of earlier books that are now somewhat out of date.[5]

One more recent attempt to break with the conventional historiography and explore alternative interpretations has been undertaken by Richard Sims in *Japanese Political History Since the Meiji Renovation*[6] which rejects the nomenclature of the "Restoration", opting instead for a wholly new term, "renovation". Sims' aim of filling "the gap between general histories of Japan and the monographic literature" is laudable but, as will be argued in this work, the term Restoration is not to be lightly rejected. Moreover, in the end the work is arguably more conventional in its narrative than the title suggests and has the added drawback of commencing from 1868, the year of the Restoration, rather than providing adequate coverage of the period of political development beforehand. Demarcating historical studies on the basis of the beginning of Emperor Meiji's rule is a common enough tendency (possibly stemming from the influence of Japanese scholarship which tends to compartmentalize historiography into *kinsei* and *kindai* periods); this is very consciously avoided in this volume.

A work that has clearly done a better job of filling the "gaps" that Sims so aptly emphasized is Carol Gluck's *Japan's Modern Myths*[7], although it remains unclear why the focus was on the latter Meiji period when so much of the groundwork for the development of national ideology was established in the second decade following the Restoration. It is also debatable whether the term "myth" ought to have been reiterated in relation to Meiji Japan when, as most scholars of nationalism will acknowledge, all modern nation states indulge in the practice of national-myth construction and Japan is perhaps merely a more overt example.

Consequently, there remains something of an unresolved contradiction at the heart of the Meiji Restoration that cannot be easily resolved by juxtaposing the conservative and retrospective drive of the Restoration with the innovative and iconoclastic aspects of the social transformation. Even contemporary commentators such as Tokutomi Sohō who was, initially at least, a fervent advocate of the Restoration as a revolutionary and in many ways counter-traditional process, remained acutely aware of this contradiction, employing the rather telling figure of a two-headed snake[8]. There were clearly contradictory forces at work in those early stages but there was also something that was holding it together, at least long enough until the disparate forces found some new equilibrium and social institutions acquired some greater degree of stability.

In order to resolve that sense of contradiction, I would argue that an essential first step is to more directly challenge the perception of 1868 as a turning point where the great leap from traditionalism to modernity took place. For the newcomer to comprehensive histories of early modern Japan, it is easy to come away with the impression that following the Restoration, feudalism was replaced by industrialism, superstition gave way to reason and science, and that, as seems implicit in many commentaries, authoritarianism commenced a slow retreat in the face of the inexorable drive of the democratic and liberal impulses of "the people".

The sheer scope and scale of Japan's transformation following the Restoration of Imperial Rule in 1868 makes it tempting to overemphasize the political novelty of the developments following the event, especially given that they seem to usher in something of a "miracle". Certainly, the achievement was extraordinary; however, the transformation is capable of explanation in terms that are less hyperbolic. The essence of the wonder at the scale of the transformation also possibly stems from the fact that it did not follow a Western pattern, or at least did not occur in the wake of similar kinds of social transformation witnessed in the Western precedents. Even so, there have been persistent attempts to trawl through the Western experience for familiar lines of narrative to apply to the Japanese case. For example, given that certain kinds of leaders and certain types of ideas have mattered a great deal over the last 200 years in Western history, the tendency has been to look for parallels to explain the Japanese case. Consequently, the leaders behind the Restoration have variously been characterized as highly cosmopolitan "modernizers" who have undertaken a program of national refurbishment according to the Western pattern.

The attempt to make sense of the Restoration in such terms has tended to obscure the very strong persistence of pre-Meiji conceptions of status, duty and morality that continued to characterize the political culture at the time of the Restoration and further on throughout the ensuing period. It has also invited assumptions that the Meiji strategy for fixing national policy amounted to more or less thumbing through the catalogue of Western institutions, whether it is in relation to military organization or to the matter of the Constitution, and then selecting the "model" to suit. As an ironic corollary, the cause of the experiment's failure has in some cases been attributed to a lack of understanding of Western models either among the leadership or alternately among the populace at large.

In any event, the magnitude of the transformation was such that it could not have been forced through in such a short time following the Restoration purely by dent of the wisdom and foresight of a few enlightened zealots or of the superiority of their knowledge of "more advanced" Western alternatives. Indeed, we cannot assume that emulation of the West in all aspects was ever on the agenda in the first place.

The other most notable instances of attempting to interpret Japan's political development through Western experience have been evidenced by a preoccupation in post-war historiography with two social movements: the "Enlightenment Movement" (*Keimō Undō*, 啓蒙運動) of the early 1870s and the "Freedom and Popular Rights Movement" which sprang up with particular vigor following the end of the Seinan War in 1877. Both these movements, while obviously significant, have been reified within the overall narrative of the early Meiji period, a point that is made particularly clear by the fact that both the terms, *Keimō* and *Jiyū Minken*, were not actually current in the parlance of those participating in events at that time.

Both these movements will be addressed in more detail in later chapters (*Keimō Undō* in Chapter 4 and the *Jiyū Minken Undō* in Chapter 5); suffice it to say that, for the most part, there are no major works produced in the first 20 years of the Meiji period that employ the word *Keimō* in the sense above. Moreover, there are no works that include the phrase *Jiyū Minken*; the closest is Ueki Emori's *Minken Jiyūron* of 1879, but it is an exception. The terms most commonly employed were *Jiyū* as in *Jiyūshugi* (自由主義) for Liberalism and *Minken* as in *Minkenron* (民権論), the general sobriquet for debates on popular sovereignty and representative government.

The first major commitment to *Jiyū-Minken* appears with the two volumes dedicated to "Liberal-Democratic Thought" in the *Meiji Bunka Zenshū*, a collection of original publications edited and compiled by a committee of leading scholars headed by Yoshino Sakuzō in the 1920s.[9] This was certainly a strong endorsement of a "Freedom and Popular Rights" nomenclature but it is interesting that even after World War II, we can find examples of how the transition in terminology was still evolving, as is indicated in one of the early editions of the *Iwanami Kōza* history of Japan where Gotō Yasushi makes the point of referring to *Jiyū* and *Minken* separately (自由と民権の思想).[10] Overall, both *Keimō Undō* and *jiyūminken undō* are phrases coined by later generations with rather particular predilections of interpretation and we would do well to at least remove them from view to examine what else can be surveyed.

Consequently, this book is deliberately reoriented away from such preoccupations and aims to reappraise political developments in terms that are closer to the intent and objectives of contemporary actors themselves. The aim is, to use Collingwood's phrase, an intellectual "re-enactment", which means avoiding the temptation to assume that the terminology employed by the Japanese intelligentsia, especially terms such as "liberalism" and "popular rights", always signified an understanding of those terms in common with their Western counterparts.[11] Needless to say, the re-enactment presented in this book will not be altogether perfect, but there would seem to be considerable merit in exploring an alternative narrative that fits more closely with the broad political conditions of the time and the aspirations of those living in it.

As early as 50 years before the Restoration, Japan was arguably already developing traits associated with proto-industrialization: a national network of transport and commerce, a sophisticated exchange economy, and the first signs of urban centers being able to draw and support large numbers of people from the agricultural sector.[12] All this was proceeding at a pace not all that removed from contemporary Europe. Of more significance, however, is the fact that the transformation was not following in the footsteps of European Humanism or Positivism.

It is the configuration of Japanese society and its ideology prior to the Restoration that must be our starting point—that and the immensely catalytic effect of the West's encroachment on Japan from the early nineteenth century onward. We must try, as much as is reasonably possible, to approach Japan's epoch of change from the Japanese perspective.

Restoration and national salvation

While accepting the various caveats on using the term as outlined in the foregoing, a key premise of this book is that "Restoration" of imperial rule remains pivotal to an understanding of Japanese national development from the 1840s onward. As is well-rehearsed in general histories, the Restoration was foreshadowed by the emergence of *Kokugaku* (国学) and *Kōkogaku* (考古学) scholarship in the late eighteenth century and, with the encroachment of the Western powers, it quickly became a core element in the ideological reformulation of that period. It has been typical to regard this outlook as revisionist and backward looking, yet it was nonetheless also part of a broader attempt to clarify the rationale for a new form of political configuration and it was already well under way prior to the Restoration proper. An added complication was the fact that the threat from across the seas gave the political situation an urgency that was quite distinct from the experience of Europe and the New World, producing a particularly emphatic agitation for the restoration of imperial rule in tandem with the drive to repel all foreign incursions by force, culminating in the *Sonnō Jōi* movement (尊皇攘夷運動).[13]

Restoration was therefore based on a long-term current of thought which had been nurtured within Japanese political discourse that did not emerge in the late 1860s. Moreover, it did not find resolution simply by virtue of the cessation of hostilities in the Boshin War (1868–9). Under the rubric of such terms as *Saisei Itchi* (祭政一致, literally, "the unification of ceremonial and political authority"), and *Ōsei Fukko* (王政復古, "the restoration to monarchical rule") the Imperial Household was to remain an important political icon in the hands of the new Meiji leaders during the ensuing decade, often being relied upon to quell popular disquiet and silence critics. This very tendency was itself also to prove as a source of the leadership's undoing as both the Emperor himself and the broad array of Imperial Household-aligned officials and grassroots activists invoked the Imperial throne to sanction actions that were increasingly opposed to the policy of the nation's new political executive.

Moreover, as the term *Saisei Itchi* makes particularly clear, the Restoration was not simply a political event, it entailed a most profound rearranging of the relation between religious institutions (what the contemporary Victorian thinker Herbert Spencer rather aptly termed "ceremonial institutions") and political institutions. In this regard (and only this regard, of course), it was a kind of "reformation". As already noted, considerable attention has been given to the *Ee ja nai ka* festivals that occurred on the eve of the Restoration and these do reflect some profound upheaval in the realm of popular religious and moral sentiment. However, they are perhaps less significant in themselves than as indicators of a temporary abeyance of an earlier order as another religio-political order swung into its place. In the case of the Emperor himself, he was to be propelled to the seat of political administration, albeit as a complete figurehead in the initial stages. This after centuries of being swaddled within the remote confines of the palace only emerging to view the ordinary citizenry during seasonal festivals where, among other things, the visitors would scoop up gravel from the surrounding grounds to sprinkle on their gardens to ward off pests. Through the Restoration, however, the Emperor traversed in popular significance from being the equivalent of the supreme shrine festival spectacle at particular times of the year to being the sovereign of the empire and direct descendant of the native deities all at once.[14]

Even so, this was not the only reorientation that occurred in the popular consciousness. For the first time, the people were introduced, more suddenly and forcefully than can be easily appreciated, to the kind of open, homogenized public political space that fealty to a central government rather than a local domain lord made possible. In a sense, it was liberating and it was the awareness of this that made the faddism of *Bunmei Kaika* ("civilization and progress") so infectious. After all, *Bunmei Kaika* was a cultural change endorsed by the government and even the Emperor himself now wore Western clothes, rode a horse and took shooting lessons. This transformation signified a reconfiguration of hierarchy away from geographically localized structures to an increasingly homogenized political space bound by the borders of the nation state, a space where more immediately negotiated relations with the power centre became possible through the development of nationally articulated modes of mass communication. Nonetheless, in Meiji Japan, this was a public space founded on Imperial sovereignty, a political fact that would be reasserted, both through the policies of certain factions within the leadership as well as through popular expressions of monarchist sentiment that found an outlet in the new nationally circulated mass media. More importantly, the capacity of the government to control what would be the political coinage of this new space would not remain unchallenged and the arrival of the agitations for popular representation along with the later agitations for more direct expressions of Imperial Rule were indicative of how precarious the government's hold on that space would become.

By the end of the 1880s we see that the realization of a more full-blooded Restoration, in political fact and deed, was precisely the direction being taken within the polity. Yet it would not be in the form of a reincarnated Ancient Court, but as relatively autonomous configuration within the national polity which would increasingly compete with the "Western-style" executive. It was an influence which spanned all levels of the national administration and almost all ministries of state, although it should be emphasized that, apart from the obvious instance of the Imperial Household Ministry, there was particularly focused support from within the Ministry of Internal Affairs, the Education Ministry and the Ministry of the Army. It also created a division that reached right to the heart of the Satsuma and Chōshū-dominated cabinets from the 1870s onward.

The Imperial Household, as both a political institution and a cultural totem, was increasingly integral to the dynamic of political contest in the two decades following the formal Restoration of 1868. Yet its significance, or rather the significance of those who aimed to employ it to reactionary or traditionalist ends, has been misunderstood to some extent.

If we take preconceptions regarding democratization and liberalism out of the equation, the general picture that unfolds is one which differs considerably from more conventional interpretations: the Restoration of 1868 was part of a protracted series of political convulsions that, if anything, intensified in the ensuing two decades. The pivotal event of 1868 was in fact a coup d'état, initially a highly localized one that nonetheless projected the nation into an unprecedented and unpredictable direction. Consequently, the Meiji leaders were not altogether the helmsmen of state that they might have wanted to appear. They were in fact constantly besieged; by disaffected *samurai* in one quarter, a truculent urban public chaffing at the persistence of the "unequal treaty" arrangements and the economic dislocation that was being caused by the influx of foreign goods in another. Meanwhile, the Emperor and those aligned to him aimed to undermine and circumvent the influence of the imperially appointed ministers of state from within the upper reaches of government. The fact that the reforming faction within the ruling oligarchy suffered two assassinations—Ōkubo Toshimichi in 1878 and Mori Arinori in 1889—along with the nearly fatal attack on Ōkuma Shigenobu in 1889 testifies to how much they were literally in the "firing line". Moreover, they were all attacked by disaffected *samurai* who were zealots for imperial rule more than advocates of Western forms of representative government.

The Meiji government was not secure or immune from virulent political reprisals, and it doubtlessly required enormous determination to steer Japan through the series of international and domestic crises that the country faced. They were dedicated reformers, yet they were not Westernizers or advocates of Radical Liberalism. They were those very modern political creatures, conservatives, albeit conservatives of a variety of hues.

Conservativism

In earlier works I have discussed the political developments of the early Meiji period in relation to political conservatism. This connection was not introduced simply for the sake of adding a new motif within an already cluttered arena of scholarly terminology dealing with this period. Given that the Meiji Restoration was not a liberal democratic event, was not directly inspired by Western traditions of Radicalism or the Enlightenment and, more to the point, did not entail the abandonment of the traditional order or the means of maintaining it but rather sought its reconfiguration, there would seem to be an eminent need to include conservatism as a central paradigm for discussing the political culture of the country and the intent of the contemporary government's policies.

As has often been remarked in the literature on political theory, however, conservatism is difficult to discuss systematically in that it seems to take on a multitude of expressions depending on the particular conditions of each society. Even so, arguably the best theorist of conservatism remains the pioneer of the sociology of knowledge: Karl Mannheim, whose great contribution was to clarify modern conservatism from traditionalism or reactionary politics. To quote:

> Traditionalist action is almost purely reactive behaviour. Conservative action is action oriented to ... a complex of meanings which contains

different objective contents in different epochs, in different historical phases, and which is always changing.[15]

Though conservatism is invariably bound to exist in some sort of relationship with the traditionalist and reactionary forces, the essence of
Mannheim's insight lies in his perception that political conservatism is
always socially and historically contextualized while maintaining a core
concern to accommodate the fluidity of social conditions generated by
industrialization. As Mannheim so astutely observed, conservatism is
a particularly *modern* intellectual counter-movement to the highly disruptive social forces inherent in industrialization, a fluid and somewhat
reactive political outlook that becomes necessary because unreflective
and unqualified tradition in its pre-modern sense is no longer completely tenable.

The point here is that regardless of the intentions of reactionaries to
re-erect a pristine "ancient" tradition, the prospect of its survival beyond
industrialization is tenuous at best, especially since pre-industrial traditions are contingent on the preservation of pre-industrial social relations. Maintaining traditions "authentically" requires the retention
of the matrix of their production more or less intact, something that
is quite impossible when the culture of the village artisan and the
relatively self-referencing folklore of the rural community gives way
to mass migration of the populace to urban centers which form the
focus of developments in mass communication and the centralized
coordination of a standardized national education system. Some degree
of survival is witnessed in some of the fine arts and performing arts
(e.g., *Kabuki* or *Noh* theatre), yet these are particular exceptions that
if anything exemplify the limits of how far traditional cultures can be
preserved despite the thoroughness with which all other aspects of com-
munal life have been transformed.

Having made this point it should be remembered, of course, that the
flux of social relations engendered by industrialization does not extin-
guish the aspiration of the former ruling class to remain in a dominant
position in society. Their survival depends on the extent to which they
manage to adapt to the new social conditions: if they adapt well, then
they retain status and considerable political influence (as in the case
of, for example, the landed gentry in Britain); if they fail to adapt and
simply strive to shore up the traditional order at all costs, then they
can be obliterated (as in the case of, for example, the aristocracy of
eighteenth-century France). However, even when the old order is obliterated, it is rare that the former traditional elements do not reassert

themselves in some way or that a new cohort of elites emulates the old structure, albeit in some hybrid sense, to replicate the characteristics of the traditional political culture. Again, France provides us with a perfect example in the figure of Napoleon following the French revolution and we can even extrapolate along similar lines to gain an understanding of the persistence of "great leader-oriented authoritarianism" in modern China and Russia.[16]

In the Japanese context, the ruling elite, the *samurai*, produced a cohort of conservative reformists who were able to adapt to the contemporary policy challenges with extraordinary vigor. The degree of determination with which they pursued these reforms creates the semblance of Radicalism that may seem inimical to conservative aims. Yet they were most definitely and self-consciously aiming to establish a new form of social order from the midst of the contemporary flux that Japanese society was being forced to undergo. And they did this not so much by simply obliterating the existing order but by attempting to refurbish it on the basis of a more ancient one resurrected from within. Of course, it cannot be assumed that the leaders of the Restoration all had a common vision of what the new political settlement should look like, nor did they perhaps even have a definite vision even as individuals. The one thing that kept them solidly together was a collective anxiety regarding the possibility of social collapse (i.e., the complete loss of social order) and the inevitable subjugation of Japan to Western colonialist powers as had been witnessed in other parts of Asia if they failed.

Consequently, I would reiterate that conservatism is a meaningful category of political discourse when examining Meiji Japan; indeed it has long seemed strange that while there is voluminous historical political analysis of conservatism in Europe and the US, there seems to have been little conception of its relevance to Japan beyond being a vague prelude to ultra-nationalism. Given that it was arguably the conservative camp that won out in the intellectual struggle between advocates of Western Enlightenment ideals and "Nativists", there is even more reason to devote considerable attention to its rationale and organizational dynamic within the broader Japanese social context.

There are, nonetheless, shades of distinction in the Japanese case that warrant clarification. Firstly, there is the high degree of diversity in the political bloc that we might characterize as "conservative" and there was not, for the greater part of the era being examined, the practice of political figures self-consciously styling themselves as such, let alone forming a distinct "conservative" political party (there being no parliament during that period). Yet through an examination of the writings and practice of certain figures in government and in the politically active urban intelligentsia, it is nonetheless possible to distinguish the core of a political outlook that was essentially conservative in the modern sense that Mannheim gives it.

Secondly, traditionalism and conservatism were more thoroughly mixed and intertwined both on the interpersonal level and the intellectual level. This was mainly due to the fact that the move from traditionalism and reactionary politics to a more dynamic mode of intellectually mediating the transformation of Japanese society was being forced through so very quickly. The oligarchy at the vanguard of the Restoration were arguably the quickest to appreciate the institutional and intellectual requirements of conservatives in an industrialized society and unitary government, the remainder were in various stages of adaptation and/or confusion. Early attempts to reconstruct pre-modern traditions, such as the ham-fisted promotion of Shintō as the National Religion in the earliest stages of reform, highlighted the ultimate infeasibility of the traditionalist approach in an industrializing society, although it did not entirely discourage the ambition to realize the ideal one way or another.[17]

Thirdly, as the new government was consolidated and the details of the national policy were clarified, there emerged a significant difference in approach within the conservative camp: two highly divergent strategies for the refurbishment of the national order were becoming increasingly apparent. The first strategy, that of the majority of the leaders among the Meiji oligarchy, was to prioritize industrialization and bureaucratic rationalization while nonetheless aiming to imbue it with a distinctive native character. It was a dynamic strategy that optimized Japan's capacity to reorganize and consolidate, and as such it was very much what Japan needed to do in order to hold its own in the international arena, but it left its proponents open to accusations of blind Westernization or even political radicalism.

The other strategy was to establish a new form of monolithic social order centered on the Imperial Household. It had enormous allure given that it had a clear proclivity with the pre-Restoration conception of social stasis inherent to the orthodoxy of *Chu Hsi* Neo-Confucianism (termed *Shushigaku* in Japan) and that it placed primacy on a native institution, the Imperial Household, rather than on an imported Western system of representative government.

I have characterized the former outlook as *progressive* conservatism; however, it might also be better amended to *dynamic* conservatism reflecting as it does the fluid conception of the social order and the more elastic treatment of tradition within the reform process. The latter outlook I have previously characterized as *formalistic* conservatism but in its place I would propose *static* conservatism, which perhaps reflects more closely the kind of social stasis idealized by such political actors.[18]

Even so, the common thread that holds them within the same political orbit is that both outlooks are not mere traditionalism but essentially modern *hybrid* adaptations that lend themselves to mass-society and mass political communication. They also both have a distinctly ideological dimension, by which I mean that they embody modes of popular discourse that provide the mental shorthand necessary for such mass political mobilization. Without ideology in this sense, the "imagined community" that is the modern nation state is untenable. Ultimately, their distinguishing trait (vis-à-vis other political movements) is to promote a stable new political order that relies on the perception—if not at times the substance—of a national political tradition and its cultural continuity.

As will be made apparent in the course of this work, the members of the progressive (or "dynamic") clique were definitely neither blind worshippers of the West nor particularly inclined to emulate Western democracy per se, yet they worked at a constant disadvantage to convince the domestic political audience otherwise. These figures would ultimately have to share the domain of governmental control with other more reactionary statesmen and officials who did not share the relative flexibility and dynamism of their view of the Japanese polity.

The latter move from political conservatism to statism was not sudden or unilinear, yet formalistic conservatism is useful for tracing the emergence of an intermediary form of political practice that ultimately fed into the successive move away from a dynamic and negotiable polity toward something more static and non-negotiable. These terms, which may seem relatively insignificant in their differences, are not employed simply to split conceptual hairs; they are employed in order to be able to discuss two similar yet ultimately inimical political approaches to national reconstruction that coexisted and ultimately competed with each other for survival in the first half of the Meiji period. This book, in that sense, is intended as an examination of the rather tragic fate of the former and a critique of the latter in that it encouraged the state to be employed in an increasingly coercive manner to compensate for the lack of compliance between the people and the "tradition" they were supposed to be embodying. More overt forms of indoctrination and repression become routine and the possibility of any citizen attempting to define the national identity on private or independent terms becomes tantamount to treason. Here, we have a picture of the early mechanism leading to full-blown Fascism which emerged in the early twentieth century.

The genesis of Meiji conservatism

The question that I have not addressed directly yet is of course as to who come within the framework of political conservatism in nineteenth-century Japan. To do that requires some consideration of the long-term trends from the late-Edo period to the Meiji period proper. The social and intellectual antecedents of conservatism run deeply through the late Edo period (and these will be given considerable attention in the ensuing chapter), but the matter is complicated to some extent by the fact that prior to the 1860s, we are looking more at the emergence of "proto-conservatism" rather than fully developed conservatism as defined according to Mannheim earlier.

The key figures in the emergence of proto-conservatism are Yoshida Shōin (1830–59), Sakuma Shōzan (1811–64) and Yokoi Shōnan (1809–69). The significance of their respective activities lies in the manner in which they severally revised the orthodoxy of the Tokugawa social order and the Neo-Confucian scholarship (*shushigaku*). Sakuma and Yokoi can be described as developing two competing conceptions of the *Wakon Yōsai* ("Japanese Spirit, Western Learning") motif and, although their personal involvement in the events leading up to the Restoration was relatively peripheral, their intellectual legacy was to be carried on and reworked by their successors. Yokoi's academy in Kumamoto was to provide a training ground for figures who emerged later in the Meiji period within the new administration. In particular, Motoda Eifu, tutor to the Emperor attached to the Imperial Household, and Inoue Kowashi, an indispensable legal specialist and amanuensis of the new government, emerge as noteworthy examples of that latent continuity. Sakuma Shōzan was also to have a slightly less direct connection to the formation of the Meiji elite through one of his "star pupils", Yoshida Shōin.[19]

Yoshida is noteworthy for the degree to which he was prepared to distance himself from the Bakufu regime and the genuine radicalism of his doctrines. His academy, the *Shōkason Juku*, which was based in the domain of the Chōshū clan which would later be a key player in the Restoration included a remarkable number of figures who were prominent in the new government from 1868 onward: Kido Takayoshi, Takasugi Shinsaku, Inoue Kaoru and Itō Hirobumi being perhaps the best known. Yoshida was alone in conceiving a new social order that entailed abolishing the traditional four castes in favor of one nation of citizens under one sovereign, the Emperor. At first sight, this might appear to be an endorsement of a democratic impulse; however, we should note that the "equality" implied by the dissolution of castes was countered by the conception of equal obligation to serve an omnipotent ruler.

Neither Sakuma's nor Yokoi's position were as radical as they might at first seem, yet they found themselves in enormous strife as a result of their views and ultimately paid for their roles in history with their lives through the assassin's sword. Sakuma was cut down by anti-foreigner radicals near Sanjō Bridge in Kyōto, his crime being to advocate the promotion of interaction with the West, albeit for the purpose of strengthening Japan militarily. Yokoi was dispatched in the vicinity of the Imperial Palace in Kyōto, primarily for daring to voice ambivalence regarding the utility of the Imperial Household in political reform prior to the Restoration.

Yoshida, as much an activist as a teacher, had been imprisoned in as punishment for sneaking aboard a foreign vessel without *Bakufu* approval in 1854 and he was finally arrested and executed for his association with a plot to assassinate a government official in 1859. Yet Yoshida's legacy was secure and his fame reached even beyond Japan, with no less a personage than Robert Louis Stevenson making a point of including Yoshida among a group of seven illustrious persons in world history.[20]

As political thought goes, Yoshida did not come anywhere near articulating the detail requisite to outline a concrete blueprint of a centralized nation state; indeed, if there is one element that ultimately binds Sakuma, Yokoi and Yoshida together, it is quite simply that they had an essentially moralistic conception of government that was inclined to give relatively scant attention to the minutiae of administrative procedure.

In the new realm of intellectual exploration that these proto-conservatives opened up, there was no guarantee that knowledge as previously enshrined would remain intact.

This is where conservatism proper comes into clear view. The various disciples of these charismatic leaders had a broader experience and were better placed to grasp the necessity to abandon the traditionalist perspective in favor of one that was politically more sophisticated. Of particular note are the students of Yoshida Shōin who went on to dominate the early Meiji government. At the same time, there were also many among the Bakufu's corps of students sent overseas to study, particularly Nishi Amane and Tsuda Mamichi, along with translators and other persons in support such as Fukuzawa Yukichi and Nakamura Masanao, who were to revise the Edo intellectual legacy just as profoundly. The legacy of this later group of former Bakufu-aligned scholars will be given particular attention in the chapter dealing with *Bunmei Kaika* wherein the clarification of an essentially conservative response to modernism will be more fully clarified in relation to their contributions to the *Meiroku Journal*.

The content of many of the contributions of these scholars indicates that despite the radical reworking of the body of knowledge regarded as necessary for the development of the Japanese nation, there was, nonetheless, no immediate necessity to abandon certain aspects of the traditional moral outlook. This tendency is more pronounced in some figures than others, but it is made apparent, particularly in the case of Katō Hiroyuki, that the traditional moral outlook could in fact be retained intact, to a point, and remain oblivious to any new practical discoveries that might emerge.[21] By the 1870s, there emerged a clearly bipolarized focus in the act of intellectual exploration; knowledge of the West would lay open realms of knowledge of the material world while metaphysically there would be an abiding dedication to retaining the moral order as it had always been conceived. Indeed, the marked secularity of the traditional moral order of the late Edo period meant that, for example, it would have far less significance to a Japanese to consider the implications of evolutionary theory than to a contemporary Christian.[22]

In connection with the foregoing, one persistent internal trait of Japanese society that needs to be highlighted as being significant throughout the period in question is the continuing prominence of the *samurai* class as the academic and bureaucratic elite, something that the maintenance of the distinction between *shizoku* (*samurai* class) and *Heimin* (commoners) beyond the Restoration attests to. Although the *shizoku* lose the greater part of their ceremonial and financial privileges following the Seinan War in 1877, they remain the de facto leaders in the world of letters and administration, at least for the next generation until a more homogenized and generically educated population comes to the fore. This has particular relevance for our understanding of the persistent divide within the so-called "freedom and peoples' rights" movement which in reality was separated into a "high" reformist movement (led in various guises and forms by the likes of Fukuzawa Yukichi, Tokutomi Sohō, Ōkuma Shigenobu and Itagaki Taisuke), contrasted with "lower" populist movements that incorporated dispossessed *samurai*, rural non-*samurai* literates and the more radical advocates of political representation and liberalism.[23] In tandem with the foregoing, there is also the persistent divide between the city and the countryside, the core of political power and the periphery, which is not profoundly altered in any substantial sense until the end of World War II.

Consequently, the moralizing tendency of the early proto-conservatives did not fade away altogether but remained a persistent inclination within the Japanese intelligentsia beyond the initial stages of the Restoration. Ultimately, it would re-emerge toward the end of the 1880s (albeit in a substantially different institutional context) as an increasingly dominant mode of discourse for discussing the nature of Imperial sovereignty and the requisites of sound educational policy. This mode of moralistic discourse found increasingly vociferous support from disenchanted advocates of the "Freedom and Popular Rights" movement in tandem with a solid core of *shushigaku*-trained Confucianists who never lost their sense of dismay and moral outrage throughout the early stages of the Restoration, even though at the time they were seemingly "yesterday's people".

By the 1890s, this constituted a disparate bloc of agitators; some being relative outsiders from the politically disinherited clans, others being disaffected *shizoku*, along with still others who were rehabilitated former Bakufu administrators and scholars. The figures given particular attention in this volume are tutors to the Emperor such as Motoda Eifu and Nishimura Shigeki, along with the clique of disaffected military heads who initiated the practice of resigning to protest against the actions of the executive, Torio Koyata and Tani Tateki being the most prominent examples. To these, we could add the civilian agitators who argued vehemently against Western-style parliamentary politics, especially the *Chūsei-ha* and their affiliates. And there was the increasing body of government officers who had come through the process of undertaking training overseas or making inspection tours of the West but returned as anything but advocates of increased imitation of Western customs and institutional practices, for example, Komuro Jutarō, a graduate of Harvard Law School who went on to agitate against the Inoue proposals for treaty revision. There were also the likes of Yamagata Aritomo, whose visit to Austria to listen to the lectures of Lorenz von Stein had similar consequences.[24]

One group that also requires considerable attention in connection to the foregoing but does not fit neatly into the camp of either the "progressive conservatives" or the "formalistic ones" is the generation of young journalists who became active in the promotion of "national essentialism" or *kokusuishugi* (国粋主義). Predominantly graduates of the new national education system, they became increasingly disenchanted with the Itō cabinet's policy of cultural appeasement toward the West in order to win concessions in treaty terms. *Nihonjin*, the journal of the *Seikyōsha*, which included Miyake Setsurei and Shiga Shigetaka, and *Nihon*, the journal presided over by Kuga Katsunan, worked together to promote a re-nativization of public discourse away from the slavish imitation of Western concepts and theories, but they were distinguished from the foregoing group by their more exclusive dedication to journalistic rather than party-political activism.[25]

Overall, there would be genuine disparity in the social status and policy aims of all these groups but they shared a common interest in agitating against the Satsuma and Chōshū oligarchy which effectively had taken hold of the key positions of day-to-day administration. The persistent proclivity toward the moralizing of the state in the person of the Emperor became the ideological basis for drawing together the non-Satsuma and Chōshū interests into a broad social movement that was to lay open the way for wresting the business of administration from trained specialists (especially, for example, in the spheres of military and educational policy) and giving it over to the hands of nationalist ideologues.

Beginnings: A prelude to re-enactment

As will be apparent from the outset of the next chapter, considerable attention has been given to a reappraisal of the international context in the late Edo period. This is quite simply because it is necessary to grasp the social and historical premises of the Restoration that in turn conditioned the emergence of a distinct political culture. Most histories highlight the arrival of the Black Ships under US Commodore Matthew Perry as being the decisive turning point in Japan's international relations and, in turn, Japan's domestic approach to reform. However, there was a much broader series of incursions by the Western powers being undertaken in East Asia, particularly from the 1840s onward, and these were fully recognized by those members of the Bakufu administration who dealt with areas of foreign trade and Dutch Studies. Indeed, emphasis needs to be redirected toward the moral outrage and panic that began to grip the section of the intelligentsia that knew enough to be concerned well before 1853, an aspect that enables us to grasp more accurately the spur behind the Restoration Movement.

The event that substantially hastened the demise of the Tokugawa system was from across the seas. Britain's full-scale hostilities with China over the opium trade from the 1840s through the 1850s were to have the profoundest repercussions on the Japanese archipelago. When the British eroded China's military superiority, they did not evoke merely a sense of China's martial failure; they were precipitating the demise of the all that was "good". It was, in a sense, a "triumph of evil". Failure to grasp this point is to miss the spring behind the fanatical hatred of Western incursions into Japan up until the Restoration and even beyond. The sense of moral revulsion did not cease to operate even as the country was being "opened up" and ostensibly "Westernized". The initial phase of exploration of Western metaphysics and moral philosophy in the wake of the Restoration was just that, an exploration—tentative, at times fearful and ultimately alienating. Grasping this aspect of Japanese intellectual life enables us to more adequately account for the essential transience Western Radicalism and the eventual return to full-blown hatred of the West in the era of ultra-nationalism.

Overall, the addition of external pressures and interference to the process of national development was to have a profound effect on the development of conservatism in Japan. Indeed, it was the issue of the "unequal treaties" first imposed on Japan in the late 1850s that was to plague the conservative bloc in the government and prevent it from being able to fully present itself to the general population as the guardians of the national interest. The advocates of responsible, gradualist policies were forced to come to terms with the increasingly rankling intransigence of the Western powers to make any substantial compromises on tariff control and extra-territoriality provisions.

We will never know just how this configuration of finely balanced conflicts of interest would have resolved themselves in the long term if left more to their own devices. It is plausible that the continuing internal economic crisis in conjunction with the increasingly self-evident impotence of the government would have forced, at a relatively sedate pace, a rearrangement of the personnel and a trade-off of status for efficiency that would have resolved the conflicts to some degree while catering to the former ruling elites' need to maintain dignity. It is perhaps equally possible that the national order might have collapsed completely and that Japan would have re-entered a phase of relative decentralization and sporadic local conflicts somewhat reminiscent of the pre-Tokugawa period. In any event, the option of letting things take their own course was no longer there.

2
Japan Within the World System: Urbanization, Political Stasis and Western Economic Expansion

Thursday, September 4, 1856.   Slept very little from excitement and mosquitoes,—the latter *enormous* in size. At seven A.M. men came on shore to put up my flagstaff. Heavy job. Slow work. Spar falls; break cross-trees; fortunately no one hurt. At last get reinforcement from the ship. Flagstaff erected; men form ring around it, and, at two and a half P.M. of this day I *hoist* the "First Consular Flag" ever seen in this Empire. Grim reflections—ominous of change—undoubtedly beginning of the end. Query,—if for the real good of Japan?

Townsend Harris, First US Consul to Japan[1]

When considered overall, I believe that although Harris now has access to the highest levels he is not one to be deeply feared. He is given to making numerous empty statements, although lamentably there is no-one within government who has the wit to understand this yet. Even so, if Harris' utterances are put into practice one by one, it will fare badly for our sacred country; if they count for nought, then all will be well.

Yoshida Shōin (7 April 1859)[2]

The predominant image of Japan during the "Isolation" period is that it was locked up and entirely secured from intercourse with Western culture. This is for the most part, and for the greater proportion of the populace, undoubtedly true. Yet by the end of the 1700s, there was a more dense concentration of medical specialists and scholars in Edo as well as in the broader Kansai region around Kyôto (the Imperial capital), who were procuring and disseminating a greater awareness of Western technology. On one level, it merely fuelled a vague curiosity for things arcane and there were many random iconic elements of Western culture that were adapted into the popular media. At the same time, the tangible applications of Western inventions undoubtedly contributed to the expansion of technical knowledge and, more significantly, a growing unease about Japan's capacity to maintain its defenses in the near future.[3]

At the turn of the century, the quality of this knowledge was of course uneven and at times inaccurate, and so the true dimensions of Western society and its military threat were not always fully appreciated by the greater part of even the literate population. There were also social diversions and political compensations enough to make a fundamental reconsideration of the world outlook unthinkable for the majority. The Edo intellectual mindset was oriented toward a confidence in an immutable and serene permanence, reinforced occasionally through the ritual inculcation of a non-negotiable orthodox oeuvre of learning, the Chinese classical texts and the Neo-Confucian teachings of Chu Hsi (*Shushigaku*). The *Shushigaku* orthodoxy enjoined all to maintain the positive virtues of benevolence, self-sacrifice and devotion in interpersonal dealings.[4] Ultimately, in practical terms, this meant simply a requirement for each person to follow the admonitions of those of a higher station. In this sense, the objective of the ideological apparatus of the Edo state was little different from that of the Absolutist monarchies of Europe; a key distinction, however, was that in Edo Japan, this ideology was underpinned by an extremely sophisticated system of political control (in certain regards it was a proto-"police state") and it was perpetuating itself despite the intensifying dislocations in society that were being generated by an increasingly sophisticated system of commerce and popular communication.[5] This is perhaps one of the pivotal differences in the experience of modernization between Japan and the emerging nation states of Western Europe; whereas in Britain (for example) the burgeoning commercial classes gradually undermined and transformed the system of aristocratic control from both within and without, the commercial classes in Japan flourished as a relatively separate entity whose influence was almost never permitted to be converted into political power. In other regards, however, the flourishing of a national exchange economy and a dynamic urban popular culture— and it was in fact exceptional in the degree to which culture was being mass produced and mass consumed at this time—was on a par with the development of popular culture in the great urban conglomerations of Europe.

Late Edo Japan was therefore subject to a profound social contradiction; it had the potential for rapid adaptive change culturally and, to some extent, economically, yet it remained firmly in the grip of a political system that prioritized political stasis. The series of fiscal crises and famines that afflicted the country from the mid-1700s onwards did not dent the resolve of the ruling class to preserve the political system; indeed, it seemed to foster a determination to more thoroughly reconstitute the Bakufu on its repressive founding principles. This aim was practically unattainable given the social developments that had already taken place over the previous two centuries and was therefore increasingly futile, yet it was a mirage that seemed no less achievable for its being apparently within reach. It would take an extraordinary degree of force to shake Japan out of this condition of political ossification.

The unraveling of isolationism

There is nothing like an object lesson to create an emphatic impact and this came with the Phaeton Incident of October 1808. The Napoleonic Wars had brought about a curious alteration in the power relations of Europe. The Dutch colonies and trading interests around the world were now under the indirect control of Bonaparte who had occupied the Netherlands, and as a result they were regarded as "fair game" by the British Navy in any quarter of the globe. The British zeal to enforce this point led the commander of a British man-o'-war, the Phaeton, to brazenly venture into Nagasaki harbor, take two Dutchmen hostage and to demand provisions. After procuring the necessary provisions in total disregard of the protocols so carefully laid down between the Dutch and the Shogunate, the British sailed off to leave the red-faced Dutch and the powerless local officials of the Bakufu to explain themselves to the Shogun in Edo.[6]

The Japanese were thus brought face to face with the kind of military force they would have to deal with if military conflict ensued between themselves and a Western power in the near future. The peasant in the countryside would hear little of the matter but the lesson was not lost on astute observers, and would spread throughout the broader urban intelligentsia, not just the officials of the Bakufu itself. Here the threat was clearly manifest and discontent with the military status quo intensified accordingly. An awareness of a potential crisis had already been cultivated from as early as the 1790s with Hayashi Shihei's *Kaikoku*

Heidan (published from 1787 to 1791); however, the Phaeton Incident focused debate on Japan's lack of preparedness under the Shogunate to withstand foreign naval incursions in a new way.

Yet naval incursions coupled with such criticism were not enough to create a crisis of political legitimacy for the Tokugawa Shogunate in themselves. The next most significant phase in the Bakufu's unraveling came with the horrendous famines of the 1830s. The government was increasingly compelled to find a decisive solution to the dislocations and conflicts that a highly urbanized society and dynamic commercial sector engendered within a social order predicated on hierarchical stasis.[7]

The directives of the government in the Tempo reforms were entirely predictable and as ineffectual as earlier attempts to eradicate social and economic unrest. Injunctions against extravagance, cancellation of *samurai* debt, and exhortations to return to the Tokugawa orthodoxy of military training and *Shushigaku* were evidence of a government that had no idea of what to do in terms of concrete economic policy. The forced repatriation of the poorest in the cities to the countryside to shore up the agrarian economy signified a steadfastly retrogressive approach. Moreover, the literal "selling off" of central control by releasing certain Daimyo from their traditional obligations to attend one year out of two in the capital, in return for a fee, was an abject renunciation one of the government's earliest and most effectual prerogatives.[8]

Even so, though the Shogunate was ill, it was not quite on its deathbed. The *samurai* class as led by the Shogun at the national level and the respective Daimyo at the provincial level was by no means ready to countenance a radical reworking of the social order.

Western overtures and Bakufu responses prior to the "Black Ships"

In the decades prior to the famous arrival of US Commodore Perry's "Black Ships" in 1853, the international situation saw a rapid succession of shifts in influence among the major maritime powers, each being beset at different turns by problems, domestic and foreign, that made continuous interaction with the Japanese government difficult. By the late 1830s, Britain was arguably better positioned than the Americans to approach Japan in that it could call on the services of Charles Gutzlaff and his Japanese secretaries recruited from among several shipwrecked Japanese mariners. However, there was too much conflict on the coast of China to enable the British to spare the attentions of British diplomatic officials let alone arrange a military escort. The rather meager overture to open relations in 1837 through an attempt to repatriate the ship-wrecked sailors on the *Morrison* simply confirmed suspicions that Japan was not at all inclined to revise its isolationist policy.[9]

The view that Japan was worth approaching but would nonetheless remain intransigent persisted throughout the 1840s. Probably, the best opportunity for making progress came with the outcome of the Opium War (1839–42) and the later conflicts that emerged over enforcing the terms of the Treaty of Nanking (1842). The Shogunate in fact relaxed its erstwhile order to expel foreign ships without exception, having given tacit consent for ships to collect provisions at certain Japanese ports. However, there was too much discontent simmering below the surface of relations between Britain and China to ever permit anything except for the small-scale overtures which were undertaken in 1845 and 1849.[10]

In the late 1840s, the Americans were keen to make headway with the Japanese government having the added incentive of formalizing arrangements for whaling ships to enter ports for refitting and resupply. They had also remained steadfastly neutral in the conflicts with China which served to put them in a much better light than the British. The British government, for its part, was in fact quite happy to assist the Americans indirectly; in 1849, Commodore Biddle was able to rely on the services of Gutzlaff and his staff when it came to the matter of trans-lating official documents into Japanese, and indeed a British observer accompanied Biddle on the trip.[11]

As for the Bakufu, the heightened sense of crisis from the Phaeton visit onwards led to the cautious pursuit of "Dutch studies" which became more extensive from the beginning of the next decade as a sense of urgency in being well-informed about Western activities and develop-ments intensified. This trend picked up even greater impetus with the arrival of the German physician Dr Phillip Franz von Siebolt at Dejima (the officially sanctioned port of entry for the Dutch and Chinese since 1641) who gave extensive instruction to Japanese acolytes while posing as a Dutchman. Engaging in this form of study was regarded with deep suspicion, even paranoia; Matsudaira Sadanobu had coined the phrase "Dutch disease" to refer to the frivolous influence of such learning while nativist ideologues such as Hirata Atsutane could only grudgingly acknowledge the utility of Dutch medicine before feeling obliged to remark on the physical deformities of Dutchmen. When von Siebolt's clandestine collating of maps was revealed in 1828, Takahashi Kageyasu, his main informant, was imprisoned and, even after prematurely dying of illness, he was beheaded to reinforce the depravity of his "crime".[12]

Dejima Island at Nagasaki proved to be pivotal in relation to the procurement and dissemination of information about overseas developments. The respective heads of trade for the Dutch and Chinese there were required to submit reports upon each visit (*Fūsetsusho*, 風説書). The day-to-day administration of the port was under the oversight of the Saga and Fukuoka Clans which had been charged with the security of Nagasaki Harbour since 1641. This position gave these clans plentiful opportunities to gain access to foreign sources of information as well as develop expertise in translation along with particular fields of application such as medicine and military technology.[13]

It was an indirect consequence of the fact that Nabeshima Naomasa (1815–71), the tenth clan head of his domain, was the descendant of the head of security when Saga was entrusted with policing the foreign vessels at the time of the *Phaeton* debacle, and he proved to be exceptionally well-informed and intent upon gleaning every advantage through the promotion of Dutch Studies and the domestic production of Western military hardware, especially cannon manufacture.[14]

During the 1830s, continuing visits and news of military incursions abroad would embolden some within Japan to commit themselves to critical comment on the Bakufu policy in print. Following the arrival of the *Morrison* and its rough send-off in 1837, Takano Nagahide published *Yume Monogatari*, a rather wistfully evasive title which translates as "A Tale of Dreams", which dared at the same time to question the wisdom of treating British overtures so shabbily. In 1839, with news of British military operations in China, the Bakufu commissioned a review on coastal defenses to which Takano and another high-ranking *samurai*, Watanabe Kazan, contributed an outline of foreign conditions. Their ostensibly positive view of barbarian practices earned them immediate censure—Watanabe was imprisoned and committed suicide in 1841, Takano evaded imprisonment and was killed by government officials while resisting arrest in 1850.[15]

The 1840–2 war between Chinese and British navies was by far the most explosive event to shake the status quo in Japan. From the contemporary Western perspective, the outcome was regarded as part of a broader march of modernity trampling underfoot the backward and despotic regimes of the Orient. It was a foregone conclusion and in certain terms "necessary". However, for the contemporary Japanese elite, it was in no way a foregone conclusion and defeat of the Chinese could only be regarded as nothing short of a cataclysm.

The first information to come through to the Bakufu was supplied, naturally enough, through the *Fūsetsusho* supplied by the Chinese and the Dutch. The Chinese documents proved to be less reliable in terms of both their depiction of Chinese misfortune in the conflict and sheer factuality. In one case, they even claimed to have captured an English princess from a capsized man-o'-war and were going to exchange the hostage for the return of territory.[16] The Dutch proved to be more factual and more comprehensive in their descriptions of recent conflict between England and China which led the Bakufu to request supplementary reports which they in turn used to test further reports obtained from the Chinese. In 1844, the Dutch Monarchy sent a document providing greater detail of the circumstances surrounding the humiliation of the Chinese as well as subsequent developments in European expansion in other parts of Asia, including British-ruled India.[17]

The information obtained by the Bakufu was technically top secret and there were very strict guidelines established to control their translation. Even so, many of the officials involved were members of either the adjoining Saga or Fukuoka clans, or persons of ability from other parts of the country, so a number of hand-copied documents were quietly disseminated finding their way to the Mito branch of the Tokugawa Clan and Senior Counsellor Abe Masahiro of the Fukuyama Clan.[18] The *Fūsetsusho* were also used as the basis of a number of pamphlets and other publications that reported on recent events in China, such as Saito Chikudo's *Ahen Shimatsu* (1843), Shionoya Tōin's *Ahen Ibun* (1847) and Satō Nobuhiro's *Suiriku Senpō Ron* (1849).[19] The dimensions of the Western threat to Japan were abundantly apparent by the mid-1840s and when H. N. Lay, the son of a British diplomatic official, accompanied Commander Glynn of the USS *Preble* to Japan in 1849, he could report on his return that the Japanese recoiled in terror at the very mention of the British.[20]

The 1850s saw a significant expansion in the amount of intelligence available to those outside the Bakufu as well. Satsuma's Shimazu Nariakira was able to obtain copies by 1852 and by the late 1850s, copies of *Fūsetsusho* could be found in the libraries of even some of the smaller clans.[21] Another important catalyst for dissemination was a *Fūsetsusho* from the Dutch forewarning the Japanese about the impending visit of Commodore Perry. Abe Masahiro, one of the Shogun's more pragmatic Senior Counsellors, consulted other like-minded Daimyo such as Shimazu and Nabeshima who, while determined to resist military incursions, nonetheless recognized the need to engage in some kind of relaxation of the isolation policy to effect better development of Japan's defenses.[22] In the wake of the formal opening in 1854, Nabeshima in particular distinguished himself by making the most of every opportunity afforded by his position of overseer of Dejima to review Western ships up close in person and to develop a detailed knowledge of Dutch studies first hand. This earned him considerable respect as a scholar (he was sometimes referred to as "the Honorable Encyclopaedia" by his retainers) and perhaps an equal degree of derision from those opposed to any dealings with foreigners. In any event, his clan's tradition of manufacturing prowess in military technology was to place the Saga faction at the forefront of the military refurbishment of the army in the build-up to the Boshin War (1868–9).[23]

The foregoing should not be taken to suggest, however, that Nabeshima or any other of the Daimyo had somehow come to be enamored with the West or inclined to regard the Western powers as an object of general emulation. For Japanese observers, the outcome of the conflict between England and China had not merely been a military disaster but a moral catastrophe. There was an assumption that the moral superiority of Chinese culture and philosophy, quite distinct from its military prowess, would ensure victory. Such an outlook was part of the fabric of contemporary conceptions of the social and moral order within Japan itself as well; the superior status of the *samurai* class was conceived of not only in purely social or military terms but also in moral ones. This order was unambiguously quietist and paternalistic, and given that there was also the added dimension of exclusive military privileges for *samurai*, there was something more emphatic about the notion that superiors were entitled to rule.

The undeniable defeat of the Chinese in 1842 reinforced awareness of the need to take more practical account of the merits of Western military technology so that the likes of Sakuma Shōzan could write explicitly of the imperative to reorganize coastal defenses along foreign lines and promote personnel on the basis of ability rather than mere status. The Dutch studies school of Itō Gemboku in Edo (initially established in 1833) began to attract more *samurai* students (including later on Fukuzawa Yukichi) as did that of Ogata Kōan in Osaka (established in 1838). Nonetheless, Dutch studies beyond the immediately applicable medical and military expertise remained a less than auspicious field of study and even an established expert in military science such as Takashima Shūhan found himself summarily imprisoned in 1842 for no other reason than being too knowledgeable for someone of non-*samurai* birth (his abilities were subsequently "rediscovered" upon the arrival of Perry in 1853).[24]

This keen sense of danger did not translate into the clarification of a clear strategy of response when the inevitable clash with the Western powers would come. There was no consensus, and so no clear line of action beyond an attempt to shore up the status quo was being followed. Members within the Senior Council of the Bakufu, such as Hotta Masayoshi, were quite explicitly in favor of opening trade with the Western powers while retaining an awareness of the need to refurbish Japanese defenses in the future. Others, such as Tokugawa Nariaki of the Mito branch of the Tokugawa Clan, were more adamant about repulsing the barbarians at all costs. It was not until the issue was forced through Perry's arrival that the Bakufu came to make a clear response.[25]

The Black Ships

By the arrival of Commodore Perry in 1853, the political ossification of the Bakufu was at an advanced stage and the system seemed incapable of operating towards any end other than the short-sighted preservation of itself. The Bakufu was a system of patronage that was bankrupt in terms of effectively managing the crises it faced, and the force that held it together was the anxiety of those who profited from its continued survival regardless of its incompetence and saw no alternative. This paralysis would intensify rather than diminish over time and indeed it was ultimately an important precondition for the success of the Restoration in 1868. However, the final resolution of the stalemate emerged in the wake of one final lockage in the system, a cataclysmic failure that would produce an abundant awareness of the Bakufu's policy paralysis and enfeeblement. The events of 1853–4 were to provide precisely such a demonstration. Unlike even the situation with the Phaeton, the arrival of the ships at Uraga could not be contained from the popular imagination—the ships were visible from Japan's largest city and were not sent packing by the Bakufu. They gave a tangible embodiment to a hostile world, and the flourishing industry of *Kawaraban* (single-page broadsheets) would ensure that arcane and incensing images of foreigners and their contraptions would be circulated by the tens of thousands.[26]

Although Britain was initially closer to being able to muster the naval forces and appropriate level of diplomatic representation to make an approach to the Japanese government, this was again thwarted by the outbreak of fresh hostilities, this time in Europe with the Crimean War which commenced in 1854. Under these circumstances, America was freer to continue to prepare for direct approaches to the Japanese government and it was a situation that the British did not particularly regard as a direct threat to their own interests. They were largely just as helpful to

Commodore Perry as they had been to his predecessor Biddle, expecting as they did no particularly greater possibility of success than on the previous occasion. When Perry returned in 1853, having delivered his letter from the American President, he had no concrete undertaking from the Japanese government other than that they would make a formal response the following year. The Treaty that was ultimately concluded in 1854 was in fact highly limited in scope and had more to do with securing permission for US ships to berth at designated ports outside of Nagasaki to obtain supplies rather than establishing full-blown trade relations. It is often forgotten that, in 1854, the British Navy represented by Admiral Stirling was able to secure more or less equally favorable terms for berthing with the added bonus of a most-favored nation clause that, theoretically at least, enabled the British to claim the same conditions as had been agreed with the Russians and the Americans. It is also highly ironic that this resulted not from a formal diplomatic initiative but through a direct enquiry from a representative of the Royal Navy who ventured to obtain an assurance from the Japanese that they would remain neutral in the Crimean conflict providing no support for the Russian navy while the British maintained the status quo. It was due to a series of interpreters' blunders that the notion was conveyed that the British were demanding blanket rights to enter Japanese ports to pursue their war with the Russians. These negotiations, in any event, led to the signing of the Stirling Convention of 1854.[27]

Britain may well have moved to capitalize on Stirling's initiative if it were not for the inveterate jealousy that Sterling's convention had stirred up among the diplomatic corps in China, particularly John Bowring, the Superintendent of Trade. There was also the fact that even with the cessation of the Crimean War, Britain again became embroiled in hostilities in China through the Arrow Incident which became a catalyst for revisiting and addressing ongoing frustration with the Chinese Emperor's determination to renege on the terms of the Treaty of Nanking.[28]

The scale and success of the military expedition conducted in China under the leadership of Lord Elgin set the stage for Britain to establish a more complete basis for establishing diplomatic relations and opening trade. Following the conclusion of the Treaty of Tientsin in 1858, Elgin led a small squadron to Edo to pursue negotiations and conclude a treaty more or less on the spot. He was of course beaten to conclude a treaty by Townsend Harris, the American Consul, who had just been through the process with the Japanese government under the Chief Counselor, Hotta.[29] However, as is well documented, Harris made frequent reference to the British threat looming on the horizon and thereby managed to cajole the Bakufu into moving more swiftly than they would otherwise have liked. Harris persuasively presented them with the option of either concluding a treaty that made concessions that were more on their own terms or having something as thoroughly unpalatable as a treaty similar to that concluded in Tientsin foisted on themselves. As it turned out, Harris was right; Elgin was content to use the US treaty as a model for the British agreement, with the notable exception of including a most-favored nation clause which Harris had left out.[30]

The British, as ever, were the main threat in East Asia; the Americans, though obviously capable of intimidating diplomacy, had shown themselves to be more amenable to adapting to Japanese concerns, and the fact that America remained steadfastly neutral throughout the conflicts of the 1850s with China spoke a great deal in its favor. At the same time, Britain and France were to confirm themselves as the scourge of East Asia through the follow-up campaign conducted in the wake of the freshly concluded Treaty of Tientsin (1858) which had Elgin reassigned to China to lead an allied force right within the walls of Peking itself in 1860.

In the shake-up that followed the conclusion of the Treaty of Amity and Commerce in 1858, Abe Masahiro resigned as head of the Council and Hotta Masayoshi took his place. For a time—and it was to be a relatively brief time—the progressive elements in the leadership were to come to the fore. Someone had to deal with the foreigners and the more rabid anti-foreign conservatives would sooner have nothing to do with them than take the place of Hotta and his chief collaborator, Ii Naosuke. Tokugawa Nariaki put the situation in clear perspective when he stated that Japan had only two options, war or some form of appeasement; when the crunch came, few leaders, even the profoundly anti-foreign ones, could bluff themselves that Japan was ready to wage war with the West. One final initiative that indicated a relative opening of the Bakufu to the West was the establishment in 1856 of a bureau to compile research materials and carry out translations of Western works, the *Bansho Shirabesho* (literally, "The Bureau for Investigating Barbarian Books"). The hasty finalization of trade treaties with America and then Britain unleashed a fury of resentment that the Bakufu could barely contain; Ii Naosuke was to pay with his life, he was assassinated in 1860.[31]

Consequently, the much vaunted "opening" of Japan in the 1850s was clearly not so much a matter of positively embracing the new realities of the world system as of making an explicit confession to political bankruptcy. It was not an enlightened choice to "embrace" the West, nor an acceptance of American "goodwill" and an enfolding of it into national policy; it had more to do with running away from the real threat, Britain. These points merit emphasis because before we talk of the coup d'état of 1868, we need to understand the preconditions without illusion. The Restoration was possible precisely because the Bakufu, despite its resources and unquestionable hold on legitimate authority, had worked itself into a position of inaction and deadlock. As with other modern revolutions, a surprising amount of success could be had by a relatively limited circle of tightly knit activists; it was not so much a reflection of individual resolve and political tenacity (though these were considerable) but rather the peculiar form of paralysis that sets in on a monolithic social system that has become redundant but has nowhere to go.

So the country was officially "opened" diplomatically for the purpose of limited trade but that was about as far as it went. The Bakufu, premised on the very notion of keeping all foreigners at bay, was now conducting a policy that undermined its very *raison d' être*. There was admittedly much that successive officials of the late Bakumatsu era undertook to transform Japan's military and intellectual capabilities but these were all too often hampered by the legacy of seclusionism the caste-based social structure. A new intellectual outlook and a new social structure were required but only a few had the wit or the will to countenance such changes; this is perhaps hardly surprising given that such an enterprise entailed the dismantling of the edifice that they were themselves a part of.

The push for meaningful change came, not unexpectedly then, from those clans who had been systematically marginalized under the Tokugawa regime: clans such as Satsuma and Chōshū in the Southwest which had been excluded from top-level involvement in national government due to their status as *Tozama*, former enemies of Tokugawa Ieyasu, the Edo Bakufu's founder.

The foregoing developments largely account for some of the responses to the West made by the Japanese government and the more outward-looking clans in the 1860s. When the Bakufu organized its first diplomatic mission overseas, it was America and not Europe that they headed for. Moreover, the unauthorized attack on British ships off the coast of Kagoshima by the Satsuma Clan in 1863 was fuelled precisely by the perception that Britain was the main villain among the Western powers and Satsuma was keen to make a show of challenging this fearsome scourge in the Bakufu's stead. In this sense, it was a moral rather than simply a military operation, an act intended to exemplify what could be done if Western technologies were actively adapted to the traditional

Japanese military structure. It was done with the clear aim of reasserting the pre-1853 orthodoxy of expelling the Barbarians and maintaining isolationism.

Nevertheless the long-term outcome of the conflict with the British once reprisals had been exacted was to educate the Satsuma Clan in the futility of such a program of retaliation. The social and political order would need to change and no amount of technology by itself would suffice. The Satsuma Clan might well have turned to the Americans for their next lead but America's position in Japan's diplomatic orbit was shaken profoundly by the Civil War and so for the next six years, the US remained in view but hardly active within Japan's internal development. It was the British that demonstrated the capacity to work with progressive and business-like elements within the Satsuma leadership and ironically the British influence on Satsuma was to have long-term implications for the future beyond the Restoration of 1868 as well.

The conceptual thaw begins

The intellectual antecedent of the new group of leaders that was to emerge in the 1860s was in fact already well developed by the 1850s. As recent Japanese scholarship has emphasized, the process of gauging the precise dimensions of the Western military threat as well as exploring the array of consequences for an attempt to integrate Japan into a unitary political structure were well thought out. Sakuma Shōzan and Yokoi Shōnan are the two figures that most clearly stand out as the leading intellectuals in the discussion of Western learning and its implications for the Bakufu order. Their achievements were in fact remarkable given that neither had any direct experience of the West first hand.[32]

Sakuma Shōzan was an exponent of Dutch learning who also had a formidable grasp of military technology. When Perry's ships lay at anchor at Uraga, he was on hand within 24 hours to observe not only the comings and goings of officials but also to make detailed assessments of the American boats' formation and weaponry. As the only technician in Japan who had succeeded in forging a cannon that could propel a projectile 2000 yards, he was well aware that the black ships were in formation and ready to open fire at a moment's notice. He also knew that lobbing shells from the ships right into the precincts of Edo castle was perfectly within their capability. The Japanese fortifications, as they then stood, only had cannon that could clear 800 yards.[33]

Sakuma was a staunch supporter of the Bakufu throughout his career and, despite censure for his unabashed advocacy of adopting Western military practice, worked tirelessly to ensure that ultimately the Bakufu would remain the dominant player in the body political. Ironically it was his thinly concealed attempt to arrange for the transfer of the Imperial court to Edo in 1864 which led to his being assassinated on the streets of Kyōto by fanatical anti-foreign Chōshū *samurai*. According to the contemporary account, he was wearing a Western cap and cloak when attacked; he apparently did not realize that he was potentially the target of such violence due to a perhaps conceited awareness that he was one of Bakufu's most important advisors.[34]

One other reason he may have felt relatively safe was the assumption that the most vehement critics of Bakufu policy, *samurai* from the Chōshū Clan, were ostensibly under the restraining influence of one of his disciples, Yoshida Shōin. Just ten years earlier, when Sakuma had rushed to Uraga, Yoshida too had made a lightening dash for Edo joining his teacher within 24 hours. Yoshida came out of the experience convinced that it would be necessary to sneak aboard one of the foreign ships and smuggle himself out of the country to observe the West first hand. Sakuma heartily approved and even wrote a poem commending his star pupil. In the end, Yoshida was unable to successfully effect a surreptitious passage out of the country; he missed the American boats which left too soon and he had no better luck when he attempted to intercept the Russian vessel that called at Nagasaki soon after.

In tandem with Sakuma Shōzan, an intellectual figure who presented also some of the most profound insights into the moral dimension of Japan's national predicament was Yokoi Shōnan. In common with Sakuma Shōzan, he was fully aware of the need to actively promote expertise in Western science and technology. Nevertheless as the lucid argument of his widely read *Kokuze Sanron* (1860) indicates, he was more acutely aware of the need to combine commercial development with military prowess. More significantly perhaps, he was preoccupied with the issue of unifying the nation on the moral level; he was aware of the role of Christianity and patriotism in forging a common identity in Western societies and equally aware that Japan as yet did not have an ethos that would function to integrate the populace in the same manner. He did not advocate the adoption of Christianity, neither was he in favor of blind Emperor worship. It seems that he had grasped the essence of the problem of modern citizenship and realized that whatever solution was adopted would have to conform to indigenous cultural imperatives. It is not so well known that the Charter Oath promulgated by the Restoration government in 1868 was in one sense a condensed summation of the *Kokuze Sanron*, being penned as it was, apart from article four which was Kido Takayoshi's addition—by a disciple of Shōnan, Matsuoka Hachirō).[35]

Given that Yokoi Shōnan was perhaps the least experienced in terms of exposure to Western society, his appreciation of the dimensions of reform requisite for the reconstruction of the nation were exceptional and his influence extended across a truly diverse array of activists and politicians even after his death. Sadly, he too was to become victim to the virulent hatred leveled at reformers which, if anything, became even worse in the immediate wake of the Restoration. Yokoi was "guilty" of being too familiar with things Western and it was alleged that his conduct had displayed disrespect to the throne. It was even rumored that he had had secretly converted to Christianity. Yokoi Shōnan was cut down while returning to his abode on the southeastern outskirts of the palace grounds in the January of 1869.

In conjunction with both Sakuma Shōzan and Yokoi Shōnan, the figure who merits particular attention is Yoshida Shōin, the founder of the *Shōkason Juku* in Chōshū which included a number of students who were ultimately to become leading activists in the Restoration government, either as military leaders as in the case of Takasugi Shinsaku and Yamagata Aritomo, or as statesmen as in the case of Itō Hirobumi, Kido Takayoshi and Inoue Kaoru.

Yoshida's major achievement was to break more decisively with the late Tokugawa *Shushigaku* tradition and articulate a formula for a new form of relationship between the citizen and the state. It was remarkably prescient in that it dispensed with the intermediary structure of Bakufu and domain, to posit the citizen as subject of the Emperor as the key political relationship regardless of political background. Moreover, as is evidenced from his memorial to the *Meirinkan* in 1848, along with his later polemic, "Words of a Madman", he was singularly dedicated to the promotion of personnel purely on the basis of ability and irrespective of social status. Yoshida had grasped the significance of the relationship between the promotion of the best personnel (*jinzai*) and the now pressing need for a centralized structure for the dissemination of knowledge. Accordingly his proposal of a new central administration and a new centre for the promotion of the most advanced learning, including Western science, was evidence of a strengthening awareness of the need for a completely new institutional structure to complement the restoration of Imperial authority. As for military organization, Yoshida can be credited with experimenting with new forms of military unit that were not drawn from the *samurai* class; even going so far as to conduct rifle drill at the grounds of his academy.[36]

One other significant legacy of Yoshida, which may seem incidental but in fact had considerable significance with regard to the successful enactment of the Restoration, was his emphasis on extensive travel, interpersonal networking, and the sharing of social and political intelligence on a regular basis. In themselves, they were not remarkable in that they were what was being commonly carried out by the Bakufu. Yoshida's masterstroke was to appropriate these activities in the non-governmental sphere. One of the key elements in Yoshida's political strategy was to employ politically independent "grassroots" activists—students, literati and the like—to form a national network for the gathering of detailed intelligence and the organizing of armed action if required. Yoshida maintained a folio of the regular missives from his widely dispersed network of students which he entitled "Flying ears, long eyes", arguably indicating that his widely traveling students (flying ears) were enabling to have far-reaching vision (long eyes). The content of the folio resembled a modern journal or newspaper and demonstrated Yoshida's capacity to garner vital intelligence even before those in the domain of the government knew.[37]

Much has been made of Yoshida's meritocratic views as suggesting that in Yoshida we have the kernel of radical democratic impulses; this is not particularly apt. His invective against luxurious living and self-idealization as a philosopher-sage/valiant warrior indicate that he had very much retained a traditional intellectual outlook. The ideological pillar of his justification for political activism was deeply rooted in Mencian Confucianism, particularly the notion of the failure of the Bakufu to fulfill the "mandate of heaven". This was not mere strategy but in fact a largely unreconstructed continuity from his earlier education.[38]

Yoshida also drew much of his early inspiration from the quasi-reformist Mito School which had a pronounced nativist and anti-foreign orientation. Accordingly, though he was able to break away from some of the formalistic prescriptions dictated by Tokugawa orthodoxy, his disciples were, all the same, fervent monarchists whose over-riding aim was the literal fulfillment of the twin aims of restoring the monarchy and expelling the foreigners.[39]

Following the Ansei purge which was initiated by Ii Naosuke from 1858 onwards, Yoshida became directly involved in organizing direct violent confrontation with the Bakufu, primarily with a plan to assassinate the police superintendent of Kyōto, Manabe Akikatsu. This plan was undone through a combination of political naivety—he tried to directly enlist the support of influential officers from the ranks of the government, and the lack of proper means and opportunity. This fanatical outlook would eventually be modified substantially by Yoshida himself but it was conspicuously persistent in the outlook of Chōshū military leaders, particularly Kusaka Genzui and Kijima Matabei.

Yoshida was arrested at the end of 1858 and eventually handed over to the Bakufu where he was interrogated and sentenced to death almost a year later. The sentence was carried out on the 27th day of the tenth month and both Itō Hirobumi and Yamagata Aritomo were on hand to accept his remains. It is not difficult to imagine that the younger stratum of Yoshida's *juku* were afforded a number of practical lessons in the need for political stealth as well as iron determination in fulfilling the aims of national reconstruction. The tragic fate of Yoshida had had easily the most impact.

The foregoing outline of the intellectual legacy of Sakuma, Yokoi and Yoshida illustrates how the initial move away from reaction and traditionalism was made towards a conception of a social order that clearly accommodated tradition within a political structure that was in essence consistent with the "modern" nation state; unitary in terms of geographic reach and central jurisdiction, as well as universal in terms of citizenship. Yet it was only a tentative first step; it was the groundwork for establishing a genuinely conservative political outlook and agenda, but it certainly did not entail the sort of administrative detail that would eventually require clarification if such a vision were to be enacted in full.

Developing a vision of national reconstruction in detail was nonetheless being initiated, as is evident from the career of Ōkubo Toshimichi, arguably one of the most perceptive and skilled politicians within the Restoration movement. Born in 1830 into a low-ranking *samurai* family of the Satsuma domain, Ōkubo was quickly initiated in the vicious politics of clan factionalism during the period of looming national crisis in the late 1840s. His father, who had been attached to a more progressive faction of retainers who supported the succession of Shimazu Nariakira, the urbane and well-read heir to the clan headship, was exiled to Kikaigashima in 1849 while the young Toshimichi was dismissed from his duties as an official archivist. Fortunately, intervention from Abe Masahiro in 1851 led to the dismissal of Shimazu Nariaki in favor of the rightful heir, Nariakira, in 1851. Ōkubo was eventually rehabilitated to office in 1853 and in the aftermath of the Black Ships, he developed a fervent devotion to the cause of Imperial rule and expulsion of the barbarians forming the "The Sincere Loyalists Faction" (Seichū-gumi, 誠忠組) with Saigō Takamori and Yoshii Tomozane.[40]

Following the death of Nariakira in 1858, it might well have been expected that Ōkubo would again find himself on the wrong side of factional infighting. However, his association with the pro-Imperial and anti-foreign expulsionists put him in a position that was not altogether removed from the sentiments of Shimazu Hisamitsu (regent to the new clan head, Mochihisa) even though Hisamitsu had been one of the main losers in the fight over succession in 1851. That earlier episode had been a tragic instance of short-sighted ambition and political jealousy poisoning the capacity of the clan to fulfil its potential; Hisamitsu seemed to have learned at least the merits of avoiding another confrontation. When confronted by open agitation of loyalists such as Ōkubo and Saigō to join other like-minded young *samurai* in Kyoto, with or without official sanction, both Mochihisa and Hisamitsu admonished them against rash action and advised them that action would happen "when the time would unavoidably come". Ōkubo listened, and managed to rein in many of his associates, others bolted the domain nonetheless.[41]

From this point onwards, Ōkubo developed a working trust with Hisamitsu, again heeding his advice not to take matters into his own hands in 1860 when fury at Ii Naosuke's unilateral endorsement of the commerce treaty was at its height. It is also from around this time that Ōkubo commenced his diary and in it we begin to see the kernel of a shrewd and perceptive observer of politics. The initial entry refers to the admonitions of Hisamitsu and follows the turn of events both within the domain and on the national scene. Ōkubo's notes assiduously note the state of play in Edo and there is reference to reports from colleagues who have returned from other "hotbeds" in the country such as the Mito domain.[42]

Of particular note in this connection is a reference to Hitotsubashi Yoshinobu (the member of the Mito branch of the Tokugawa Clan destined to become the last Shogun in 1866) and apparent approval of the view that "[w]hile the main aim of expelling the barbarians springs from a spirit of loyalty which grieves at the desecration of the Imperial realm by foreigners, there is also the policy of Hitotsubashi who advocates the strengthening the country within all the better to strengthen the country without". This is remarkably prescient of Ōkubo's more mature views regarding national policy following the Restoration; in many ways it could be summed up as the prioritization of internal affairs over international ones, as indeed the refusal to assent to the proposed invasion of Korea in 1873 and the prioritization of the formation of a Ministry of Internal Affairs in the same year illustrates.[43]

Apart from such fragmentary observations, however, there is nothing quite as substantial as a blueprint for national reform. Clearly Ōkubo saw some potential in the prospect of Hitosubashi becoming a more effectual reformer of the Bakufu, and this most likely gave some impetus to accepting the possibility of a merger between the Imperial household and that of the Shogunate (*Kōbugattai*, 公武合体) as advocated by Shimazu Hisamitsu. Otherwise, the news of the assassination of Ii Naosuke before the Sakurada Gate is related with a combination of surprise and perhaps even some disquiet; there is certainly no sense that he relished things having taken such a bloody turn. The country was in crisis and clarification of a policy of national reconstruction was what was needed.

It is no surprise that out of the foment of unrest that engulfed the country in the wake of the Treaty of Amity and Commerce (1858) that clarification would be slow in forthcoming. But undoubtedly, the most important formative influence on that process would be found in the experiences of the young *samurai* who ventured into Western society for substantial periods for training and social reconnaissance.

Experiencing the outside world

Experience of the West following the partial opening of the country came in many guises and through a variety of opportunities. In the first instance, students sponsored by the government to journey to the West for training and tuition would seem to have all the advantages but that was not altogether the case. Ironically, it can be argued that it was the coterie of young men dispatched to Western Europe and America by the Satsuma and Chōshū Clans, without official government endorsements, and without the same degree of financial support that came through the experience more keenly awakened and more practically skilled to take up the challenges of national reconstruction.

Research and the dissemination of knowledge of Western learning had remained under the close control of the Bakufu which had always been highly selective regarding the spheres of enquiry that would be condoned or otherwise restricted. There was a degree of openness towards the adaptation of Western techniques in the visual arts, and indeed in the demimonde there was even a certain faddism associated with the employment of Western regalia or day-to-day implements for novelty's sake. However, Dutch learning was the officially endorsed avenue of serious enquiry into Western technology and arts, and it meant that right up until the early 1860s, the brightest and best within the fraternity of Bakufu-sponsored intellectuals would be expected to be masters of Dutch first and any other language as a bonus skill. Apart from the obvious appeal of medical expertise, they would be required to focus on arts with military and defense applications: navigation, metallurgy, astronomy and mathematics.

When the first major Bakufu-sponsored mission visited the US in 1860, English was spoken by a precious few and with considerable limitations. Even by the time of the second mission to Europe in 1862 at the behest of the English representative, Alcock, and his French counterpart, de Bellecourt, there were few persons who had a tolerable working knowledge of English. Fukuzawa Yukichi was one of the more experienced hands in English but even he relied on a substantial degree of backup from a Dutchman living in London at the time of the visit to augment the notes that would form the basis of the final report on the Mission in Japanese. Fukuzawa was to quip that the Mission was managed in the manner of carrying the policy of seclusion around Europe.[44] By contrast, the experience of the Satsuma and Chōshū students was substantially different and it was to have a decisive influence on their respective outlooks whether they were to enter government or engage in pure scholarship.

The clearest illustrations of how the Bakufu's elite leadership and intelligentsia struggled to come to terms with the imperative of the age are provided by the formal missions that were dispatched to America and Europe in 1860 and 1862, respectively.

The main reason for the 1860 Mission to the US was to enact ratification of the 1858 treaty. In the intervening two years, the counter-winds of conservatism had swept those that had originally been involved in negotiating the settlement out of favor so that by 1859, the Mission was to be led by a relatively inexperienced high-ranking bureaucrat, Shimmi Masaoki, who was supported by a former governor of two treaty ports, Muragaki Norimasa.[45] The brief for the Mission was quite simply to complete the process of ratification as quickly and as quietly as possible; there was a large entourage of retainers and dignitaries and a relatively small number of specialists in either technological matters or Western languages. There were representatives from non-Tokugawa and non-Fudai clans included in the party, including Chōshū and Tosa; however, all members of the mission were subject to the watchful eye of superintendents who were appointed for the express purpose of ensuring that none exceeded the brief or engaged in questionable activities in either word or deed. Such constraints, along with the addition of a curfew of six in the evening for all diplomatic staff, would prove to be a major obstacle to any attempts to engage in serious investigation of American society and practices.

The Mission departed from Yokohama on 13 February 1860 on the USS *Powhatan* landing at San Francisco on 29 March. Several diaries remain from the pens of the leaders of the expedition but what these records reveal is an abiding disdain for Western customs (including the inexplicably deferential treatment accorded to women), a propensity to whine about food and an anxiety to avoid awkward social occasions as much as possible.

The Americans, to their credit, laid on lavish entertainments and the warmest of public receptions—albeit mixed with a predictable degree of vulgar curiosity—at almost every city. Some members of the Mission, especially those lower down the hierarchy were occasionally able to engage in some light-hearted socializing or compile genuinely useful records based on factories or institutions visited. However, once the main purpose of the visit, the ratification of the 1858 treaty, was concluded, the Mission refused invitations to visit Niagara and Boston and embarked (ironically) on the USS *Niagara* which set out on 29 June from New York to take the party all the way back to Japan via the Suez. After a brief stopover in Batavia, the Mission returned via Hong Kong to Yokohama. The stop in Hong Kong would enable all in the Mission to be acquainted with the unadorned news of China's ultimate humiliation at the hands of Elgin who had entered Peking and razed the summer palace to the ground. Upon the return to Yokohama on 9 November, there was no fanfare and little ceremony; the "dirty business" of dealing with Western powers was not something to be advertised and the upper-ranking members of the Mission could congratulate themselves on having survived the trials of the last months to return to proper food and a hot bath.[46]

In stark contrast to the Mission to the US, the voyage of the *Kanrin Maru* to San Francisco and back in the same year demonstrated what could be achieved when the aforementioned constraints on contact with foreigners were relaxed to some extent. The ostensible purpose of the trip was to wear-in a new steamer/sailing vessel that had been procured from the Dutch by the Bakufu. A compliment of 96 Japanese was accompanied by 11 American sailors under Lieutenant J. M. Brook when it left Uraga on the 10 February. Katsu Awa was ostensibly in command but the fact was that the practical sailing was undertaken at first by the Americans while the Japanese struggled to find their sea legs and discover what their respective routines and duties would be. By the time of arriving in San Francisco on 17 March, the Japanese crew were deemed fit to handle the ship by themselves and after a period of refitting the storm-damaged boat in dry dock, they set out again for Japan on 9 May, arriving back later that same month.

Of particular interest in this voyage is that it was not over-laden with officialdom, it contained a number of technical and linguistic specialists (including Nakahama Manjiro and Fukuzawa Yukichi) and it enabled an extended period of time of informal contact with their American counterparts. The quality of information compiled by such a group, quite apart from the practical skills they were able to further develop, were to constitute a significant example of how Japan could take steps forward in equipping itself with the hardware and personnel requisite for national self defense. The pity of the matter is that the lesson was not learnt and many of the constraints that existed in the case of the 1860 mission to the US were replicated in the case of the 1862 mission to Europe.[47]

The main objective of the 1862 mission was to ratify the trade agreement that had been concluded with Britain some four years earlier. However, internal dissent in the wake of signing the accord, which had burgeoned from 1860 onwards, led to consideration of attempts to postpone the opening of ports at Hyogo and Niigata along with the cities of Edo and Osaka. There had been numerous attacks on public or private figures that were perceived as having compromised with the barbarians. Apart from Ii Naosuke's assassination in March of 1860, there was the nearly successful attempt on the life of another Senior Counselor, Ando Nobumasa, in February of 1862. There was also an intensification of attacks on foreigners; Townsend Harris' secretary, Hendrik Heusken, was killed in January of 1861 and there was also an attack on the British legation in July of the same year which led to the wounding of Laurence Oliphant, the former secretary to Lord Elgin.[48]

Both the British envoy, Rutherford Alcock, and his French counterpart, Duchesne de Bellecourt, were eager to see a top-tanking delegation visit the capitals of Europe to dispel mistrust, enlighten the Japanese elite, and of course to thereby smoothen the way for commerce, including orders for military hardware. Alcock, who was an "old hand" of China, was particularly eager to facilitate a more positive response towards foreign powers by fast-tracking the Bakufu's awareness of the fruits of industry and Japan's precarious position in world affairs. Accordingly, he even ventured to advise the Bakufu on who should lead the mission. Predictably, the Bakufu was less than inclined to send anyone that was either of excessively high status or overly enamored with the notion of trading with the West. The responsibility for heading the mission was given to Takenouchi Yasunori, a foreign affairs commissioner *Gaikoku Bugyo* a safe pair of hands for an unfavored job. Matsudaira Yasunao was a younger and relatively progressive deputy but with the customary addition of Kyōgoku Takaaki as *Metsuke* (superintendent), there was little chance of anyone senior delving into anything beyond that which was strictly outlined in the Mission's instructions.[49]

Among the party of 36 that was assembled for the mission, only 6 had been on the earlier ventures to the US. Four, including Fukuzawa Yukichi, were to serve as translators although it is not clear how proficient they were in English or French as opposed to Dutch. Matsuki Kōan, formerly of Satsuma, was also a valuable addition although officially he was listed as a medical specialist. Alcock was clearly anxious enough about the Mission's capacity to interact with their hosts in Europe that he sent along a young British interpreter, John Macdonald, to ease their dealings along the way.[50]

The Mission was away from 21 January 1862 until 29 January 1863 (arriving in Marseille on 3 April and leaving Lisbon on 25 October). After a relatively brief stop of just over three weeks, the Mission headed straight to Britain in order to get a satisfactory outcome on the issue of postponing the opening of the additional ports and cities. They found, somewhat to their disappointment, that Alcock had not arrived back from Britain yet and so there was a wait until the end of May to establish the terms that had been freshly negotiated at Edo; the opening would be postponed for a further five years.

During the extended stay in Britain, there were ample opportunities to travel further afield than London and on occasion they were taken. To some extent, Alcock's aim of forcing the Bakufu elite to come face to face with the dimensions of Britain's industrial as well as military might was largely achieved. However, the senior members of the delegation persisted in avoiding evening engagements, made few attempts at communication beyond the absolutely necessary and maintained a steadfast fixation with aspects of British society that had military implications. They could confess to being impressed by what they saw at the International Exhibition in Kensington yet seemed determined to be less than impressed by Britain as a whole. The food was unpalatable, the people more disorderly and the streets dirty. The reception in Paris, by contrast, had been far more to their liking as the French government had gone out of its way to greet the mission with a degree of pomp.[51]

The pattern established in the first few months of the mission was retained for the remainder of the journey. There was certainly greater fanfare and enthusiasm in Holland, Prussia and Russia for the visitors but since there were no pressing diplomatic issues to conclude (with the exception of discussing the border issue of Sakhalin with Russia), the personnel found themselves caught up in a familiar series of receptions, military reviews as well as brief visits to the likes of hospitals and factories.

By late summer the expense of keeping the mission on an extended stay was beginning to weigh on the resources of the mission's sponsors and so it was with rather unseemly speed that the mission was whisked from St Petersberg via Prussia and France to Portugal. The delegation was even required to walk from the station to the quay at Rochefort before embarking on a ship for Lisbon.[52]

The diplomatic legacy of the mission is fairly clearly definable in that it got the rather unpalatable business of ratifying the trade accord out of the way while achieving a postponement of extra port openings without too much difficulty. The intellectual legacy is harder to quantify for the reasons already alluded to. First, there was the language barrier which the capable but, nonetheless, not-altogether-proficient linguistic specialists struggled to overcome. Dutch was still the first foreign language for all the language specialists and even Fukuzawa Yukichi was given to jotting notes in Dutch rather than English. Second, the constraints on movement placed on the more capable personnel in the mission meant that all observations would be, of necessity, ad hoc and in need of supplementation later on from written sources, if indeed these could be procured. There is evidence that a considerable amount of the material collated on British matters was in fact drawn from the verbal commentary supplied by an anonymous Dutch doctor who had been living in London.[53]

The ensuing report of the mission's journey came to amount to quite a substantial set of documents, but they were not broadly published and indeed the authors knew the dangers of exposing themselves to criticism (or much worse) if it seemed that they had too positive a view of the nations they had visited. As for the Bakufu itself, it remained an institution whose organizational culture was increasingly ossified and incapable of substantial adaptation.

Given the increasingly obvious policy paralysis of the Bakufu, things began to be taken out of their hands at the initiative of forces both within and without. In early 1863, the anti-foreign factions within the Bakufu in league with the Chōshū Clan and sympathetic members of the aristocracy in Kyōto conspired to have the government revoke the opening of the ports and, with no less than an Imperial order from the throne, set about actively driving out the foreigners (cf. *Uchiharai Rei*). The date set for this action was 10 May; however, the only attacks mounted were by the Chōshū gun emplacements on foreign ships traversing the Straits of Shimonoseki. This debacle led to an even more humiliating about face as British and French ships were permitted to re-enter Yokohama and in the following month, the former anti-foreign factions were purged from government.[54]

At the same time, the Satsuma Clan was locked in an acrimonious dispute with Britain over reparations for the murder of English subjects near Yokohama the previous summer (i.e. the Namamugi Incident). As is well documented, the brief naval bombardment and occupation of the gun emplacements at Kagoshima in July of 1863 set about an earth shift in Satsuma policy. Some satisfaction was taken from the "trouble" they had caused the British during the engagement; however, it was a pivotal moment of realization about the magnitude of the task ahead of the country if it was to meaningfully establish independence from the Western powers.

The speed with which the reorientation of the Satsuma Clan was effected in practice was remarkable. In August, the Satsuma Clan in league with the Aizu Clan from the North fought with Chōshū *samurai* and drove them from the capital. The Satsuma leaders also began to develop more extensive ties with British interests, both diplomatic and commercial, as they set out on what was increasingly an independent initiative. Alcock, who returned as the British envoy at the beginning of 1864, was well and truly exasperated by the about face of the Bakufu in response to anti-foreign pressure and saw in Satsuma the opportunity to develop an important partner for ensuring that the road to open trade would remain open once and for all. The powers were also once more leaning on the Bakufu with thinly veiled threats posed in references to the French and British occupation of Peking in 1860 which led to them being given leave to forcibly reopen the Straits of Shimonoseki (this they completed in early August).

The Chōshū Clan, for their part were not standing still either. Under the leadership of Kusaka Genzui and other fervent "Loyalists", Chōshū forces moved in several columns to converge on the Imperial capital, Kyōto. The aim was to wrest what seemed like exclusive control of the court away from Satsuma and to confront the Bakufu head on. In what was later termed the Kinmon Gate Incident, the Aizu Clan, in alliance with a smattering of pro-Bakufu small players and a relatively small detachment of Satsuma warriors routed the Chōshū forces conclusively. An Imperial edict was issued for Chōshū to be militarily punished by the Bakufu, ostensibly for bringing arms right into the inner precincts of the city and, in effect, attacking the Court itself. This order the Bakufu gladly "complied with" and, given that it was an Imperial edict, Chōshū had little choice but to accept its punishment.[55]

However, the Bakufu was perhaps lulled into a mistaken sense of having retrieved its position politically; the fact was that its success was achieved only with the aid of certain key clans, including Satsuma under Shimazu Hisamitsu, who had interests not entirely consonant with that of the Shogunate. Moreover, a new force in the military and political affairs of the Chōshū Clan was about to be unleashed by a new wave of activists, most of them former students of Yoshida Shōin. In particular, there was Takasugi Shinsaku who returned to Chōshū after a surreptitious reconnaissance of Shanghai in 1862 and quickly moved to establish the *Kiheitai* militias, essentially non-*samurai* army units equipped with the latest Western weapons. Despite a short hiatus in the wake of Bakufu's punitive expedition of late 1864, Takasugi re-emerged explosively in a domain coup d'état that swept away the former conservative leadership and opened the way for other former associates at the *Shōkason Juku,* such as Itō Hirobumi and Inoue Kaoru, to take an active role in clan politics.

Moreover, at this time, there was also a growing realization among the Satsuma leadership, including Ōkubo Toshimichi, that it would be futile to support the increasingly fragile Shogunate. An amalgamation of Shogunate and Imperial Household seemed less palatable given that the Bakufu seemed intent on taking exclusive control of the Court while at the same time making ongoing concessions to the Western powers (including the opening of further ports).[56] More significantly, the coterie of non-Bakufu-aligned loyalists who were moving around the country and developing wider contacts in places like Chōshū and Tosa (in Shikoku) were beginning to reveal unexpected common interests.

Sakamoto Rōma from Tosa was a significant go-between for various anti-Bakufu agitators and, after meeting with Yokoi Shōnan in Kumamoto, even managed to meet key players in Satsuma politics such as Saigō Takamori and, most likely, Ōkubo Toshimichi as well. There was also the unanticipated benefit of several prominent aristocrats who had been exiled from the capital for their associations with Chōshū, particularly Sanjō Sanetomi and Iwakura Tomomi, who became pivotal links in the Court when the time came for Restoration in full. Sakamoto was eager to see the two clans join forces, but there were—quite understandably—deeply held suspicions between the two clans. The offer of procuring weapons from the English on behalf of Chōshū seemed the perfect means of demonstrating goodwill and dispersing enmity. It was no easily achieved allegiance but by the January of 1866, the alliance was sealed.[57]

Sensing, quite rightly, the danger in these new developments, the Tokugawa Clan pushed for a Second Punitive Expedition. Despite Ōkubo Toshimichi's best efforts to dissuade the Court from assenting, a formal Edict was issued to that effect. Support from Satsuma, and most other significant clans was not forthcoming despite the edict. Consequently, the Bakufu went alone: the Bakufu forces were routed on all fronts despite superior numbers; the game was up militarily. As a result, 1866 turned out to be the year when the Bakufu under the Tokugawas was demonstrably defunct as the sole arbiter of power in Japan. Moreover, the attitude of even formerly fervent Imperial loyalists such as Ōkubo was profoundly shaken; following the Bakufu's abortive "punitive" expedition Ōkubo was more selective about who he approached in the Court, and he was more forthright in his view that the Shogunate had to be fundamentally revised.[58]

There was, however, some way to go before a new echelon of leaders would step to the fore and take charge of national affairs. The crucial phase of developing personnel for the post-Bakufu government involved a new approach to engagement with Western societies, one which roundly dispensed with the facile formalism and xenophobia of previous Bakufu and *Sonno Jōi* iniatives.

The training grounds of Europe and America

Satsuma had two exceptional scholars of Western learning who had served in the Bakufu. Godai Tomoatsu was a specialist in geography and gunnery who had smuggled himself to Shanghai in 1862 (along with Takasugi Shinsaku of the Chōshū Clan) to observe production facilities there first hand. The other was Matsuki Kōan who arguably had the more extensive experience in having accompanied the Bakufu mission to Europe in 1862. Both famously allowed themselves to be "captured" by the British after the Kagoshima bombardment in order to get a closer look at the ships. From the early 1860s, they had increasingly devoted their energies to the service of Satsuma rather than the Bakufu. Godai being especially instrumental, with the aid of a Scottish merchant in Nagasaki, Thomas Glover, in formulating a complex plan for sending Satsuma trainees to England for extended stays while commercial ties independent of the Bakufu's trade strictures were developed. It is a relatively neglected fact that the classic enunciation of the Meiji reform's twin aims of "wealthy nation, strong army" were in fact first clarified and expounded upon in memoranda from Godai Tomoatsu to Shimazu Hisamitsu, the head of the Satsuma domain. Godai's insight was that the Western powers' strength was born out of a complex interaction between commerce, industry and rational military organization. Commerce, in the sense of engaging in the exchange of goods in an open market, he realized, could be relied upon to take care of itself to some extent; industry was another matter and he was quick to identify how the sheer breadth of Europe's industrial complex had made the development of the military complex possible.[59]

Based on Godai's and Matsuki's recommendations, the Satsuma Clan's own delegation of students set out covertly from Japan in the spring of 1865 ultimately arriving in London on 21 June. After an initial shake-down period, they were moved into lodgings in pairs with a view to pur-suing study in scientific subjects at University College, London University (with the exception of two who were sent to Paris to study medicine).[60]

The group in England benefited from its connections with Thomas Glover's brother James as well as the long-standing goodwill that had been built up in the past between Matsuki Kōan and Laurence Oliphant (a veteran diplomat in the Far East previously alluded to, whose wounds at the hands of would-be assassins in 1861 seemed to have no bearing on his willingness to help the Japanese). Unlike the Bakufu students, they were not overly constrained by protocol, curfews or the predilec-tions of Bakufu officials.

An example of just how the culture of constraint could foil the best of intentions is illustrated by the activities of a group of Bakufu stu-dents who set out for the Netherlands just as the Takenouchi mission was wending its way back from Europe to Japan via Singapore in late 1862. The main objective was to send military personnel and artisans that would undergo training in relevant military and industrial facili-ties until a new steamer which had been ordered by the Bakufu had been completed. Accompanying them were two 33-year-old scholars from the *Bansho Shirabesho* who were under instructions to attend the university at Leiden to study matters pertaining to law, government and economics. Their tutor, Simon Vissering, was quick to disabuse them of any illusions they might have retained about the utility of studying in Dutch; he put them straight on to the leading British Utilitarians and the French sociologist Auguste Comte. Unfortunately, they had little choice but to remain in Leiden and returned to Japan on 13 February 1866, having completed a rather cloistered sojourn "away from the action", so to speak.

By contrast, the naval officers had a slightly broader experience due to their being sequestered in Dutch military facilities and their having to wait a considerable time until the steamer that the Bakufu had ordered was completed in December of 1866. The likes of a naval engineer such as Enomoto Takeaki, who managed to develop good relations with his Dutch hosts and was even employed from time to time as a roving emis-sary of the government in military procurement matters, was later to reach no less than the position of Admiral of the Bakufu fleet (this was another example of what untrammeled investigation of Western society could achieve and yet it was all too often the exception).[61]

The Chōshū Clan had also dispatched students, including Itō Hirobumi and Inoue Kaoru, to England in June of 1863. However, they suffered from a lack of quite the same connections as the Satsuma students had, relying as they did on the shipping company Jardine Mathesons without the additional support of diplomatic connections. Through a lack of communication they were forced into the rather unpleasant option of working their passage to England. Upon arrival, their circumstances improved and they were in fact the forerunners of the Satsuma students in settling into lodgings and preparing to matriculate into University College. However, Itō and Inoue, the two figures destined to play significant roles in government following the Restoration, were only in England long enough to gain a rudimentary grasp of English before they took it upon themselves to return to their home domain as quickly as possible and attempt to persuade the leaders of the clan that the looming military confrontation with the Western powers in 1864 should be avoided.[62]

Taken as a whole, the students of Satsuma and Chōshū fared better, in the sense of gaining more from their experiences overseas, precisely because they were not embedded in diplomatic missions or cloistered in narrowly regulated living conditions. The Satsuma mission was arguably more successful because it was more thoroughly conceived, actively recruited the best young scholars rather than soliciting volunteers and kept the number of officialdom to a minimum. Much of the Satsuma success was also due to the presence, during the initial stages, of Godai Tomoatsu and Matsuki Kōan who were able to ensure that the practical objectives of the study tour would be attained. They were also able to act as go-betweens with commercial and diplomatic interests in England and Belgium to facilitate the procurement of machinery and military hardware for the Satsuma Clan.

Perhaps in recognition of the need to emulate the Satsuma and Chōshū initiatives, the Bakufu sent two groups of students overseas: one to Russia in 1865 under Yamanouchi Sakuzaemon and another dispatched to Britain in late 1866 to study at London University under the tutelage of a former chaplain and naval instructor of the Far East Fleet, the Rev. William Lloyd. The former group had initial designs of studying technical and scientific subjects while in Russia, but soon found that quite apart from the difficulties of conducting daily life in the Russian language, most of the materials for study were after all drawn from the other centers of learning in Europe.[63]

The latter group fared somewhat better but suffered to some extent from the rather excessive constraints placed on the students while lodging under Lloyd's roof. Their opportunities for extracurricular contact were limited and therefore they made slow progress. Some of the students sought lodgings in separate locations but were forced back at the behest of the Bakufu. The group was being "chaperoned" by Kawaji Taro, a well-connected 23-year-old scion of a former advisor to Hotta Masayoshi in the 1850s, along with Nakamura Masanao, a 35-year-old Confucian scholar turned *Rangakusha* (Dutch Studies specialist). As will be discussed in the succeeding chapters, Nakamura was to have success as the translator of several classic texts of Victorian political thought (including J. S. Mills' "On Liberty"); however, his primary task at this time seems to have been that of acting as an intellectual *Metsuke* (superintendent) for the students.[64]

The ineptitude of the Bakufu in such matters was perhaps further exemplified by the dispatch of a delegation and exhibition to the Paris Exposition of 1867. It was triggered by being upstaged by Satsuma who had already negotiated with the French to have their own independent exhibit included. In a somewhat ad hoc fashion, the Bakufu sought to trump the Satsuma "upstarts" by sending no less than the Shogun's younger brother, Tokugawa Akitake, a boy of 14. The party of 20 included Mukoyama Ichiri, the new envoy to France, Tanabe Taichi, a veteran of an earlier trip to France in 1864 and Shibusawa Ei'ichi, who was later to emerge as one of the most prominent entrepreneurs of the Meiji period. There was also a bodyguard of seven Mito *samurai* who hailed from the Mito branch of the Tokugawa Clan that was one of the fiercest opponents to opening the country. Consequently, little of substance was achieved apart from "saving face", and the sojourn in France, if anything, apparently increased the Bakufu's distrust of the French.[65]

By 1866, however, the time allotted the Bakufu was more or less over. The sealing of the alliance between Satsuma and Chōshū brought together the two clans most eminently prepared to steer the country towards making the kind of reforms necessary to establish Japan on a sounder commercial and military footing. From a geopolitical and diplomatic viewpoint, it was also clear that in the build-up to the Restoration, it was still Britain that was the main player in the Far East. Godai and Matsuki were particularly prominent in seizing the opportunity to "sell" the clan as an alternative to the existing Bakufu government, sometimes pursuing this independent diplomatic line with extraordinary pluck, as illustrated by the determination to send an exhibit to the Paris Exhibition in 1867. The masterstroke was in arguing that Satsuma was intent on honoring the terms of the commercial treaty in a fashion that the Bakufu would not, and perhaps could not, do. Here they demonstrated that they understood not only the *realpolitik* but also the language and conventions of international relations in the mid-nineteenth century. Consequently, when the Restoration was initiated on 3 January 1868, the nearly unanimous declarations of "neutrality" from the Western powers—with the obvious exception of the French government which had thrown its support most decidedly in favor of the Bakufu—was in fact a clear diplomatic endorsement for the Satsuma- and Chōshū-led factions to formalize a new power arrangement.

The intellectual foundations of the Restoration

The success of the Satsuma and Chōshū Clans' drive to topple the Bakufu and implement the Restoration was not merely the product of diplomatic and military maneuvring. The aspect of that ascendancy that requires particular attention is the intellectual one. Knowledge and experience of the outside world was not merely individually transformative but fed into the extremely focused and rigorous analysis of Japan's options in the near future for avoiding colonial servitude. Observing the West "on the ground"—capturing the dynamic of Western societies in all aspects and all at once—yielded insights and gave pause for reflection. Concluding that military conflict was doomed to fail was perhaps the easiest conclusion; it did not in itself, however, present a detailed solution to the question of what to do instead of going to war. Those who spent the longer time at close quarters in the capitals of Western Europe, particularly London and Paris, were to gradually identify key areas for making concrete initiatives for reform and development. There was perhaps not so much mystery about what lay at the root of Western social advantages; when the former Satsuma student and later Imperial envoy to Britain, Mori Arinori, concluded towards the end of his stay in England in 1884 that there was not so much to be learnt from the West and much to be avoided, he was not being facetious.[66]

The essential lessons from the Western experience were immediately practical and not always necessarily bound up inextricably with European culture. If we were to venture to list them (not in any particular order) they would be as follows:

(1) A centralized government administration that held a seamless authority in all parts of the national territory.
(2) A centrally amassed tax fund that was paid in cash and redistributed through central government bureaus.
(3) A conscript army recruited irrespective of class.

(4) The development of an industrial complex to underpin the military.
(5) The endorsement and promotion of commercial culture as a prerequisite of magnifying the scale of exchange in goods and services.

The first alteration to Japanese society that such a list dictated was the dismantling of the caste system. There could no longer be a portion of the population exclusively dedicated for military service any more than the same could be said to hold for those engaged in commercial activity. The next imperative was to obliterate the multi-tiered construct of *Shinpan*, *Fudai* and *Tozama* Clans replacing it with a unitary governmental space. The other pressing need was to ensure that all tradable objects that were not properly delineated as units of exchange could in fact be so delineated and transacted in cash. This applied to an array of activities, most clearly the buying and selling of land. It also theoretically related to the state's amassing of taxes; these needed to be assessed on the basis of assets quantifiable in cash figures and collected in cash.

These changes seem obvious enough in contemporary circumstances and they seemed to be of obvious use to the Japanese observing Western society in the 1860s. And despite appearances, given the persistence of "feudal" social arrangements, Japanese society was in a configuration that was conducive to the fulfilling of many of those requirements at a surprising swift pace. It could be administratively centralized relatively quickly. It already had an extensive exchange economy that channeled extraordinary volumes of cash; tax and trade in rice was an unusual hangover from the past but was increasingly not the economy's all-defining commodity.[67] Of greater difficulty would be the dismantling of *samurai* privileges in order to forge more meritocratic modes of recruitment to both the military and the government bureaucracy. These too, however, were not intractable.

Of particular importance in connection to these imperatives and their potential resolution is the fact that they did not in themselves automatically imply the need for a democratic mode of representation, nor the adoption of a humanist or Christian teleology of the universe. Naturally, there were many who regarded parliamentary institutions as a necessary accoutrement for a "civilized" nation, but very few of the leading Satsuma and Chōshū students came back advocating the immediate adoption of such a political system. Indeed they had spent long enough in Western societies to recognize the negative aspects of such arrangements, including the capacity for complete breakdown as was graphically illustrated by the Civil War in the US.

It should of course be acknowledged that Christianity as a moral code impressed many of the students, some converting while overseas and undertaking intense religious training, as was the case of the young students from Satsuma who accompanied Laurence Oliphant to the US in 1867. Yet this too seemed to be a relatively fleeting influence in most cases, and the capacity for Christianity to undermine resistance to Western encroachment was also well noted. Even so, the likes of Itô Hirobumi and Ōkubo Toshimichi had no strong objection to Christianity per se and were instrumental in having the ban which had been enacted during the Restoration revoked within four years, ultimately succeeding in doing so through the "education" of the more intransigent critics who joined the Iwakura Mission to the US and Europe in 1871.[68]

In any event, those with direct experience of the West were still woefully few and apt to be regarded with suspicion. As has already been alluded to in connection with Sakuma Shōzan and Yokoi Shōnan, the slightest perception of disloyalty to the Imperial cause or excessive affinity with Western culture was regarded as grounds for violent retribution. There was also the constant danger of assassination by pro-Bakufu agents, as was demonstrated by the appalling murder of Sakamoto Ryōma, one of the key go-betweens in the early negotiations between Satsuma and Chōshū as well as being one of the leaders of the pro-Imperial reform movement within his home domain of Tosa.

The fate of such figures highlights one of the most fundamental premises of the Restoration Movement; it relied on the deliberate cultivation of the belief that a new political regime with the Emperor at the centre would emerge and that the dilatory response of the Bakufu to the Western powers would be replaced with swiftly meted out "justice", in effect the wholesale expulsion of foreigners from Japanese shores. It was therefore not a thoroughly integrated movement for enhancing the opening up of the country, neither was it particularly reformist in its most immediate aspect. The expanding of ties with the Western powers was the last thing on the minds of many of the coup d'état's "supporters" and there was certainly no seamless and unified front being maintained by the four key clans lending their military weight to the event.

The core of the key political protagonists, especially Ōkubo for Satsuma and Kido for Chōshū, had a relatively clear notion that reform of a monumental order was in store for the country. They were reinforced in their convictions through extensive consultation with veteran scholars of the West and the small band of young *samurai* who had ventured overseas and come back to rebuild the country. But these people were in a decided minority, convinced of the need for change but unable to count on their followers to share in the same store of perceptions. Often there was a deliberate cultivation of the assumption that expulsion would follow the restoration of Imperial rule. The fact that such a drastic line of action was untenable was kept quietly under wraps and not spoken about openly except within the inner circle.[69]

We can assert that Ōkubo, Kido, Gotō and Iwakura were the possessors of extraordinary political vision, one that had been quietly developed over the previous two decades through accumulated experience and experimentation. This entailed not so much a knowledge of mere history and technical facts but more an awareness of the capacity of their society to develop along a trajectory which would not neccessarily follow the Western precedent. In this sense, they were, in varying degrees, possessors of a distinctly *sociological* imagination; they were not attempting to Westernize Japan but reform it in order to harness an increased commercial and industrial capacity to a fully integrated nation state. This they knew could not be effected simply by imitating the West; the aim was to *emulate* its development, something which was in fact quite another matter. It is at this point that they parted company decisively with reactionaries and traditionalists to become the possessors of a distinctly modern conservative outlook. In fundamentals, they could agree on the most basic aims of the need to consolidate political power in the name of the Emperor and to refurbish the nation so as to make it capable of withstanding Western encroachment. But that was about as far as the agreement went—they were inhabiting an almost different planet when it came to the praxis of how this would be achieved—nonetheless, utilizing the fire and determination of the *Sonnō Jōi* movement was an indispensable vehicle, albeit an extremely volatile one, that they had little option but to utilize to the full.

One of the greatest tasks of the post-Restoration phase of reform would in fact be the act of convincing the greater mass of the people that changes hitherto inconceivable would now have to be accepted in short succession. The other great task was to keep the Western powers convinced that whatever reforms that were being pursued in Japan would not prejudice Western "interests", primarily trade, but also the development of a political likeness to the Western institutions with, if at all possible, the widening of Christian influence.

One might well ask how such a small group of political activists managed to hold sway over such turmoil and emerge more or less intact. The best clue that presents itself seems to lie in the precedent of 1854 when the initial accession to Western diplomatic demands was formally articulated: then, as in the case of the Meiji Restoration, there was easily a majority who were incensed by the current imposition of the Western powers and fervently of the belief that "moral regeneration" would be the key to revitalizing Japan's defenses and reasserting independence. But if presented with the option of taking the reins of government and implementing a range of policies that would immediately fulfill those aims, most, if not all, would balk; they were forced to concede that they did not have an adequately practical conception of how to go about it. The lower-ranking *samurai* leading the anti-Bakufu forces seemed to know what they were on about and, in one sense, no one else was game to take the task on. This would give them a free hand to some extent but it also meant that they had very few reserves of goodwill to work with.

Consequently, the "authority" which the new government of 1868 claimed for itself was founded first on a loose coalition of "new model" troops, some of them experienced and others less so; there were the economic and technological advantages that the clans that held sway over these forces enjoyed and of course they had cemented a relationship with the resurgent Court in Kyōto, a relationship that was to have ever increasing significance. As the following chapters will go on to explore and develop, the Imperial Household was to become perhaps one of the most significant elements in the entire Meiji political edifice. It has been customary to discuss the emergence of Imperial authority as largely something that existed and expanded according to the dictates of expedience under the superintendence of Satsuma and Chōshū oligarchs. The boy Emperor is depicted as largely a powerless figurehead. While that may well have been the greater part of the political reality so far as the person himself was concerned, certainly up until the end of his youth, the institution of the Imperial Household was quite another matter.

The sheer precariousness of government authority in the early years of the reform phase made reliance on charismatic authority an increasingly expedient and compelling tool in the struggle to impose a new centralized political order. It worked because it presented the new government in the role of restoring Japan to its origins, its historical essence—an integral part of the *Sonnō Jōi* movement's aims. It enabled the new government to be seen as "giving" with one hand while of course it was—with varying degrees of subtlety—very much "taking away" with the other. It was a balancing act, a political sleight of hand that worked well in the initial critical stages; and once used it became tempting to employ it again at later stages as well—the most obvious phase being the 1880s in the lead up to the promulgation of the

Meiji Constitution in 1889 and the issuing of the Imperial Rescript on Education in 1890.

The problem, however, was that charismatic authority will tend to function in ways inimical to regular and rational government; the person that mediates that authority can also rise to wield it more self-consciously and with greater independence, or, for the same token, those who have a stake in the Imperial Household either to promote its power in its own right or to employ it as a countervailing force against the government can emerge as a separate entity within the body politic. This latter outcome is indeed one of the key contentions in the latter part of this book but it suffices at this stage to say that the latter emergence of the Imperial throne as a major force in later Meiji politics and beyond had the kernel of its origin in the Restoration and even before. The fact that Mutsuhito was a minor upon succession should not lead us to forget that Kōmei, his rather irascible and forthright forebear, was a key player in the taming of Chōshū and a highly influential figure in the country's affairs prior to the ultimate move away from the Bakufu.

There was therefore an inherently charismatic aspect to the event, one that might even be profitably referred to in the classical sense of "enthusiasm", that requires some more substantial incorporation on the theoretical level. Perhaps the abiding difficulty has stemmed from the attempt to make sense of the Restoration purely as a rational political phenomenon, in the sense of being the consciously and systematically mediated result of dealing with purely political dictates and imperatives. There is no clear resolution that the Restoration presents in such terms. As has been discussed at some length in the introductory chapter, the Restoration entailed a parallel reformation of the relation between political and ceremonial institutions; it was the unavoidable corollary of the coup d'état once the Satsuma and Chōshū leaders committed themselves to the full employment of the *Sonnō Jōi* movement.

Finally, it is perhaps needful to further emphasize what this reformation of the worldview did not entail. It was not a democratic revolution. It was not a blanket conversion to Western ways of living and seeing the world. It was not a rejection of traditional authority altogether but rather a *redefinition*. Eventually, it would become apparent to a broad stratum of Japanese society that it was actually possible to cut your hair in the Western style and not lose all sense of Japaneseness or patriotism. It was equally still possible to retain one's disdain for foreigners; however, one would no longer go out of one's way to kill them. Status as a *samurai* (*Shizoku*, 士族) was clearly still important, but it was clearly becoming less so; as a point of fact, carrying two swords had already proven to be less likely to guarantee financial security for *samurai* for a considerable time before the Restoration. And now, Japan was a land of the ancient deities under the descendant of the supreme deity; through this, the entire population was converted from mere vassals stationed within a seemingly endless tiers of status to subjects with one clear, unitary political and moral objective.

This "reformation" had clearly been brewing for some time, particularly in the more built-up urbanized centers of Japan. The Restoration of Imperial rule as it was initiated in the January of 1868 was not in itself going to accomplish the full working out of its potential direction. There was certainly no guarantee that the forces at work would lead to altogether positive or constructive outcomes. The complex multitude of factors had to be weighed, judged and acted upon; policy had to be formulated and implemented. The genius of the Meiji leadership lay in the ability to read the general direction of the changes and steer the Japanese polity with some success towards a stable and tenable resolution. As will be discussed in the next chapter, that balancing act was not over within the first two years or even the first ten after the Restoration. Instability was a constant threat and in some cases only extraordinary resoluteness in moments of crisis averted catastrophe.

3
The Meiji Coup d'État

The dire position of the Bakufu brought about by the miscarriage of the "punitive" campaign against the Chōshū Clan in mid-1866 was to be compounded by the unexpected death of the Shogun Tokugawa Iemochi at only 21 years of age. Hitotsubashi Yoshinobu was the clearly preferred successor to the Shogun, but it was not an accession that could simply be rubber-stamped, especially since it would require the consolidating of support within the various branches of the Tokugawa Clan and, even more importantly, it would require the formal assent of the Emperor Kōmei.

Yoshinobu managed to extricate the Bakufu from the conflict with Chōshū by obtaining an edict from the Emperor to cease the campaign thus enabling him to turn his attention to more central matters. Ōkubo Toshimichi feared that Yoshinobu would develop a stronger connection with the court as the process of determining succession to the Shogunate ensued. These fears were confirmed as Yoshinobu played out accepting the succession as long as he could, largely with a view to accentuating his indispensability to the Bakufu but also as part of developing precisely the sort of rapport with the court he would need to take up the role of Shogun effectively. Eventually his appointment was formalized at the beginning of 1867.[1]

However, yet another unforeseen turn of events complicated the situation. The Emperor Kōmei died soon after appointing Yoshinobu Shogun; he was aged only 36. Up until the death of the Emperor, the possibility of some sort of arrangement that would accommodate the continuation of the Bakufu was still very much in the offing. However, with his death and the accession of a boy Emperor, Mutsuhito, the opportunity for anti-Bakufu factions to pursue a more radical path of political action became apparent. Yoshinobu did not help his situation in that he moved early in 1867 to push through the opening of Hyōgo port, despite the firm opposition of the majority of the most influential Daimyos in the country. This was the last excuse that Ōkubo Toshimichi and Saigō Takamori needed to move toward a fully wrought plan to topple the Shogunate and re-establish a monarchical government (*Ōsei Fukko*, 王政復古) in Kyōto. Naturally, it was not a course of action that Satsuma could achieve by itself; Chōshū would need to be substantially involved in the military aspect, and support from a wider array of clans such as Tosa in Shikoku and Geishū in Hiroshima would help to consolidate the cause.[2]

Approaches were made on two fronts: on the one hand Ōkubo, Saigō and Komatsu Tatewaki submitted a petition to their strongest supporters among the aristocracy in Kyōto—Nakayama Tadayasu, Ogimachi, Sanjō Sanetomo, Nakamikado Tsuneyuki—wherein they outlined the "crimes" of the Shogun and the need to take extreme action "for the survival of the Imperial realm".[3] At the same time, Ōkubo moved to formally secure the support of the Tosa Clan through Gotō Shōjirō in the June of 1867. Initially there seemed to be broad agreement on a plan of action: Satsuma would deploy troops in Kyōto while Chōshū moved up to Osaka to the South. The Tosa and Geishū Clans would then submit a petition to the Shogun suggesting that he resign from the position of Shogun and convene a national council of Daimyo. But as Ōkubo moved around the country to coordinate the tie-up between Satsuma and Chōshū with Kido Takayoshi, it became apparent that Tosa was much more inclined to submit the petition without the deployment of troops in the first instance. Ōkubo reluctantly agreed, but wrote a series of memoranda to Iwakura Tomomi about the need to pressure wavering elements at court and to push Gotō back to his original undertaking. He also wanted to have a secret edict in place authorizing force against the Bakufu, along with a formal proclamation of the Restoration at hand when the time to act would come. Finally, he astutely maintained contact with the foreign consular representatives, especially the British through Matsuki Kōan to Ernest Satow, and made preparations for them to be summoned to the Imperial capital following the proclamation.[4]

The petition to Yoshinobu was submitted by Gotō's faction to the Senior Counsellor Itakura Katsukiyo on 3 October. In the meantime, Imperial "permission" to topple the Bakufu was secured later the same month and it was now clear that Satsuma and Chōshū would proceed to the military option regardless of how the petition to Yoshinobu worked out.[5] Yoshinobu relinquished his title of Shogun early in November.

From this point, discussion moved to the political "rehabilitation" of the Chōshū Clan enabling their re-entry to the Imperial capital along with the reinstatement of Iwakura Tomomi and Sanjō Sanetomo to high office. The former Shogun was also now being referred to as something akin to a criminal, and avenues of "punishment" for his betrayal of the throne began to be discussed. For Yoshinobu's part, he seemed resigned to the fact that by losing control over the Imperial court, he had lost the means to salvage the Bakufu, but he did not accept the move to sideline him without resistance.

It is also the case that there was a continuing representation of the Tokugawa family in the new political arrangement in the person of Tokugawa Yoshikatsu, the head of the Owari Clan. Moreover, the representative of the Tosa Clan, Yamanouchi Toyonaru, was also significantly in favor of leniency toward the Bakufu. Not that this was likely to ensure the Shogun's reinstatement; it merely sustained the possibility of avoiding complete political oblivion.[6]

So the Restoration was teetering on the brink of realization; any number of things could have happened to thwart the plans of the *Ōsei Fukko* alliance (Gotō Shōjirō was particularly prone to having second thoughts), but the careful coordination of the key players both at the court and in the Domains by Ōkubo, and the highly detailed plans for locking down key areas of the Imperial capital drawn up by Saigō Takamori ensured that the plan proceeded without serious impediment.[7] The Imperial Restoration was formally announced on 9 December with a document that provided a full outline of the structure of the new government. All the top ministries were assigned to members of the aristocracy with the lower-ranked echelon of advisory counselors from the various clans being listed thereafter. With considerable irony, the representatives of the three clans at the centre of the Restoration were listed last.[8]

Tokugawa Yoshinobu withdrew to Osaka Castle to avoid all-out war; however, the depth of resentment toward the Satsuma and Chōshū forces among Bakufu loyalists, particularly the Aizu and Kuwana Clans from the north, was fierce and not easily defused. There was an uneasy period of stasis as the reality of the momentous change sank in and even Iwakura began to become anxious about the way things might turn out. However, when forces from the pro-Bakufu Shōnai Clan encircled the Satsuma military compound in Edo in late December, full-scale conflict seemed inevitable. It broke out on 3 January 1868 at Toba and Fushimi to the south of the Imperial capital and marked the beginning of the series of battles referred to as the Boshin War.[9]

The fighting that erupted between Satsuma-Chōshū forces and Bakufu forces quickly provided a fresh lesson in the superiority of the training and equipment of the new model army. Though outnumbered almost three to one, the Imperial forces sent the Bakufu militias flying within the space of two days of fighting. This undoubtedly convinced Yoshinobu of the futility of attempting to withstand the new government in the West and Osaka Castle was relinquished without a major military engagement. Following a spate of relatively brief encounters on the outskirts of Edo, the formidable castle of the Eastern metropolis was prepared for defense. Ultimately however, this fortress was also relinquished without a protracted campaign. Saigō Takamori, directing the siege and fusillade of the castle, was almost immediately in negotiations with the former Shogun and his retainers to determine the terms of surrender. In the end, a relatively lenient resolution was agreed upon and implemented; the former Shogun and his entourage removed themselves to the Mito Clan lands in the northeast while Yoshinobu's successor took over the castle, formally presenting it to the Imperial forces on 4 April.[10]

A fascinating glimpse of the restoration from an outsider's view is provided by the memoirs of A. B. Mitford,[11] a young career diplomat who distinguished himself in the service of Harry Parkes, the British consul. Mitford was not of the status of either Satow or Parkes but devoted his considerable writing talents to depicting the bathos and occasional brutality of the crossover period, with personal sketches of some of the key players and the most sensational events. On meeting with Tokugawa Yoshinobu immediately prior to the demise of the Bakufu, he notes the exceptional civility and dignity of his host who insisted on presenting Parkes with an artwork that the Englishman happened to admire on the wall. This is contrasted with an excruciatingly poignant description of the soon to be deposed Shogun accompanying his troops from Kyōto to Osaka, his figure slumped forlornly in the saddle with a length of dark cloth entwined about his head. This in turn is contrasted with the vivid description of fearfully attired *samurai* bands seeming to rove the area under a multitude of leaders, scarcely concealing their contempt for the foreigners and in some instances actually succumbing to the temptation of violent confrontation.

One particularly bloody episode was the attack by Tosa troops on unarmed French sailors landing at Sakai. Eleven in all were killed or wounded, and once the perpetrators and their apparent leader were identified they were duly ordered to perform *seppuku*. This they did, with Mitford and Parkes actually being at hand to witness the solitary act of the alleged leader in the confines of his cell. The others were to perform their sentences before French military observers in public. The bloody ritual was punctuated by the screaming of curses at the French as each warrior disemboweled himself. This was evidently too much for the French to endure at any length and so a stop was made at the eleventh *samurai*.[12]

Even when Parkes was to be the first foreigner to have an audience with the Emperor, Mitford was there to accompany him (Satow was ironically regarded as ineligible due to not having been presented to the British Queen). Their first attempt to wend their way through the ancient capital to the palace grounds ended in farce as two masterless *samurai* attacked the convoy with the aim of assassinating Parkes. Nine personnel were wounded but miraculously none fatally. Their next attempt to meet the Emperor was more successful and Mitford's detailed description of the relentless rain, drenched courtyards and a 15-minute audience with a 16-year-old Mutsuhito, his teeth blackened and eyebrows shaved, whispering utterances to an intermediary who relayed them on his behalf, is particularly memorable.[13]

The instability and danger evident in the aforementioned account must have been even more keenly felt by those in the Restoration leadership who were attempting to control the outcome of such wild forces. Certainly they were building on a momentum toward a political resolution that had been in train for some 15 years, yet they were also the bearers of a vision that could not be easily imparted to even their own supporters let alone the population at large. An indication of just how vulnerable Ōkubo felt at the time about the new regime is illustrated by his little-known proposal to shift the Imperial court to Osaka, all the better to consolidate the military position and liaise with foreign diplomats. It was not met with any enthusiasm, but is instructive nonetheless.[14]

It is also perhaps tempting to depict Yoshinobu as a weak-willed commander. Yet there was more than mere military prowess that he was contending against. The new army was now under the formal command of a member of the Imperial family, Ninnajinomiya Yoshiakira, who was styled as a Shogun (the title relinquished only months earlier by Yoshinobu himself) with the Imperial brief of toppling the "rebels" toward the throne. Moreover, the army was presented with a flag of the Imperial colors graphically signifying that an attack on the bearers of the flag was an attack on Imperial authority.[15]

Consequently, the predominantly Satsuma- and Chōshū-led forces were not merely a re-equipped army in a technological sense but a primary example of how the reform of the configuration between the political and ceremonial was being carried out in practice. The victorious troops of the battles at Toba and Fushimi were reviewed en masse by the Emperor in person and drank ceremonially blessed sake, arguably prefiguring the emergence of future militaristic practices. This was an irresistible new combination and Yoshinobu knew it to be such.

The perceptiveness and sense of resignation in Yoshinobu was not, however, immediately shared by all his followers. Determined resistance to the government was encountered in the surrounding areas of Edo at first and then, even more trenchantly, among the central northern Clans of Aizu, Echigo and Oū. Serious defeats were inflicted on the Imperial forces on several occasions yet given the perpetually fragmented character of the opposition forces, the overall tide of the war was moving in the new government's favor.[16]

The Powers, as has been alluded to previously, maintained strict neutrality, which was as much as giving tacit consent to the new government. A new ironclad, the *Stonewall*, imported from the US by the Bakufu was impounded by the Americans before being delivered, ostensibly in the interests of "neutrality"; however, once the decisive battles had been fought and won on the mainland, the US government relented and delivered the *Stonewall* to the new government forces. It was with this that they were able to complete the task of quelling the last pocket of resistance in Hokkaidō under Enomoto Takeaki.

Reconfiguring the state

The end of open hostilities was the end of the coup d'état's first phase. Having established military control over the entire country, the government now had to turn to matters of detail with regard to national policy. We should appreciate the fact that as yet there was no clear consensus on what concrete institutional changes would accompany the Restoration. In line with the avowed return to the Ritsu-ryō system of the eighth century, the Dajōkan was re-established and Ministers of the Left and Right, along with the superintendent Dajō-daijin, were duly appointed, all of them nobles of course. Shintō was resurrected from out of the miasma of centuries of religious syncretism and a discrete ceremonial practice established through the *Jingikan*. Nonetheless, the sheer magnitude of the gap between ancient "practice" (or what was known of it) and the contemporary political and social reality produced inevitable shortfalls, blank areas and backtracking. Itō Hirobumi and Ōkubo Toshimichi were at one point given somewhat contrived noble titles to enable them to participate in government deliberations at court. Court attire was also determined according to conventions over a thousand years old. Buddhist institutions were literally ransacked as a part of the process of reasserting the pre-eminence of the Shintō faith over the later "foreign" import.[17] And there were large numbers of armed malcontents, both within the Imperial army and the body of the now politically disenfranchised supporters of the former government, who were expecting the new government to unleash the fury of the ancient deities on all foreign interlopers forthwith.

Ōkubo and Kido pressed on with consolidating the perception of the new regime as a new form of centralized government that would transcend the old clan structures. The Charter Oath which was promulgated on 17 April 1868, was ostensibly an undertaking sworn by the Emperor before the ancestral deities and can be seen as a vehicle by which they consciously aimed to highlight precisely the new character of the state and the relation of the people to it. The oath consisted of five articles as follows:

(1) To consult widely and decide all matters through debate.
(2) To unite the hearts of all people regardless of rank to fully consider the proper way forward.
(3) To require all persons, from government officials to the commoners, to follow their chosen vocation without faltering.
(4) To discard the useless customs of the past and act according to the just way of heaven and earth.
(5) To seek knowledge throughout the world in order to strengthen the foundation of Imperial rule.[18]

There was a clear commitment to an inclusiveness and social dynamism that would have been inconceivable under the Bakufu. The new leadership was attempting to convince those outside the Satsuma and Chōshū Clans that the new government would not simply be another Bakufu, as well as sending out a clear message that Japanese society would be reconfigured according to a more effective standard of utilizing the nation's human resources. It also signaled that the world would be a place to seek new knowledge, implying of course that foreigners and foreign countries were no longer to be rejected, so long as it was in the interest of the realm.[19]

Incidentally, it should be noted here that a commitment to inclusiveness does not automatically imply an accommodation of demands for Western-style institutions of representative government. As the *Seitaisho*

(政体書), which was released soon after the text of the Charter Oath was made public, illustrates, the emphasis was on confirming the sovereignty of the Emperor and the authority of his ministers, with explicit reference to the fact that the "minor authority" of personal interests should not conflict with the "major authority" of the Imperial government.[20] The emphasis was on harnessing the potential of the entire population toward the enhancement of Imperial sovereignty and national strength; these were not intrinsically democratic or liberal imperatives in themselves.

The end of the hostilities on the mainland in the November of 1868 ushered in a period of relative quiet in political developments. The military brains of the Boshin War, most notably Saigō Takamori, returned to their home domains in the West while Ōkubo Toshimichi and Kido Takayuki attempted to cement the credibility of the new regime in the face of residual domestic hostility in the East and an as yet not altogether convinced foreign community. Ōkubo himself seemed to slip into the new ways of conducting affairs with ease, traveling to Edo by British steamer and dining at a Western restaurant. He ensured that the new Emperor also came out of the cloister of the palace, arranging for him to visit both Osaka and Edo in person. This was undoubtedly aimed at transforming the perception of the Emperor as a modern sovereign as well as accentuating the Emperor's connection to the new government.[21]

Nevertheless the calm was violently disrupted early in 1869 with the assassination of Yokoi Shōnan near the grounds of the Imperial palace in Kyōto. It highlighted the continued risk posed by disgruntled *samurai* and, although Ōkubo's diary suggests that he took it in a characteristically stoic fashion, the event nonetheless had a major impact on him. Ōkubo turned his attentions to refining the structure of the new administration, establishing an Office of Internal Affairs (*Naimukyoku*, 内務局) and gradually laying the foundations of what would be the most significant initiative of the government since the restoration itself, the abolition of independent clans and their replacement with Prefectures (Haihan Chiken, 廃藩置県).[22]

In order to press ahead with these reforms, the heads of the Satsuma and Chōshū domains were summoned to Edo but only the head of the Chōshū clan arrived. Saigō also refused to attend. Ōkubo and Kido made extensive attempts to personally cajole the disparate factions to rally round the government in Edo but found that mutual suspicion and conflicting conceptions of how the new government should function kept them away. The essence of Shimazu Hisamitsu's and Saigō Takamori's reluctance to return ultimately stemmed from the realization that the Restoration was no longer simply a Satsuma affair. Ōkubo had made a point of involving people of talent regardless of their clan affiliations, and to a large extent he acted on that undertaking in good faith. The deadlock continued well into 1870 but was ultimately broken through the dispatching of Iwakura as the Emperor's personal envoy to deliver a personal command for their attendance in Edo. Both Hisamitsu and Saigō relented.[23]

It is significant that here, as in previous cases, the Imperial "will" was to prove a decisive factor in resolving otherwise insoluble differences. The effectiveness of the Imperial decree was also backed by the astute move to entrench the new government in the East at the seat of the former Bakufu. The decision was taken early to discreetly move the Imperial court from Kyōto to Edo, which was to be renamed Tōkyōto (the Eastern Imperial capital). It was not a move that was welcomed by the nobility, nor of course the body of Restorationists who regarded Kyōto as the logical choice for an Imperial government, but it was logistically sensible and made the emphatic point that whatever shape the government would take in terms of constituting a Restoration, it would nonetheless be a fully centralized *national* administration, something that was, strictly speaking, unprecedented. Satsuma and Chōshū may well provide the military spine in the new regime but that was not the same as constituting the government.[24]

Ōkubo and Kido were also remarkably faithful to the aim of fulfilling the undertakings made in the oath. The *Kōgisho* (an assembly of the nation's clan representatives numbering in excess of 260 persons) was established for the debate of matters of state and included representatives of each domain. It is also fair to say that both Ōkubo and Kido burned their bridges with the old domain structure in one way or another during the period following the cessation of war. Their commitment to a new form of central government was clearly demonstrated through the move to have domain lands formally "returned" to the Imperial throne in the July of 1869 (*Hanseki Hōkan,* 版籍奉還). But perhaps, a more telling example is provided by the restructuring of the national army. The Chōshū army was a particular case in point; despite the successes achieved over a number of years by this close-knit domain-based entity, there was a determined trimming of its personnel and a review of the command structure during the Boshin War that made it clear that the old, almost parochial, basis of military service was no longer the norm. Substantial numbers of veterans—the aged, the less able and the less disciplined—were shed in favor of enhancing the discipline and overall professionalism of the national army. Dissension, which included an open revolt in Chōshū, was mercilessly quelled and punished by none other than Kido Takayoshi himself. The resultant force was reformed and re-stationed permanently in the new national capital.[25]

As this process of redefining the nature of central government was being pursued in the military sphere, a parallel process of refining the organs of government was also under way. Initially, the supreme authority within the Restoration government lay, theoretically at least, with the noble-born Arisugawanomiya Taruhito who held the position of *Sōsai* (総裁) from December 1867 until July 1869. Under him were assorted members of the aristocracy and hereditary feudal domain chiefs, the Gijō (議定), who were to act as a complementary delibera-tive body. Beneath them were the Sanyo (参与) essentially counsellors of low rank, who in some cases had dual roles as consulting officials to the upper institutions. The irony, of course, was that this lower level of government, at one time or another, contained the main players of the new regime, from Ōkubo and Kido to the next generation of leaders such as Itō Hirobumi and Inoue Kaoru.[26]

In July of 1869, a major restructuring of the institutions of state was carried out; the former largely unworkable system of ministries based more or less directly on the ancient administrative code was substan-tially expanded with separate ministerial jurisdiction for finance and internal affairs. The *Sōsai* Arisugawa was replaced by Sanjō Sanetomo in the position of *Udaijin* (the Minister of the Right, a title retaining the terminology of ministerial positions within the *Dajōkan*) while the *Sanyo* were also restyled as *Sangi* (参議) which later formed the basis of the *Sangiin*, an institution that was to remain in place until the establish-ment of the cabinet system in 1885. The formal unification of the army and navy into one centrally integrated command structure occurred in the October of the following year with a Ministry of Construction being established at the same time.[27]

All these administrative initiatives formed an important backdrop to the transformation of a Satsuma- and Chōshū-led military alliance into a genuine central government. Iwakura's effectively ordering the head of the Satsuma Domain to attend the court in Tokyo in December 1870 was the first test of the new government's capacity to wield this new form of authority. The assassination of Hirosawa Saneomi at the begin-ning of 1871 did not auger well for future stability but by mid-1871, the new government was ready for a second push of reform that would fulfill in practice the formal undertaking of the Charter Oath to facili-tate the full participation of the citizenry in national life regardless of birth; something that also ensured that Ōkubo and Kido were destined for a violent collision with the defenders of *samurai* privilege.[28]

The events of mid-1871, which in some instances have been referred to as a "second" coup d'état, were preceded by the blanket dismissal of all *Sangi* except Kido along with the appointment of Saigō Takamori as a new addition. Sanjō Sanetomo was re-titled the *Dajōdaijin*, and new Ministries of Education and Justice were established. More significant, however, was the formal process of abolishing the domains and establishing prefectures in their stead. The groundwork for this had been established through the formal return of lands and people to the Emperor (*Hanseki Hōkan*) the previous year, but the promulgation of a new law covering registration, the *Koseki-hō* (戸籍法), did not in fact emerge until the April of 1871. It was one thing to grasp military control of the country and bring sovereignty into one focal point around the Emperor but quite another to establish centralized organs of government that would exercise authority in the name of that sovereignty supplanting the former relatively disparate patchwork of domain administrations.[29]

Another matter of considerable significance that arose during this period was the abolition of the *samurai* prerogative to wear swords. The first government member to dare suggest that the custom be discontinued was Mori Arinori from Satsuma who submitted a memorandum to the *Kōgisho* in the August of 1871. The proposal was rejected unanimously and, before long, Mori had to flee to his home domain to escape assassination. Nonetheless the government succeeded in passing legislation to gradually disarm the *samurai*, starting first with those who were strictly speaking non-*samurai* by birth but awarded the right to wear the two swords as a special token of recognition for exceptional service. Thereafter, the abolition of the wearing of swords for all except government officials and military officers, and the requirement to dispense with the traditional hairstyle in favor of the Western style haircut was forced, though in line with the broader reforms of the armed forces. With officers of state now compelled to conform to these requirements, there was little leeway for ordinary citizens to not follow suit.[30]

It was this that enabled the general citizenry and military classes to coexist in the civilian setting without too overt a dislocation; professional soldiers in England would wear civilian clothes when not on duty or at formal functions, a fact that astounded earlier *samurai* commentators on their first visits to that country. The former Satsuma and Chōshū students who had spent time in such social contexts overseas understood the implications well and it is therefore not altogether merely coincidental that the *samurai*'s traditional right of bearing arms in public was revoked during the same phase as the army's realignment toward a centralized authority. The *samurai* backlash was totally predictable but the logic of proscribing the practice was also irresistible; sword-bearing was officially banned within the year.[31]

By late 1871, the new configuration of the polity had been set, or at least adequately solidified, to give the new government the appearance of permanent, palpable legitimacy. The "return" of the domain registers to the throne brought the national administrative structure into the same compass of sacred association that previously had been limited to the new model Imperial army. The Emperor was now permanently in the new capital, and the government was now ostensibly a fresh entity constituting a fundamental break from the previous political order.

All the foregoing developments were to enable the new leaders the opportunity to step back and ponder over their next initiatives in developing national policy in detail. In many regards, it would prove more difficult to attain a consensus on this than on political arrangements on the macro level. There remained a substantial impetus driving toward the establishment of a reincarnated ancient Imperial model of government, within which the promulgation of a new exclusively Shintō state orthodoxy and a new model priesthood was to be realized. However, the more practically minded leaders such as Ōkubo and Kido, along with those who had had first-hand experience of the West such as Itō Hirobumi and Inoue Kaoru, were aware of the essential folly of attempting to fulfill the imperatives of a modern state on the basis of such archaic and essentially illusory foundations.[32]

It is at this juncture that the decisive break between the political core of the Restoration leadership and the reactionary or traditionalist cultural elements in the Restoration Movement in general comes to the fore. The relation between the state and ceremonial institutions which had been primarily promoted in terms of complete integration (*Saisei Itchi*, 祭政一致) was being revised toward a configuration that prioritized the needs of the state as a modern governing system; the Imperial Household, the revived ancient ceremonial office of the Heian Court, the *Jingikan*, and the new State Shinto were being put to one side as the business of government took precedence. It was a decisive revision of the earlier revivalist aspirations of the original Restoration Movement as expressed in terms such as *Ōsei Fukko* (王政復古) and *Fukko Ishin* (復古維新), which denoted an unambiguous renaissance of the ancient.

At the same time, however, one aspect of the original Restoration agenda that could not be so easily put in abeyance was the issue of redressing the situation with the "unequal treaties". The fact that the Western powers could not be summarily driven out even by the new Imperial army was well and truly apparent, yet there were still substantial proportions of the nobility and the *samurai* class who regarded the re-attainment of full military and diplomatic independence as the crucial measure of the new government's worth and ultimate legitimacy.

Accordingly, a rather astounding initiative was undertaken toward the end of 1871 to, in effect, send the very highest officials of government to tour the Western powers en masse. It was a move that made sense in terms of addressing the residual resistance to the nation's administrative reorganization as well as being seen to be acting on the imperative to revise Japan's relations with foreign powers. It was also an important exercise in cementing the conclusion in Western perceptions that the new government was indeed a legitimate one and "here to stay".

The Iwakura Mission

The Mission was to be headed by Iwakura Tomomi himself with Ōkubo Toshimichi, Itō Hirobumi and Kido Takayoshi in his company. The contrast in the manner with which the Mission was planned and executed, compared with earlier Bakufu initiatives, was substantial. On this occasion, someone who could genuinely negotiate as a minister plenipotentiary had been sent as the delegation's head. The delegation included high-ranking officials such as Itō Hirobumi who had first-hand experience of living in the West and the ability to communicate in English. Mori Arinori whose talents in such regards were exceptional had already been dispatched to the US as charge d'affairs. The Mission was also not overwhelmingly top-heavy; apart from the official entourage of 46,[33] it included 60 young persons of talent, many of whom would remain overseas to continue their studies (including three young women who were to attend Vassar College). This mission, unlike any previous one, was well-focused on garnering a broad array of cultural as well as military and technical intelligence; the need for a better understanding of what made Western societies function on a broad institutional and cultural level was at last acknowledged and being acted upon by the nation's leaders.

The Mission departed from Yokohama in December of 1871, arriving in the US on 15 January of the following year. Before departing, Iwakura Tomomi was presented with a letter from the Emperor which outlined the Mission's essential aims: to pursue the renegotiation of the "unequal treaties" that denied Japanese autonomy in relation to tariffs and legal jurisdiction over foreign nationals, to promote better relations with the

Western powers and consolidate international support for the Imperial government, and to engage in the exhaustive investigation of Western societies to gain an understanding of their technology and institutions. It had been decided to approach the West via the US first for the reason that America remained the foremost partner in international intercourse in terms of trade and they could arguably rightly expect a considerably more accommodating reception there than in Britain or France. Mori Arinori, now the charge d'affairs stationed in Washington, had made substantial progress in cultivating goodwill with the Americans, having cooperated with Joseph Henry in arrangements for a US geographical expedition in the vicinity of Japan and even managing to lobby Congress to release the funds procured from the Japanese government over the Shimonoseki Indemnity and have them returned with a view to establishing a modern library.[34]

It was perhaps understandable then that once the Mission landed in the US, they felt there was some real possibility of making a quick resolution of the treaty issue. Itō and Mori were instrumental in persuading Iwakura to pursue full negotiations in Washington. Unfortunately, however, the inexperience of the delegates was quickly exposed; Hamilton Fish, the then Secretary of State, while accommodating of the proposal to commence negotiations in principle, found to his dismay that the letter entrusted to Iwakura by the Emperor did not actually provide him with adequate credentials to pursue full and conclusive negotiations on the government's behalf. A letter fulfilling that requirement was quickly dispatched (indeed Itō raced back to Japan to retrieve it in person).[35]

Nonetheless, by the time these formalities were dealt with, other difficulties arose on the basis of the most-favored nation status of the Western European powers. Fish could not commit the US to conclusive revisions without liaising with his European counterparts. He also did not want to appear to be pre-empting any such negotiations by committing to a new arrangement prematurely. The Japanese side proposed a draft treaty that the US could sign after which a round of comprehensive and concerted diplomacy could be undertaken in Europe. Fish declined.

Consequently, the Mission got off to a rocky start so far as the diplomatic question was concerned, due to inexperience and misjudgment. It was not necessarily a mistake to engage in such discussions; however, the limitations of the possibilities should have been more fully understood and a great deal of wastage of time could have been avoided.

One point in relation to the diplomatic issue that merits re-emphasis here is the fact that the unequal treaties remained an important sticking point in domestic politics. For many, the Restoration had been all about revising such insults and though dissatisfaction toward the government on this issue had not erupted into armed revolt, the potential was still there and the leadership was well aware of it. It was just as much this factor as well as "bad advice" that contributed to the premature attempts to obtain a resolution. Realistic observers appreciated that such issues were unlikely to be easily resolved any time soon but, in any event, the initiative of the international Mission had been overtly linked to treaty matters through the Emperor's letter and the public perception that the Mission would act upon such concerns was enough to buy them some goodwill. As the next two decades of unrest indicate, the treaty issue was always a matter of profound popular interest and one of the most useful accelerants for maximizing popular political clout.

Quite apart from diplomatic initiatives, however, it was by no means a waste of time to have the opportunity to examine American technological developments and cultural institutions in more depth. Those not engaged in diplomatic work pursued detailed investigations of every manner of social phenomena, from factories and schools to the practical workings of the Congress.

The long-term reflection of the Mission's investigations in the US was the participants' less-than-enamored view of American political institutions, a perspective which was nonetheless counterbalanced by their being highly impressed by America's educational institutions. There was an eminent pragmatism about American scholarship which resonated with Japanese concerns to achieve concrete improvements, particularly as they related to commercial and technical education, and so it should not be so great a surprise that when the first major initiatives in national educational reform were being undertaken by the government in the latter half of the 1870s, there was the unmistakable reliance on the American model as a guide to curriculum and educational administration.[36]

The transit to England was smooth and the Mission landed in Liverpool harbor on 17 August after setting out nine days earlier. The sojourn in England was arguably a happier one; the distraction of the diplomatic issue was laid to one side and the senior members of the delegation who were by now much better versed in diplomatic protocol prepared for what lay ahead. The stay in Britain was also an extended one but this seems to have been largely by choice (the lengthy absence of the Queen from London was naturally of some consequence but it did not require an extension when a return visit from the continent was a feasible option). Britain remained the industrial nation *par excellence*, and no opportunity to travel far and wide within the realm was turned down.[37] Moreover, the Meiji delegation, unlike its Bakufu predecessor ten years earlier, was able to present a much more sophisticated and engaging public image. With the exception of Iwakura, most of the senior delegates were already accustomed to being attired in Western costume and, as has already been alluded to, a number of them had more than passable abilities in conversational English.

The Mission crossed over to France on 16 December which constituted the start of an extensive tour of the leading nations and capitals of the continent. Two months were spent in France, compared with three weeks in Germany, three weeks in Russia and a number of much shorter sojourns in Sweden, Belgium, the Netherlands, Switzerland and Italy.

The transit to continental Europe was to represent something of a fundamental shift in perceptions and evaluations of the West. Firstly, the West as a monolithic cultural entity would cease to be a plausible construct; very profound differences in historical development, language and religion made themselves obvious, the more so as the delegation ventured to Europe's eastern and northeastern extremities. Secondly, the depth of mutual suspicion and rivalry would be amply evident, perhaps nowhere more obvious than in the battle-scarred monuments of Paris that had succumbed to damage during the Franco-Prussian War two years earlier. Thirdly, the Mission would be presented with a very different view of how religion influenced the political and moral landscape of Western societies, providing instances of thinly concealed exploitation and manipulation of the masses who in the worst cases were encouraged to remain superstitious and ignorant. Nonetheless, the role of religion in the likes of Britain and America was recognized as relatively salutary due to the fact that it did not hinder commercial and educational progress or prop up an indolent and essentially parasitic aristocracy.[38]

Overall, the continental experience confirmed the significance of commerce and education in promoting national prosperity and a high degree of "civilization". France was recognized as the great centre of manufacture in Europe and remarkably resilient to the impositions of reparations following the Franco-Prussian War precisely on that account. The widespread exposure to the public of traditional artifacts and treasures in museums, along with the latest discoveries in the natural world and realms of scientific discovery through zoos and expositions were also noted for their educational capacity.

Yet the patterns of achievement were extremely uneven. Civilization was relative even within the "West" and, as Kume rather astutely points out, some of the most advanced achievements of these societies were in fact astonishingly recent (within 40 years in cases such as the steam engine). The key seemed to lie in achieving a balance between commerce and agriculture, machinery and labor and the right amount of government coordination and legal backup to enable the entire system to function smoothly. He even highlights the significance of advanced systems of transport and logistics management, noting how various countries, whether Holland in relation to its maritime power or Germany with its new control over the inland waterways of the Alsace-Lorraine region, formed the basis of exponentially expanding trade. This was not some unfathomable mystery but an eminently employable model well within the grasp of Japan if the resources and energies of the nation could be focused on the task.[39]

Among the "dangers" to be contended with, Kume highlights the threat posed by the willful and uneducated masses clamoring for "representation" and "liberty", especially as exemplified in the likes of the Paris Commune. Republicanism was viewed with frank suspicion and held up as evidence of the need for qualified admiration of the Western example. Nonetheless, Kume did identify the need to promote an independent and well-motivated populace recognizing that the fruits of civilization could not be attained on the basis of the tradition that the paternalistic mode of government maintained in the east. This is not the contradiction it seems; intellectual independence and self-motivation do not automatically imply radically representative forms of democratic government (indeed the electoral franchise in Britain at that time was substantially limited).

This is an important point to make given that the conclusion might be drawn that those who were involved with the Mission or later returned to Japan after extended periods of study overseas could not help but be impressed with Western representative political institutions and a burning desire to recreate them in their homeland.

In tandem with the Kume record, we should also note the output of Japan's first official diplomatic representative in the US as charge d'affaires, Mori Arinori. During his two-year sojourn, he produced a number of short works, mainly in English, including a general overview of the US entitled "Life and Resources in America". The aspect of this work that should receive greatest attention is the frankly critical appraisal of the American political system. Given Mori's famous (or perhaps "infamous") proposal to make English the *lingua publica* of Japan, his forthright criticisms of endemic corruption and procedural inefficiency tend to be neglected. The condition of the American Republic at the time of Mori's tenure as charge d'affaires, and of course the Iwakura Mission's transit, was one that reflected the excesses of the post-Civil

War settlement, including the attempted impeachment of Andrew Johnson, along with the scandal surrounding the ostensibly popular yet politically inept Ulysses S. Grant. It was precisely while Mori was in Washington that various political "rings", including the infamous "Tweed ring", were exposed as being thoroughly enmeshed in influence peddling and vote rigging, even at the highest levels of state.[40]

Consequently, the response to the Western "models" on offer was at once far more ambivalent and nuanced than tends to be realized; and not without good reason in some cases. Ironically, it was actually those who had little or no experience of the West who were the most ardent advocates of direct imitation. Prime examples are Tokutomi Sohō and Itagaki Taisuke, the government actually paying for the latter to visit Europe to see and find out for himself, confident that such an experience would cool his ardor for immediate reform.

We also cannot assume that this ambivalence toward Western political institutions signified a reactionary impulse or unreconstructed authoritarianism. As Mori's investigations of American society were to demonstrate convincingly, the effective functioning of representative political organs and civic institutions relied in great part on the education and character of the citizenry. This could not be replicated in Japan in a matter of months or years but would require a longer strategy. Ultimately, therefore, the main dictate was to find a way of establishing an infrastructure that would conform to the essentials of the Western commercial and administrative model while retaining a degree of continuity with existing traditional institutions; in this regard, there was no departure from the essential premise of the Restoration. In other respects, the expectation was that the Japanese people would have to evolve into a populace capable of sustaining such a dynamic and internally regulated system.

Consequently, one of the overarching results of the Iwakura Mission was to clarify the dimensions of what obstacles lay ahead for the full implementation of a centralized government with a nationally integrated citizenry. It would not simply be a matter of establishing key government institutions and delineating legal boundaries; a new form of national culture would also have to be developed and it would be the education system that would play a central role in achieving this aim.

A national culture

The question of what manner of culture would complement the new social order established through the virtual disestablishment of the domains and the *samurai* class arose as a clear issue that participants in the freshly opened up spheres of public discourse took up with a passion. It is this context that provides the springboard for what we latter discuss under the rubric of "Bunmei Kaika", a term commonly translated as "Civilization and Enlightenment" and associated most often with the *Meirokusha* which was established in 1873 some time after the Mission's return. In the following chapter, I will argue in some detail why the use of such terminology is unhelpful to our understanding of this transitional period; however, before undertaking to clarify the contemporary significance of *Bunmei Kaika* (or *Kaika*) in specifics, some broader consideration of the social and cultural developments in the wake of the Restoration is necessary.

From 1869 onward, a movement to clarify the dimensions of a new sphere of cultural and political negotiation was already well underway, and not altogether with results that the new government would condone. One of the best introductions to where the impetus and essential character of the movement derived from has been expounded by Kosaka Masaaki. In a post-war work, re-edited and published as *Meiji Shiso Shi*,[41] he masterfully outlines the transformation of the worldview that occurred in the years immediately following the Restoration. He depicts how public sentiment, which was still firmly grounded in notions of reverence for the Emperor coupled with the fanatical aim of expelling foreigners from the country came to be transformed to the extent that the public were embracing the program of opening the country and cultural refurbishment a mere three or four years later. The year 1869 was when Yokoi Shōnan was brutally assassinated on a Kyōto street by Tsuge Shirozaemon for disrespect to the Imperial throne and collaborating with foreigners, and that was perfectly in keeping with the dominant values of the *samurai* and indeed a greater proportion of the public at the time. The same year was also when the national administration took a great leap backward into the ancient past with the rebirth of the *Taihō* Code.

Kosaka defines the decisive turning point away from the retrospective movement as 1871 with the implementation of the policy to abolish the Domains and the promotion of the *Dajōkan* above the *Jingikan*. More importantly, he notes the transformation of the daily lives of people in the cities: the first railways, the first postal services and, for the broader population, the implementation of (notionally at least) a national education system and a system of military conscription. The ultimate mark of personal transformation was, naturally enough, the cutting of hair in the Western style. None of these things are of course causally sufficient, but they indicate more precisely how the new-model Japanese citizen was beginning to emerge out of the chrysalis of the Restoration.

In reality, the lives of those living in the countryside varied to some extent depending on their proximity to major urban centers or profitable commodities; a substantial proportion, however, were to witness the effect of an influx of foreign-made goods that would drive many of the traditional artisans and manufacturers into penury, while also draining the nation of gold and silver reserves that were the main recourse for obtaining foreign currency. The urban public would experience the negative impact of opening the internal markets as well but there was the consolation of new commodities and conveniences that had the undeniable capacity to enthrall the popular imagination. There were tangible signs of "progress" in the form of new public buildings, post offices and railway stations—as well as new urban shopping precincts (such as the one at Ginza) with the newly established network of gas lamps. There was also the hitherto unimaginable convenience of new forms of transport such as the postal steamer and—albeit in relatively limited geographical cases—the railroad. There were new modes of communication such as the daily newspaper and the telegraph. It did not particularly matter that not everyone could afford to personally utilize or experience these inventions in their personal lives, what mattered most was that it gave concrete expression to a new form of national lifestyle.[42]

The initial newspapers were extremely limited in geographical reach to the major urban centers of Kantō and Kansai, yet they gradually came to be emulated in the countryside toward the end of the1870s. The advertisements of the first mass-produced newspapers were limited in the scope of their content to steamship companies and luxury items thereby suggesting that their readership was far from being among the urban rank and file. By contrast, private consumption did undergo an extraordinary degree of transformation through the proliferation of the distinctive packaging for daily items, especially the cans and bottles that were increasingly being produced en masse locally. These were relatively simple personal items that could be obtained by ordinary persons for daily use and were remodeled in a manner that fused traditional Japanese printing techniques with the Roman alphabet and foreign iconography.[43] Early examples are found in the packaging of medicines and cosmetics but later on, this came to include a boom in the consumption of matches and soap, two other items that were produced in substantial quantities domestically from the mid-1870s onward.

Of equal significance to this was the fact that the Meiji Emperor himself had been remodeled and repackaged as a modern sovereign. He and his retinue were presented in early Meiji prints predominantly in Western dress. He now rode a horse and dined on Western cuisine.

If the Emperor himself was undergoing these changes, it must have seemed little short of disrespect to not do likewise. It should also be noted that there was a decidedly military emphasis in the new profile being given to the throne. The Western attire was almost exclusively that of a military commander, the horse riding that he undertook was actually part of a daily regimen of training that included shooting practice and parade ground drills. This was part of the deliberate "trade-off" of traditional forms and customs for the appropriation of Western military prowess, always one of the practical military objectives that unpinned the *Sonnō Jōi* movement. The regimen of military training was actually Saigō Takamori's idea and it provides an insight into how his conception of what Restoration meant for national reconstruction differed in subtle ways to that of Ōkubo and Kido.[44]

In conjunction with these changes among the commoner public and within the court, there was also a transformation of the intellectual outlook of the urban educated public, a significant portion of which was lower-ranking *samurai*. In this regard, Fukuzawa Yukichi is rightly highlighted as being one of the primary exponents of redefining that outlook. To use Kosaka's terms, Fukuzawa mediated a "transformation of life's purpose" within a new social arrangement where ability would count for much more than rank, not in absolute terms, but significantly enough to make the iron cage of unwarranted privilege disappear.[45] Indeed there would be opportunities for *samurai*, and even the more able members from non-*samurai* castes, to find new vocations in either the newly formed system of national administration or the newly expanded horizon of the national economy, made possible as it was by the newly expanded network of cultural interaction.[46]

Fukuzawa's other significant contribution to the new cultural movement was that he was one of the first to use the term *Bunmei Kaika* in print. That is not to say that there were not other cases than his, as it is clear that both terms were separately current prior to Fukuzawa writing *Seiyō Jijō*. Fukuzawa was a pamphleteer and popularizer par excellence, yet he was not the only one to enjoy publishing success and one also needs to bear in mind the fact that employing a phrase to denote a new social movement is not the same as actually creating it. Indeed the terms *Kaika* and *Bunmei Kaika* had a separate life among the popular urban press where, perhaps quite surprisingly, the tone was at times derogatory and derisive.[47]

Conseqently, *Kaika* was not exclusively concerned with the adaptation of Western technology and culture but was, perhaps more significantly, tied up with the clarification of an *indigenous* cultural reconfiguration. We are perhaps too quick to assume that by "Bunmei", the Japanese were referring to Western civilization. This was undoubtedly the case for some writers at the time (as well as a considerable portion of the reading public); however, we ought not to forget that, since the words "Bunmei" and "Kaika" were current before the Restoration, they had an intrinsic domain of meaning much broader than the post-1868 circumstances might tend to suggest.[48] Naturally the fount of that learning up until the Bakumatsu period was predominantly Chinese. With the opening of the country and the accommodation of non-Chinese letters into the first rank of study, certainly the purview of the term was transformed, but not altogether.

To locate the evolution of these words within the context of the milieu that Kosaka so vividly conjures up, especially in the sense of moving from profound seclusionism to an embracing of the outside world, we can even interpret "Bunmei Kaika" as the opening up of *Japanese* civilization, particularly in the realm of culture and learning. *Bunmei Kaika* was primarily a cultural movement, not a political movement; it was the intellectual correlate to *kaikoku* (開国), opening the country.

Additional insights into the nature of this transformation of the world of letters in modernizing societies is provided by Ernest Gellner's *Nations and Nationalism*, one of the rare expositions of modernization that accounts for the transformation of culture in the age of industrialization and nationalism without recourse to ethnocentrism. Gellner aptly accentuates how a certain universalization and meritocratization of the mode of educating emerges in tandem with the rationalization of other aspects of industrialized societies. The imperative of the modern nation state is simply to meld the populace contained within a given geographical area to the seamless (i.e., unitary) state apparatus that exerts exclusive authority over it. This process of integration is inevitably complicated by religious and ethnic factors but what ultimately matters is that *somehow* an ethos of identification with the state is achieved; this is an open problem that each potential nation state has to resolve, and when it does so it often achieves it imperfectly, albeit on its own terms and largely in its own unique way.[49]

The key contention here is that this phase of cultural redefinition mediates a transition from elite-to-elite dissemination of knowledge—the maintenance of a "high tradition" of education and cultural reproduction—to a mode of discourse that is altogether more homogenous, open and standardized; yet at the same time, this does not presuppose the necessity of a liberal or universalist content to that education.

The *Bunmei Kaika* movement was in essence the first stage of clearing the way for this melding process to come into effect. Whether the content of the new discourse was liberal or reactionary, universalist or particularist, is naturally of interest yet it remains secondary to the matter of creating the preconditions for developing a truly homogeneous *national* culture.

Internal reform: Rebellion and conservatism

The year 1873, when the Iwakura Mission returned from its overseas tour, was to become a key turning point in the development of both the infrastructure of government and a national culture. But it was a phase that would be marked by an extremely turbulent phase of internal unrest. As is well documented, the caretaker government under Saigō Takamori had managed to keep the new mandate in tact, but at the same time the most prominent leaders of *shizoku* class who had been at the forefront of the military campaigns of 1868 and 1869 had begun to develop an agenda independently of the absent ministers of state. Mention has already been made of the crisis that confronted the government in the immediate aftermath of the Boshin War which was resolved in 1871 with the dissolution of the domains and the establishment of the first genuinely centralized organs of government. The neutralizing (or rather circumventing) of clan-aligned militias was naturally a vital step in fulfilling that objective, but the *shizoku* were far from being a neutralized force in the nation's culture and local politics.[50]

The origin of that influence lay in the fact that *shizoku* were a class that combined the privilege of being armed in public with exclusive access to higher education and so it should not surprise us that even though they may have lost certain outward signs of the status through the banning of wearing swords in public, they continued to take the lead in administration, business and education. The government for its part knew all too well that there were limits to how far they could marginalize this class, the retention of *shizoku* as a separate classification from the general citizenry *heimin* being more than merely a cosmetic gesture of appeasement. The "defeat" over the wearing of the two swords was not the end of the matter so far as the future fortunes of that class were concerned. Many *shizoku* were capable of apprehending the military reality that the day of the sword had largely passed, yet this did not automatically mean that they ceased to retain a sense of inherent status or notion of superiority vis-à-vis the other classes. Their "brief" had altered somewhat but the essential dimensions of their moral universe remained unaltered.

The inherently elitist, fragmented and disruptive force of this class was still part and parcel of the government that was left behind by

Ōkubo and Iwakura at the end of 1871; in fact, it is arguable that with Saigō Takamori at its head, there was bound to be a pulling away from the national vision that Ōkubo and Kido had begun to set in place through their earlier reforms. Saigō was a crucial figure in so far as militarily securing the new regime was concerned; however, he lacked an administrative understanding of the new nation-state and could not extricate himself from sentimentalism about the *samurai* tradition and, at times, the virulent irrationalism that underpinned the anti-foreigner movement in the lead up to the Restoration.

The subsequent emergence of the policy to invade Korea was the logical extension of the mentality of those who had resisted the abolition of sword-bearing only a year earlier. There was in fact a fairly long precedent of advocacy for such a move, from the writings of Hayashi Shihei in the late eighteenth century up to even Yoshida Shōin who was the mentor of so many central figures in the Restoration. To attempt to comprehend it as a purely diplomatic or military proposition is to miss the fact that it had become one of the central motifs of the *Sonnō Jōi* movement some time before 1868 and that it was, as such, an integral element in the strategy to indict the Bakufu for its failure to project Japan's military prowess not only against the foreigners at home but in direct competition with the foreign powers overseas as well. The only difference for the advocates of the invasion of Korea in 1873 was that they were no longer aiming to undermine a Bakufu but rather a government that was perceived as having betrayed the "true" aims of the *Sonnō Jōi* Movement.[51] The 1873 political crisis that erupted following the Mission's return was therefore simply a further installment in the continuing struggle to neutralize an element within the body politic which was inimical to centralized authority.

Ōkubo terminated his participation in the Iwakura Mission early, returning to Tokyo on 26 May with the aim of reasserting influence over the course of events. He was to find, however, that his long-standing friendship with Saigō was not going to have any bearing on the outcome. As was Ōkubo's style, he attempted to placate his adversaries while awaiting an avenue of resolution that would avoid open conflict. When Iwakura and the remainder of the core leadership of the government returned in mid-1873, deliberations led to the decision to quash the notion of sending an expeditionary force to Korea. Fresh from their review of Western nations, especially their military installations and administrative structures, it was clear that the enormity of the task of nation state building ahead of them could not be delayed for the sake of pursuing petty aggrandizement vis-à-vis Japan's Asian neighbors.[52]

The ostensible catalyst for the planned invasion of Korea had been a perception of "disrespect" that was generated by Korea's refusal in 1868 to accept the position of Mutsuhito as an Emperor apart from the Chinese monarch and vocal criticism of Japan's "westernization". To the advocates of a military expedition, this was a profound matter of national honor that struck right at the root of the Imperialist aspirations of the Restoration in 1868. When it became apparent that Ōkubo, Kido and Iwakura would not sanction such a move, Saigō resigned his government post and returned to Satsuma in disgust. Other like-minded objectors also resigned from the government and began to agitate against Ōkubo and Iwakura through the popular press, the most famous instance being the resignation of Itagaki Taisuke, Etō Shimpei, Gotō Shōjirō and several other former members of government who issued a memorial on 18 January 1874 calling for the immediate establishment of a popularly elected government (*Minsengiin Setsuritsu Kengensho*, 民選議員説建白書).[53]

This incident is often portrayed as one of the pivotal events igniting the Freedom and Peoples Rights Movement which is arguably erroneously characterized as part of the "universal" trend toward popular representation as seen in Europe at the same period. However, as Fukuchi Shigetaka aptly emphasizes, it is not entirely accurate to regard the ensuing founding of the Aikokuto (Patriots' Party) in 1875 or the later nationwide "Freedom and Peoples Rights Movement" as being analogous to Western political movements. They were self-consciously cultivated and led by the more articulate and disgruntled elements within the *shizoku* who retained a sense of the right to chastise the government for ostensible "betrayal" of the Imperial cause, an attitude based more on a notion of inherent authority as *samurai* than being grounded in the Western-sounding doctrines they were promoting.[54]

In early 1874, resistance took a violent form with the attempted assassination of Iwakura Tomomi by Tosa "loyalists". This was followed soon after by a full insurrection led by Etō Shimpei and Shima Yoshitake centered in Saga, just north of Kumamoto. Ōkubo reacted with characteristic calmness and dispatched the Imperial Guard and the Imperial Artillery Corps to suppress the rebellion and arrest the leaders. The campaign was relatively brief and both Etō and Shima were arrested in nearby Satsuma where they had fled in the hope of finding support from Saigō Takamori; on this occasion, it was not forthcoming.[55] This was, in one sense, the first serious test of the new national army since reforms immediately after the Restoration and they had proved to be thoroughly successful. Ōkubo had reason to be satisfied, and the comments in his diary following his attendance at the trial of Etō indicate perhaps a hint of over-confidence.[56]

Having secured his mandate and, for the time being, Saigō's tacit coalescence, Ōkubo set to work to resolve issues pertaining to the consolidation of internal administration. His arguments against invading Korea had included the consideration of international factors and Japan's still under-developed military capacity; however, the main emphasis was put on the need to prioritize internal reform (*naichishugi*, 内治主義).[57] In the first instance, he dealt with the issue of the most appropriate form of government for Japan in a memorandum on the constitutional options available to the country (Rikkenseitai ni kansuru Ikensho, 立憲政体に関する意見書) which was produced at the height of the conflict over the Korean question. It is a document of some length that provides a discussion of the merits and demerits of monarchy and democracy followed by an outline of how Ōkubo conceived that the Emperor and the other organs of state should function.

The recommendations are strikingly prescient of the Constitution that would be produced in 1889; the Emperor would have supreme authority to appoint ministers, to convoke or dissolve parliament, initiate legislation, and so forth. The major difference is that parliament in Ōkubo's draft would be allocated a predominantly consultative role, an issue that was to engender considerable debate in the ensuing decade. There was also the notable inclusion of a clause that, in effect, exempted the sovereign from responsibility for his government's mismanagement, the kernel of Imperial "inviolability".

Considerable debate has been conducted over whether Ōkubo intended to advocate an autocracy or a gradual shift toward genuinely representative institutions of government.[58] It is clear that he felt that for the time being, a degree of autocratic rule in Japan was unavoidable and he specifically refers to the unrest and violence of the French Revolution as a lesson in how democratic forms of government can lead to disastrous outcomes.[59] The following passage merits particular attention:

> There is no task more pressing at this point in time than the discussion and clarification of our national polity [国体]. Whether we like it or not we must give order to these discussions and not rush to adopt the systems of government found in the countries of the West. We have an Imperial House with and unbroken lineage and a people with a degree of enlightenment. We must give full consideration to

the merits and demerits that this circumstance provides and proceed to draft our laws accordingly.[60]

Ōkubo was advocating a middle course of reform that would build on the existing traditions with the implication that a more open form of political arrangement, which he specifically lauds in the preface, would be realized in due season. This clarifies the conclusion that the experience of observing Western forms of government had brought him to; Japan was not ready for a republican democracy, and pure despotism also would not do. His insistence was that "forms of government should be established in a way that is consistent with the customs and disposition of the people as they have developed since ancient times". Accordingly, in Japan, a more sophisticated form of gradually adjustable arrangement between the Sovereign and the people mediated by a flexible Constitution was what the times called for.

Ōkubo's view of governmental reform as set out in the foregoing document was to become a far-reaching road map for future developments. We see here the kernel of the political outlook that would be more explicitly articulated as a policy of "gradualism" under Itō Hirobumi in the early 1880s. The term employed was "zenshin no Shugi" (漸進の主義)—expressing the principle of gradual progress—and, as will be examined in much greater detail in the ensuing chapters, it signifies the unequivocal emergence of precisely the form of dynamic conservatism that was discussed in the introductory chapter.[61] Ōkubo, while breaking with simplistic traditionalism and the atavistic undercurrent of the Restoration that spawned the plan to invade Korea, was outlining a practical rationale, a "soft realism" for proceeding forward; one that would not deny the possibility of liberal reform but also one that would prioritize political order on the basis of a distinctly conservative outlook.[62]

As part of the drive to give the government the institutional wherewithal to handle such reform, the Ministry of Internal Affairs was established in November 1873 with Ōkubo as the first head. Various commentators characterize this development as either the beginning of a phase of "despotism" or even in some cases as the beginning of the government's move toward constitutional democracy. Undoubtedly, Ōkubo's position as Minister of Internal Affairs gave him precisely the oversight required to coordinate the maintenance of public order. At the same time, however, it also became a crucial means for coordinating the development of commercial initiatives and industrial projects that were recognized as being integral to Japan's overall capacity to compete internationally. His authority as Minister was also to enable him to tackle the last vestiges of *samurai* privilege, the receipt of government stipends.[63]

The revoking of the stipends that the *shizoku* had remained in receipt of since the fall of the Bakufu constituted an obvious fiscal burden that the government could not hope to service; such expenditures were untenable while carrying out major reforms of the national infrastructure at the same time. One solution was to abolish the stipends outright but even then Itō and Ōkubo realized that some kind of financial "incentive" would need to be offered if the policy was to gain any political traction whatsoever.

It was with the aim of raising a substantial loan in the US to facilitate a one-off compensatory payment to the *shizoku* that Yoshida Kiyonari, one of the original Satsuma students dispatched to England along with Mori Arinori and Terashima Munenori (formerly known as Matsuki Kōan), traveled to Washington in mid-1872. The Iwakura Mission had already moved on to Europe by this stage and it was Mori who remained in Washington as the Japanese charge d'affaires. Yoshida knew Mori well from the time they had spent together in the religious commune run by Thomas Lake Harris near Lake Erie but it seems even he did not count on Mori taking issue with the policy of raising funds in the US to abolish the stipends and even taking to the local American press to label the proposal as nothing short of "robbery". Undoubtedly this incident led to Mori's recall to Japan the following year and he was, as would be expected, not able to have any influence on the outcome; Yoshida succeeded in raising the funds on the government's behalf and so began the slow but certain dismantling of the financial basis of *shizoku* privilege.[64]

The incident with Mori indicates particularly well just how sharply opinion could be divided even among the Satsuma and Chōshū oligarchy. Also, the fact that Mori, the one who had initially been one of the first to advocate the abolishing of the *samurai*'s right to bear swords, could nonetheless regard the status of the *shizoku* as inviolable speaks volumes about the residual strength of the *shizoku* legacy even among the government's chief advocates of reform.

The official move to formally terminate the stipends for *shizoku* came in 1876; it meant almost certain financial catastrophe for many, even though instantaneous impoverishment was not the immediate result. Within a year, there was an armed uprising centered in the southwestern domains of Satsuma and Kumamoto led by Saigō Takamori. The rebels were outnumbered and outgunned. Moreover, just as in the case of the former Bakufu armies, they also bore the stigma of being branded enemies of the Emperor. Eventually, Saigō was later to become a symbolic figure epitomizing traditional warrior virtues, but for the time being, he was consigned to official ignominy.

The emergence of Saigō as a "folk-hero" in the late 1870s was the result of the new media operating in the public arena producing unexpected consequences. The most powerful medium was in fact a very traditional one, the *Nishiki-e Shimbun*, essentially Ukiyo-e style illustrations depicting contemporary events, (the more sensational the better). These gave impactive visual representation to episodes that had captured the popular imagination while providing brief written commentaries alongside.[65]

Saigō's later hagiography, despite official disapproval, was an intriguing instance of how counter-establishment figures could be appropriated by the popular press to put disconcerting pressure on the government, although it was only so long as they had some measure of traditional status and virtue as well. There are arguable parallels in the basis of celebrity for Itagaki Taisuke, a noted general of the Restoration who resigned from government over the refusal to send a military expedition to Korea in 1874, along with the much later posturing of Tani Tateki in 1886 when he too resigned from his position in government as the Minister for the Army over the Inoue Kaoru's plans to compromise with the foreign powers over the issue of extraterritoriality.

The actions of Itagaki Taisuke, Etō Shimpei and so on, in submitting a petition calling for the immediate establishment of an elected representative assembly was evidence that *Kaika* could produce in the public domain all manner of disruptions, a matter that was of concern not just to the government but to any intellectual who placed value on the orderly improvement of Japanese society. This was an important contextual premise for the emergence of the *Meirokusha* which will be examined in the following chapter.

The *Meirokusha*: An intellectual aristocracy?

As proposed earlier, *Bunmei Kaika* was primarily a movement concerned with enabling the establishment of a new intellectual arena for the clarification of the content of the new form of *national* culture—along with the essentials of national identity and the necessary preconditions for "good" citizenship—rather than a grand "Enlightenment" project after the European mould.

We should also note that the *Bunmei Kaika* movement was not altogether the consolidated intellectual movement that it might appear.

It was at one and the same time both a popular "fad", in terms of the emergence of new fashions of clothing and new dietary trends, as well as a common watchword among the intelligentsia, indeed anyone who could gather like-minded persons into an association and scrape together the funds to actively participate in the aforementioned cultural arena. As such, it would attract contributions from persons with all manner of perspectives, often with people of divergent political outlooks vying to take possession of the same terms and concepts for their own interest group.

So far as the *Kaika* of pure popular culture is concerned, readers will find engaging and informative commentary in the work of Asukai Masamichi or Susan Hanley.[66] In the following chapter, however, attention will be focused on the members of the *Meirokusha* and their contributions to the Meiroku Journal. There is already a considerable amount of literature dealing with this society and its output but it merits further attention nonetheless. The first reason is that it clearly illustrates the transformation of public discourse away from high culture, the relatively exclusive traditions of classical Chinese scholarship (and even "Western Studies" for that matter) toward more inclusive and accessible modes of exegesis and debate. The second is that it exemplifies the multiplicity of political outlooks that could be accommodated within this process. The third reason lies in the fact that a considerable proportion of the *Meirokusha* members, far from being protagonists of Enlightenment in the Western sense, actually turned out to be key intellectual players in the move toward conservatism during the 1880s. In this sense, the *Meirokusha* also provides a primary illustration of how assumptions of Enlightenment aspirations among Japanese intellectuals during this period have come to be deeply embedded in historical commentaries despite a lack of consistency with the primary sources and the latter political trajectories of the participants. As will be discussed at some length in the next chapter, the common concern was to refashion educational, academic and moral discourse in the *national* interest and, if indeed that is the case, then it is the conservative turn that should be the key axis of our enquiry.

4
Mass Media and the Development of Civil Culture

In parallel with the developments outlined in the foregoing chapter, there was a palpable transformation occurring in the sphere of mass communication, a process that the government might well have liked to consider it was able to control, as it seemed capable of doing so in most other areas of conduct. However, this dimension of Japan's post-Restoration cultural development was to prove more complex an issue to engage with. Ironically, the push to encourage the emergence of broadly disseminated daily newspapers and journals was very much initiated by the government itself; newspapers were a distinctive accoutrement of Western societies and had clear benefits from the point of view of—potentially at least—developing an avenue for government-coordinated programs of mass education, civilian regulation and propaganda. In practice, however, this was not easy to achieve.

The popular press in Japan, naturally enough, built on the precedents of mass-produced single-page broadsheets and gossip columns, the *kawara-ban*. As mentioned earlier, these publications presented condensed and visually stimulating material related to the sensational happenings of the day, whether serious (as in the case of incidents involving conflicts with Westerners) or scandalous from a social perspective. They were almost invariably "unauthorized" and therefore anonymous, so that they were given to inaccuracies, inconsistencies, slanders, plagiarism and other relatively lowbrow tendencies. It was no wonder then that the better-educated members of the citizenry, primarily the *shizoku*, were inclined to view such avenues of communication with disgust.[1]

There were notable exceptions though. Fukuzawa Yukichi was particularly intrigued by the phenomenon of mass-produced newspapers in the West and wrote about them enthusiastically in his account of his experiences in Europe and America in the early 1860s.[2] Some of the first serious attempts at producing Western-style newspapers were mainly from Western expats residing in the major cities. There is the well-known anecdote of how John R. Black attempted to educate a Japanese shopkeeper about the merits of the newspaper. The shopkeeper was impressed with the quantity of information contained in the publication and surprised that the publication would be forthcoming almost everyday—but he couldn't see the need for it. Slowly, however, more Japanese would begin to see the merit of producing such publications and there was a public that was eager to take them up once they were available.[3]

An important technical innovation that made the quantity and quality of information for a daily imprint tenable was the introduction of the telegraph. It is not often given perhaps the weight it deserves but it was arguably as pivotal to the Restoration government's success as the introduction of Western weaponry. The telegraph network provided instant intelligence of happenings at vast distances; this, coupled with a burgeoning transport system by rail or steamer, gave a small and well-equipped force the potential to react swiftly in concentrated ways that rebels could not counter. By the late 1870s, this system was about to transform mass communications in the country.

The first newspapers were generally four pages long and divided into three sections: *kanrei* (official notices), *shinbun* (news updates) and *zappō* (miscellaneous news and commentaries). Most publications eventually developed an editorial column (*shasetsu*) wherein the political predilections of the editorial staff would be given free rein. Some commentaries obviously came from well-educated persons either anonymously or under a pseudonym.

There was a fundamental distinction between the more highbrow publications oriented toward the urban intelligentsia and the more lowbrow publications that fairly shamelessly aimed to cater to a less elevated sort of curiosity. The cost of the highbrow publications was in fact quite prohibitive for the average urban dweller, and more often than not access was had through government offices and schools which would underwrite a subscription for common perusal. Naturally, given that these were state-run institutions, there would be little choice but to subscribe to publications that were sympathetic to the government.[4]

Some publications bucked the distinctions. For example, the *Hiragana E-iri Shimbun* commenced as a thoroughly lowbrow publication that prioritized the *zappō* sections that frequently contained salacious material with images to match. Eventually, this publication would evolve into a pro-government and more elevated publication, seemingly as it came to model itself on the British *Illustrated Times* model. *Yomiuri Shimbun*, which took its name from one of the other terms for *kawaraban*, started out as neither altogether lowbrow nor highbrow, but actually quite distinctive in its focus on timely and informed reportage on events of national and international significance.

In the longer term, however, a considerable number of newspapers came to be relatively inexpensive mass-circulation imprints that cultivated a critical view of the government and popular discontent, especially among the *shizoku*. Ironically, the development of newspapers gave the relatively voiceless cohorts of Bakufu sympathizers and deposed bureaucrats an avenue for articulating sharp criticism and common action. Predictably, these publications came to be censured in an increasingly draconian fashion by the government.[5]

Within the relatively uncharted territory of mass communication that was emerging in the mid-1870s, there is one publication which has garnered considerable attention, primarily as it has been accorded a pivotal role in the development of linguistic and discursive models for later developments: the *Meiroku Journal*.

The Meiroku Journal

The *Meiroku Journal* was the flagship publication of the *Meirokusha*, or Meiji Six Society (so named to commemorate the society's establishment in the sixth year of the Meiji Emperor's reign). It was initiated by Mori Arinori of Satsuma upon his return from serving as charge d'affaires in the US from 1871 to 1873. The commonly accepted account is that he approached Nishimura Shigeki for his support soon after his return and that on 1 September 1873, ten of the most significant specialists in Western Studies gathered as Charter Members, including, apart from Mori and Nishimura themselves, Fukuzawa Yukichi, Tsuda Mamichi, Nishi Amane, Katō Hiroyuki, Mitsukuri Shūhei, Mitsukuri Rinshō, Nakamura Masanao and Sugi Kōji.[6] As such, it could be described as a collection of veteran scholars of the West, and the curious aspect of the society's composition was that the overwhelming majority of the members were not from Satsuma or Chōshū, but were formerly at the core of Bakufu scholarship of the West before the Restoration. Fukuzawa Yukichi, Nishi Amane, Tsuda Mamichi, Nakamura Masanao and Mitsukuri Shūhei, all had obtained the opportunity to study in the West under the auspices of Bakufu missions. However, following the Restoration, they were all offered opportunities to assist the government and, with the notable exception of Fukuzawa Yukichi, they accepted such invitations quite readily.

It is common in conventional accounts of the Meiji period to highlight the *Meirokusha* as being at the forefront of the "Japanese Enlightenment", a term based on the phrase *Keimō Undō* (啓蒙運動), and this characterization is broadly accepted by both Japanese and non-Japanese historians to refer to the phase of intellectual development in the early Meiji period spanning from 1871 to the late seventies.[7] The other term associated with the cultural developments of the period, *Bunmei Kaika* (文明開化), is commonly translated as "civilization and enlightenment", and is used more or less interchangeably with *Keimō Undō* (啓蒙運動) to unambiguously generate associations with the eighteenth-century European "Enlightenment".[8]

A further complication in this mix is the propensity to posit Fukuzawa Yukichi at the centre of this group as a presiding "Voltaire" figure. Certainly Fukuzawa's contribution to the world of letters in Japan from the late 1860s onward was substantial and his significance as a master disseminator of a new mode of discourse on the West was indeed unparalleled, but the fact that he only contributed three essays to the Journal in the entire time that he was involved with the society should give rise to doubts about such a characterization.

Nevertheless the merit in revisiting the *Meirokusha* lies on two points: the fact that it was a pioneering publication for the promotion of academic debate on genuinely difficult contemporary issues (such as the opening up of the interior to foreigners and the dangers of "free trade") and also the fact that it was an important vehicle for a number of former Bakufu *Yōgakusha* to develop opportunities to expand the scope of their activities both academically and politically thereafter.

However, in order to examine these facets on their own terms, it is necessary to demolish some of the unhelpful preconceptions that have persisted in a great deal of the commentary on the society to date.

"Enlightenment": *Keimō* or *Kaika*?

Intellectual historians who have dealt with the European Enlightenment will of course readily concede that this field of study is vast, diverse and almost impossible to nail together into one integral whole. Of course, this has not deterred many scholars from attempting to do so. While "Enlightenment" may well be understood as a broad historical phenomenon in Western intellectual development, the notion that it can be traced from particular intellectuals in European society of the late eighteenth century and then be extrapolated into a picture of a universal whole is, in any event, problematic. The Enlightenment in Europe was an intellectual movement that grew in response to a radical transformation of fundamental social relations *in Europe*. That certain figures in various parts of Europe clarified the implications of this broader social and cultural transformation for their own particular readership is evident. Therefore the point that needs to be retained in mind is that these were, and always have been, particular articulations specific to the peculiarities of the political, economic and religious configurations of each country. The Enlightenment, far from being a universal given, has always been profoundly contingent on time and place.

The cultural contingency of Enlightenment is something that has been better understood and better expounded upon in recent times so that, for example, we can refer to Roy Porter's excellent depiction of an "English Enlightenment" which, quite significantly, retains plausibility despite the absence of contemporary intellectual colossi as emerged during the Scottish, French and German Enlightenments. Porter points out the oft-neglected fact that the French *philosophes* were apt to quote Bacon and Newton as luminary predecessors and even the encyclopaedist Diderot was chiefly inspired by the earlier Chambers Encyclopaedia.[9] Certainly, Porter's work is not free from controversy but the essence of his approach lends us a useful tip on how to approach intellectual developments in the early Meiji period. In essence, we ought to examine the output of this period more properly within the context of earlier indigenous literary and scholarly traditions, considering them on their own terms rather than attempting to find a "match" with a prefabricated ideal type. There is no historical necessity that there should emerge in the Orient a correlate to the Western event. The Western movement has itself been reified into mythic proportions and it can only be counterproductive to conflate that mythology with world history and thereby create a correlate mythology in the East. Japan did have a genuinely bourgeois (i.e., *urban*) world of literature prior to the Restoration, as is adequately attested to by the sheer volume of publication sales for the urbane novel, ukiyo art and poetry.[10] What it did not have, however, was an unfettered tradition of *belles lettres* or pure scholarship; if you were a scholar, you were forced to—at least superficially—adhere to the Tokugawa-endorsed orthodoxy, *Shushigaku* (朱子学).

This particular tradition of circumscription of intellectual enquiry was a distinctive precondition to intellectual activity in the late Edo and early Meiji periods, and redefining that tradition was a distinctive premise of what those engaged in *Bunmei Kaika* were trying to achieve.

We ought not to assume that they were attempting to emulate the West, but should accept that they might well have been trying to clarify contemporary cultural imperatives on their own terms, employing Western motifs as and when appropriate. Consequently, the output of the *Meirokusha* serves as a particularly instructive example of how that process of clarification was being worked out.

Given the currency of the "Enlightenment" terminology in contemporary academic literature, one might well assume that this was precisely what those active both within and without the *Meirokusha* were eager to emulate. The fact is, however, that the founding Charter makes no reference to Enlightenment per se, simply stating that the broad purpose of the society was that of gathering to discuss matters of contemporary national significance and thereby contribute to an improvement in education and morality. There is no invocation of Western precedents with a view to emulating the Western tradition and the more we look into the substance of contributions of the *Meirokusha* members, the more we discover that they remained relatively indifferent to the eighteenth-century continental Enlightenment. Their interests and debates were often at odds with the compass of liberal "Enlightenment" concerns.[11]

It becomes imperative, therefore, to roundly dispel the association of *Bunmei Kaika* with *Keimō* (啓蒙, "enlightenment"). The fact is that the term *Keimō* was rarely employed by the intellectuals in question; indeed it does not occur even once in the entire output of the *Meiroku Journal*. *Bunmei Kaika* itself was also used sparingly while the term almost invariably employed was *Kaika*.[12] A broader examination of the listing of publications for the early 1870s from the *Meiji Bunka Zenshū* reveals that in fact very few publications used the term *Keimō* in their title, and of those that did the subject matter and purport belong to the notion of providing a basic introduction to a practical subject. Indeed, it emerges that the term *Keimō* was current in the late Edo period among traditional scholars in precisely denoting a work introducing a generic field of study. A typical title would tend to be something like "Sūgaku Keimō Sho" (数学啓蒙書), "An Introduction to the Study of Mathematics".[13]

So, when was the term first used in relation to the *Meirokusha* and the *Bunmei Kaika* movement in general? It seems that perhaps the earliest substantial instance of making a direct association between the European Enlightenment and *Bunmei Kaika* in Japanese is in the work of Ōnishi Sōzan (also known as Ōnishi Hajime, 1864–1900). Ōnishi was a specialist in ethics at Tokyo Imperial University who later went on to write in theology and establish a substantial reputation as a literary critic. Two years before his death in 1900, he produced an extremely influential essay in the *Kokumin no Tomo* (October 1898, no. 362) entitled "Keimō Jidai no Seishin wo Ronzu" ("A Discourse on the Spirit of the Enlightenment Age"). In it, the term *keimō-teki shichō* ("the Enlightenment-style intellectual current") is used to describe the intellectual activity of the 1870s and Fukuzawa Yukichi is singled out as being the primary exponent of that trend.[14] We should note that this is not historiography but literary criticism; it is a form of characterization for effect rather than a statement of fact and, to be fair to Ōnishi, the dominant tone of the essay is to be self-conscious of this. It should be noted, moreover, that the introduction of the term did not signify an unequivocal acceptance. Later literary writers were prepared to run with this idea in an increasingly uncritical fashion, but historians remained ambivalent. In any event, when Natsume Soseki made his famous speech at Wakayama in 1911 criticizing the prevailing notions of "progress" in Japan, he referred exclusively to *Kaika* and not to *Keimō*.[15] At some point, however, the *Keimō* association in historical commentary came to be more broadly accepted by established historical commentators; the likes of Kōsaka Masaaki and Ōkubo Toshiaki both raise the association of *Bunmei Kaika* and *Keimōshugi*, yet at the same time acknowledge the problematic aspect of the connotation.[16]

We do not get the first full-blown references to *Keimō Undō* as a form of historical truism until the immediate post-war period in the writings of, for example, Maruyama Masao or Matsumoto Sannosuke. In both cases, it is noteworthy that their enthusiasm for the Enlightenment association has been combined with an equal enthusiasm to posit Fukuzawa Yukichi at the centre of that movement.[17] The respect that Maruyama and other post-war scholars have articulated for Fukuzawa's legacy is, in certain regards, understandable but over-emphasized, and revising his involvement in the *Meirokusha* is something that needs to be done in order to examine *Bunmei Kaika* and its proponents in the *Meirokusha* more directly.

Re-evaluating Fukuzawa's role within the *Meirokusha*

It is still commonplace for commentators to gravitate toward Fukuzawa Yukichi in their discussion of either *Bunmei Kaika* or the *Meirokusha*. But for anyone who has had even a cursory look through the pages of the journal, the thing that springs immediately into view is that Fukuzawa was, at best, a peripheral contributor to the journal and what he did contribute was not exactly exceptional in terms of perception or philosophical exposition either. Fukuzawa was in fact putting his main efforts into works that were being published separately through his own university (Keiō Gijuku) of which *Gakumon no Susume* and *Bunmeiron no Gairyaku* are some of the most famous examples. Indeed, he was contributing in a much more prolific manner to his own journal, the *Minkan Zasshi*, rather than to the *Meiroku Journal*.[18]

A great deal has been made of this activity outside the *Meirokusha* as indicating a commitment to intellectual independence and a reluctance to be too deeply associated with a coterie of figures who were almost without exception in some form of government service. But as his essay on the occupation of scholars reveals, and as was quickly noted and publicly commented on by his *Meirokusha* colleagues, Fukuzawa retained a curiously paternalistic view of government and a rather limited notion of what intellectual independence should denote in practice. Also, as Nakanome Tōru has observed in some of the most recent research on the *Meirokusha*, the remaining charter members of the group were always aware of the clash of interest between their public offices and private opinions. The fact remains that they were remarkably forthright in their political opinions and did not shrink from the political controversies at hand during the period of the *Meiroku Journal's* publication.[19] It might even be argued that Fukuzawa was not necessarily the leading exponent of Western civilization within the *Meirokusha*, nor perhaps even within Japan during the *Meirokusha's* existence, yet we have inherited a tendency to regard Fukuzawa as being the intellectual exemplar of his generation.[20] It would of course be an overstatement to suggest that Fukuzawa was not an integral participant in the *Bunmei Kaika* phenomenon; nevertheless it has been necessary to dispel the over-idealized view that has been promoted so that we can reassess the legacy afresh.

Overall, then, the only terms used by mainstream historians from the eighties right up to the Taishō Period were *Kaika* or *Bunmei Kaika*. This was indeed the legacy that continued right down to the figures at the centre of the *Meiji Bunka Kenkyū-kai* who later collated the "Bunmei Kaika" volume for the *Meiji Bunka Zenshū* (明治文化全集). In general, they exhibited a marked indifference toward the apocryphal use of *Keimō*, and a review of their collectively administered journals, *Shinkyū Jidai* and *Meiji Bunka*, indicates a general attachment to presenting the facts and avoiding sentimentality.[21] Certainly, when Yoshino Sakuzō outlined his motives for compiling the collection in a brief essay there was no sign of any desire to indulge in hagiography or sentimentalism; he was quite simply anxious to see that the most essential and precious resources for later historians would be made permanently retrievable before they, and more importantly, the knowledge pertaining to their context, was lost for good.[22]

Yoshino was not alone in this outlook. Ishii Kendō, the compiler of the *Meiji Jibutsu Kigen* (明治事物起原),[23] was also disinclined to indulge in hagiography, indicating, incidentally, a particular skepticism regarding Fukuzawa Yukichi's legacy. When referring to Fukuzawa's claim to have come up with the idea of the *Jinrikisha* while observing a pram in the US, he dismissed the claim commenting wryly that Fukuzawa was "always one to make himself out as the originator of things".[24] Osatake Takeshi, whose background was in law, also stood out as a singularly thorough and objective commentator.[25]

Kaika

The foregoing contextual discussion clears the way for us to explore distinctions and interpretative nuances that have not been explored adequately to date. As mentioned earlier, "civilization" by no means denoted that of the *West* exclusively; it just as often denoted the possibilities of refurbishing Japanese and Chinese civilization, the West providing an auxiliary source of knowledge. Indeed when we examine the output of the *Meirokusha*, we see that for most *of these* scholars the objective was to re-conceptualize Japanese culture and Japanese notions of civilization, not slavishly explore Western culture and society as though it were the non-negotiable model toward which Japan must be transformed.

In the above connection, it should also be noted that by the 1860s, many western contemporaries in the English-speaking world were beginning to discuss human social development in precisely such dynamic and contextualized terms, particularly as their social and historical outlook had come to be profoundly infused with the dynamic and quasi-scientific rubric of social evolutionism. And anyone devoted to the study of English at that time would most likely be exposed to the writings of Herbert Spencer: if not his *Social Statics*, then his more accessible works such as *The Study of Sociology*.

Japanese scholars such as Yamashita Shigekazu have outlined comprehensively the scope with which the Spencerian oeuvre was appropriated by the new generation of intellectuals following the Restoration. There was, of course, no single "take" on Spencer's writings. Intellectuals engaged in the Freedom and Peoples' Rights Movement were prone to latch on to some of the earlier writings of Spencer where his 1840s Radicalism was to the fore. Others in academia and government were drawn to his writings on sociology and ethics focusing, arguably in a manner more consistent with the man himself, on the gradualist and integrational aspects of his sociological outlook. Figures such as Toyama Masakazu and Ariga Nagao, who later both became instrumental in promoting Spencerian sociology at Tokyo Imperial University, were developing their interest in the subject at precisely this time. Mori Arinori, who incidentally was particularly significant in this context as the founder of the *Meirokusha*, was also profoundly influenced by the Spencerian outlook.[26] Fenellosa, and Morse before him, are also well known to have been rather fervent disciples of the Spencerian gospel of social evolution (Fenellosa was also particularly instrumental in promoting Spencerian sociology during his relatively brief stint as professor of politics and ethics at Tokyo University).[27]

The foregoing list of figures does not indicate the strict limits of the influence but rather the veritable tip of the iceberg. Civilization was increasingly being understood as a continuous, relative and not even necessarily predetermined process, though there would be some institutions—political, economic and cultural—along with certain ethical constraints, particularly as they related to the capacity for free and responsible conduct, that were broadly accepted as part of a progressive program of civilizational advance. These institutions, given the social organicism inherent in the evolutionary sociology being employed, would be valued more for their socially integrative and invigorating potential rather than in some traditional *Humanistic* sense. In other words, the people expounding the gospel of civilization in the *Meirokusha* who had any substantial exposure to contemporary British and American thought, were more likely to be self-consciously defining themselves as social scientists rather than as eighteenth-century literati.

This was the discourse of civilization and progress current in the (English-speaking) West that was increasingly the focus of inquiry for the leading intellectuals in the *Bunmei Kaika* movement. I would not conclude that they had their conceptions of *Kaika* shaped predominantly by that contact; it is more accurate to say that social evolutionism provided precisely the culturally neutral (relatively speaking) and dynamic framework necessary to systematize discussion of issues in Japan's program of national refurbishment without having to accept Eurocentric conceptions of liberty and rationality hard-wired in place.

This brings us back to one key contention, namely that the term "enlightenment", especially with a capital "E", had no place in the translation of *Bunmei Kaika*. David Huish appropriately refers the persistence of the Enlightenment association as a "heuristic device".[28] Yet one could perhaps go further, even the "civilization" in *Bunmei Kaika* is of relatively limited relevance, because in so many contexts, only the word *Kaika* is used by itself. Under these circumstances, we are left with the core concept of *Kaika*, an "opening up" that might well be rendered simply as "progress" or "improvement".

Howland raises many of these issues in his book *Translating the West* but he stops short of arguing for the rejection of the "Enlightenment" association as stridently is proposed here.[29] The term "enlightenment" was of course still part of that discourse but even as Howland himself acknowledges, it was used primarily verbatim in English and with the same indeterminate nuance of something culturally or morally elevated. The term was certainly in use at that time but not with an overt consciousness of eighteenth-century connotations; it was, for want of a better way of putting it, a throwaway cliché for public speakers. The thing that contemporary English-speaking intellectuals discussed earnestly was "progress" in the sense of promoting the scientific advancement of social institutions according to a conception of social evolution, not the ad hoc dispensing of high culture or "enlightened" manners.[30] Indeed it could be said that we can find a measure of how thorough a particular intellectual figure's grasp of the contemporary English-speaking intellectual milieu was precisely by establishing how far they were inclined to discuss the dynamic implications of the evolutionary model; if they were quoting Buckle and Guizot (or Bacon and Newton) rather than Smiles and Spencer, one could conclude that they were either working with stale material or were perhaps simply more interested in the literati-oriented concept of enlightenment rather than the Positivist approach to civilization. The point here is that the evolutionary conception of progress was precisely how more sophisticated Japanese intellectuals in the *Kaika* movement came to conceive of progress, and they did so in that manner because it enabled them to conceive of progress outside of predetermined cultural models.[31]

For the sake of avoiding reification, it should be emphasized that "progress", so defined, did not imply a blind adoption of Western concepts. The Japanese had their own terms and were adequately clear in what they meant by them. Kōsaka's commentary can be invoked to clarify where that "indigenous" perception sprang from, and we would do best to keep that to the forefront of our contemplation of the *Meirokusha*; otherwise we will fall into the error that Howland so appropriately lambasts: the error of assuming that we can find precise parallels that mean exactly the same thing in Japanese as another term in English.

The remainder of this chapter examines the *Meirokusha's* output in the *Meiroku Journal* in some detail to establish how far the above observations regarding the Japanese perception of "civilization" and "progress" apply. It will hopefully be adequately demonstrated that a European conception of "Enlightenment" was not dominant among the contributors, and, if so, then we may accept that we should let the "Japanese Enlightenment" label fall away. If we find that some other distinct perception of civilization and culture was dominant, then we would do better to clarify it. We may of course still conclude that some momentous intellectual movement was in progress but if it is not an "Enlightenment", then we must call it by another name.

The Meiroku Journal contributors

While it might constitute an act of oversimplification to attempt to categorize participants of the *Meirokusha* into groups with distinct outlooks and interests, it will nonetheless make the task of clarifying the overall direction of the *Meirokusha's* output easier. As already alluded to, one of the most fundamental aspects of the *Meirokusha* is the fact that the charter members were overwhelmingly students or employees under the former Bakufu. As such, most of them were scholars of orthodox Confucianism first before they were scholars of the West. Nishimura Shigeki, who arguably enjoyed one of the most prestigious careers as a bureaucrat among the former Bakufu intelligentsia within the *Meirokusha*, made his name initially in the study of Neo-Confucianism and indeed this remained a major source of success throughout the remainder of his career.[32] Even Nakamura Masanao, who distinguished himself with the celebrated translations of Samuel Smiles' *Self Help* and J. S. Mill's *On Liberty* had an early reputation as an exceptional scholar in the orthodox school of *Shushigaku* （朱子学） and so it should come as no surprise that he made a point of arguing in favor of classical Chinese scholarship in the *Meiroku Journal*.

There were other commonalities that impinge on the character of this group. Being former Bakufu scholars, their opportunities for study of the West were sometimes hindered as well as helped. Nishi Amane and Tsuda Mamichi were to discover rather rudely that Dutch learning was a rather secondary avenue to the study of the leading countries of the West and, although they stand out as having rather singularly profound exposure to philosophical and scientific currents at the time, they retained a rather idiosyncratic conception of them. Nakamura's experience was reasonably substantial but his primary role consisted in chaperoning some Bakufu students in England from 1866 to 1868. Mitsukuri Rinshō moved from Dutch Studies into a French specialization, ultimately joining a Bakufu delegation of students to France in 1867. By contrast, Nishimura Shigeki, who had in fact requested an opportunity to visit overseas, was ultimately denied permission to go.[33] Katō Hiroyuki's major moment of exposure was the receiving of an emissary from Prussia in 1860; otherwise he had no direct experience of the West. Kanda Takahira and Sugi Kōji were the same.[34]

In many ways, therefore, the credentials and expertise of the *Yōgakusha* were shaped by their Bakufu-sponsored activities and it is possible to distinguish a difference in the quality of their contributions based on the peculiarities of their experience. To make a broad distinction, it is possible to argue that those who had substantial exposure to Western institutions of learning developed the more sophisticated outlook on civilization, often actually departing from pure translation to move on into independent intellectual and professional endeavors. Nishi Amane was certainly exceptional in this regard and the same can be said for Tsuda Mamichi, Mitsukuri Rinshō and Mori Arinori. Compared with their contributions to the *Meirokusha Journal*, the essays penned by, for example, Katō Hiroyuki, Mitsukuri Shūhei or Sakatani Shiroshi are not exactly innovative or exceptional.

Fukuzawa Yukichi and Nakamura Masanao present a profile quite different altogether. Their position within the *Meirokusha* can be explained in terms of being former Bakufu employees, men of ability, but nonetheless not altogether given the best opportunities by their patrons. Fukuzawa Yukichi certainly had substantial exposure to Western countries as he was employed as a translator during voyages to pick up ocean-going vessels that had been procured by the Bakufu in the US (in 1860 and 1867) and he was part of a delegation to Europe in 1862.[35] It is important to note, however, that unlike Tsuda, Nishi, Mitsukuri Rinshō, or even Mori for that matter, he was not dispatched by his patrons for formal study overseas. Fukuzawa was an able linguist who nonetheless struggled to gain kudos among the Bakufu elite. This possibly explains why he was preoccupied with collecting substantial numbers of books (without the express permission of his patrons) to stock the library of the *Juku* that he would set up as his own upon his return.

Much of what can be said about Fukuzawa can also be applied to Nakamura who engaged in a rather intriguing parallel set of activities both before and after the Restoration. Nakamura had a similar degree of exposure to the West but again it was more as a "minder" than as a scholar, pure and simple.[36] In parallel with Fukuzawa's Keiō Gijuku, Nakamura established the Dōjinsha academy, an institution that in fact rivaled Keiō during its existence. In parallel with Fukuzawa's publishing success with *An Encouragement of Learning* and *An Outline of Civilization*, we have Nakamura's arguably equally significant translations of Smiles and Mill. Nishimura also went on to publish a series of essays in the *Meiroku Journal* entitled *Seigaku Ippan* which were a series of expository tracts on Western civilization very similar to Fukuzawa's *Seiyo Jijō*. It is hardly surprising, then, that as it was said that Fukuzawa was the "Saint of Mita", Nakamura was correspondingly referred to as the "Saint of Edogawa".[37]

The point of discussing Fukuzawa and Nakamura in this vein is simply to highlight a fundamental premise of their literary output; to succeed as a mass circulation popularizer of Western culture was, among other things, extremely lucrative, indeed it was their livelihood, a business venture as much as an intellectual undertaking. Naturally, that was not their sole motivation in their activities but it remained an important practical concern that should not be ignored.

Consequently, we can perhaps broadly divide up the most prolific and influential contributors as follows: there are the *Yōgakusha* veterans who constitute the "elders" of the *Meirokusha*—Nishi Amane Tsuda Mamichi and Katō Hiroyuki. The merits of their contributions vary greatly but, with the possible exception of Tsuda, their intellectual purview remains essentially antiquated. Then there are the new bureaucrat intellectuals, Mori Arinori, Mitsukuri Rinshō, Shimizu Usaburō, Kanda Takahira, Tsuda Sen and Sugi Kōji. They are generally the "next generation" of *Yōgakusha* who are increasingly becoming specialized professionally and becoming more strictly Positivist and pragmatic in intellectual outlook. In contrast, there are the members of the *Meirokusha* who display some aptitude for the discussion of Western concepts and institutions yet remain firmly entrenched morally and intellectually, in the legacy of the late-Edo Neo-Confucian orthodoxy: Nishimura, Sakatani and Kashiwabara. Finally, there are the entrepreneur-scholars, Fukuzawa Yukichi and Nakamura Masanao. They have exceptional skills in rendering English texts into a new style of Japanese that is lucid and engaging. Their intellectual outlook is often more conservative than the publications suggest and if we were to look for a thoroughgoing philosophical basis for their opinions, we would find that it is surprisingly undeveloped.

Veteran *Yōgakusha*

Nishi Amane was one of the most prolific contributors to the Journal (next to Tsuda Mamichi's 29, he submitted 25 articles in all) and as such he deserves special attention. It should not be altogether surprising that the figure who was one of the oldest members and one of the two first Japanese scholars to undergo rigorous intellectual training in the West should preside as something of a "senior colleague" in proceedings. His is the first contribution and, arguably, one of the most controversial; he advocates substituting the Chinese and Japanese scripts with the Roman alphabet (with some cunning accommodations added). It is testament to the good-natured adversarialism of Nishi, and indeed the generally open spirit of the *Meirokusha* that Nishi's essay appears side by side with Nishimura's rebuttal.[38] This was, after all, one of the primary aims of the society—to promote open and critical academic discussion, not create an arena for "sages" to unilaterally pontificate.

Nishi was also, naturally enough, in the thick of criticism of Fukuzawa for his veiled broadside at the *Meirokusha* from his own newspaper in his "Essay on the Role of Scholars".[39] And once this matter was dealt with, in the next issue he was straight in with a withering critique of the former *Sangiin* minister's advocacy of an elected assembly.[40] In this essay, we see the precursor of what would be Nishi's dominant style: a care for the precise definition of terms, a fondness for analogy (unfortunately sometimes doing himself a disservice) and a capacity for wry and self-deprecating wit in debate.

This rather distinctive style stems from having been inculcated (perhaps idiosyncratically) with the academic ethos of the West. Unlike contributors such as Nishimura Shigeki or even Nakamura Masanao, we encounter a mind that has taken possession of an outlook that enables him to not merely talk about Western things but to do it in a "Western" scientific way through deduction and induction.[41] It is also to his great credit that he employs examples from both Western (both ancient and modern) and East Asian classical texts. The result is sometimes curious but it has integrity.

For example, in the series of essays published on the theme of "Knowledge" we find that Nishi is more focused and more clearly philosophical in approach. The first installment in Issue Fourteen (July 1874) is a typically florid exposition on the subject replete with metaphors such as the battle between Reason and Wisdom, Knowledge the terrain and Scholarship the means of war. It has a familiar taxonomy of the constituent parts of wisdom—talent (才) and ability (能) mediated by understanding (識)—along with a challenge to the conventional use of the term "principle" (理) in Neo-Confucian scholarship by postulating a fundamental division between principles of the objective natural world (物理) and innate principles of the subjective world (心理). The next installment (Issue Seventeen, September 1874) explores the relation between knowledge and wisdom, eventually alighting on a more fruitful discussion of the way that knowledge has evolved to become not the province of any single great thinker, but part of a systematically organized whole held in common by many. The next two essays expand on this theme by detailing how this emerged in the West through the development of a culture of investigation based on observation, experience and proof and how sciences and the arts (学術) could be furthered by two particular methods of investigation, the deductive and the inductive. Using the example of the investigation of water, he outlines how induction forms the basis of hydrology while deduction enables the development of technology through hydrodynamics. Nishi seems to be gearing up for an encyclopaedic exposition of the categories of knowledge but in the end, in Issue Twenty-five, he settles for an exhaustive exploration of all the sub-branches and sub-disciplines of knowledge that pertain to language, including poetry, prose, grammar, rhetoric, linguistics, philology and a host of others, literally too numerous to mention.

As an exposition of Western learning, this was clearly informative for the specialist but, perhaps as a reflection of a realization that he was losing his audience, so to speak, he began to develop other subjects, including such varied topics as "Personal Obligation" and "Secrets". These were essentially almost literary reflections on matters such as the practical conundrum presented by Japanese moral sentiments which Westerners found difficult to comprehend and Japanese found even more difficult to escape, or the need to dispense with obscurantism in scholarship and develop transparent leadership in government. The other essay of particular note outside the two aforementioned series is one that took up the issue of permitting foreigners to reside within the interior of the country. The purport of the argument is simple enough: having opened the country it was not an option consistent with that policy to place limits on foreigners' travel and the inconveniences that might conceivable arise (including fights between a Westerner's dogs and Japanese dogs), problems that could be minimalized through government regulation. However, the argument is couched in two fairly convoluted discussions of how to resolve the issue through deductive and inductive reasoning which, if anything, weaken the impact of his assertions.

Overall, there is genuine erudition apparent in Nishi's contributions and the idiosyncrasy of his arguments should not distract us from this. He is also a genuine universalist though not a Westernizer, as his discussion of the "Three Human Treasures" amply displays. Moreover, he has not lost touch with his Confucian heritage by any means. For almost every reference to a Western precedent, there is also a Chinese parallel presented as well. Indeed, the vehicle he chooses to present the matter of egotism versus altruism is Mencius' story of two brothers, one unwilling to shed a hair for his neighbor, and the other hairless through having shed every hair for his fellows.

Of greatest purport here, however, is the fact that Nishi, for all the encyclopaedic tendencies of his broader scholarship (such as the *Hyakugaku Renkan* of 1870–1 and *Hyaku-ichi Shinron* of 1874) makes no attempt to espouse associations with the French encyclopaedists. As Havens outlines very thoroughly in his monograph on Nishi, the nearest Nishi gets to the French tradition is Comte; by far the strongest influences, as is evidenced further by his notebooks, is the proclivity for contemporary English language sources and thinkers such as J. S. Mill and G. H. Lewes.[42]

In the final summation, Nishi emerges as a very erudite and entertaining contributor to the journal, but he was arguably not quite the New Model intellectual that was needed for post-Restoration Japan. He was much further into a vein of scholasticism than the hard-headed and practical line that Mori envisaged at the commencement of the Society. It is little wonder, then, that a scholar like Fukuzawa Yukichi wasted little time in responding to Nishi's essay on foreigners' travel and made fairly quick work of the more arcane aspects of it (to be discussed later).

A *Meirokusha* member who has been relatively neglected despite being the most prolific contributor and producing work of considerable interest and merit is Tsuda Mamichi. Tsuda was born in the same year as Nishi, and accompanied Nishi to Europe for studies in the Netherlands. Being of the same age and having a similar degree of exposure to Western Studies, one might well expect that Tsuda would share some of Nishi's Patrician temperament. What we find, however, is one of the most vigorous, independent and intellectually rigorous contributors to the society.

Tsuda's initial contributions (following the rebuttal of Fukuzawa's Essay on the Role of Scholars) clarify his *partie pris* with regard to Western civilization as lying emphatically with an English (and especially Protestant) conception of it. In the article entitled "Methods for

Promoting Social Progress" (my translation for "Kaika wo Susumuru Hōhō wo Ronzu"),[43] he outlines a vision of the diffusion of practical knowledge from the West which he conceives as being capable of acceleration with the addition of a degree of Protestant Christianity (although he is cautious about the dangers of bringing in excessively conservative or doctrinaire missionaries). In a flurry of fairly prolific output over several months, Tsuda explicitly expresses his attachment to many of the contemporary touchstones of British liberal thought; an argument in favor of free trade ("In Opposition to Protective Tariffs"), a plea to maintain freedom of the press ("On Desiring Freedom of the Press"), an invective against torture,[44] along with a slightly curious and anecdotal rejection of excessively gaudy ceremonial attire.[45] In his eighth essay ("On Transportation", June 1874), he elaborates on the significance of a highly developed transportation system and points to the fact that England's enormous wealth has historically stemmed from its ability to create and maintain an extensive international maritime network. In one further essay from the same period, we also see the genesis of a Positivist attitude to the world that would ultimately mature into a thoroughgoing Materialism in his later career.[46]

It would be a mistake, however, to assume that Tsuda was an unreflective or uncritical advocate of British liberalism or parliamentary institutions. In the five-part series entitled "On Government" he singles the Japanese monarchy out as an exceptional and intrinsically valuable political institution which ought to be maintained as part of Japan's cultural tradition. Indeed he is highly critical of those who advocate the demolishing of tradition in the name of progress and this is essentially the basis of his argument in the third installment against the proposal in the former *Sangiin* members to establish a parliament in Japan. In the fourth installment, he calls for a thoroughly transparent and rationally administered government but that still does not prevent him from conceiving of the nobility, the *samurai* and wealthy taxpayers as constituting the most likely first echelon in a parliamentary electorate. Moreover, in a related essay entitled "On Imagination" he cautions his readers against investing in an illusory conception of liberty without knowing its true worth or without having an understanding of what it means in practice.

If anything, this cautionary attitude toward the diffusion of Western influence becomes more strident as time goes on. Using the pen name "Tengaishi" he describes the dangers of Oriental powers ("Yellow Dragons") biting and devouring each other to the benefit of the "Sons of White Emperors" (see "Earthquakes", Issue Seventeen, September 1874).

In the next essay, he is even dismissive about the "rough and shallow" culture of America, referring to Ernest Satow's corrective of the contemporary perception of English Studies (英学) as actually being closer to "American studies".[47]

The remainder of Tsuda's contributions either revisit familiar themes such as freedom of speech ("On the Press") and the need to abandon antiquated legal practices ("On the Death Penalty") or wade in to the debates that were particularly current in the second year of publication; the issue of foreigners residing in the interior ("Travel by Foreigners Within the Country"), the question of the detrimental effects of Japan's terms of trade ("On the Trade Balance") or the issue of the respective rights of men and women ("The Distinction Between Husbands and Wives" and "On Destroying Prostitution").[48]

Overall, the latter contributions maintain a consistent advocacy of the free trade and relatively extensive opening up of the country to foreigners. Nevertheless Tsuda becomes increasingly cautious in the way that he raises these issues and, as already remarked, he never lost sight of the potential for harm emerging from such interaction either. Rather intriguingly, we also see a marked increase in his willingness to use classical Chinese texts as part of his general mode of exposition. This reflects, if nothing else, his willingness to engage with other members of the Society more on their own terms (certainly we have already seen that even Nishi was rather fond of quoting Chinese classics and we find that for a number of contributors, there is a residual proclivity with this tradition despite the ostensible "Western Studies" credentials of the membership). Tsuda's output actually rather neatly indicates the transition after the first year from a form of unilateral discursive style to a more polemical and dynamic mode of engagement in the second year, and it is a transition he makes with relative ease. Even so, the *Meirokusha* articles are perhaps more significant for their promise than their substance; his best was arguably yet to come.

Katō Hiroyuki, being one of the more senior members but also having some of the most limited exposure to the West first hand, presents quite a different picture to more vibrant figures such as Mori, Tsuda and Nakamura. His first contribution was the first to take issue with Fukuzawa over his essay on the role of scholars. Katō had every reason to take the essay personally as he matched Fukuzawa's typification of the *Yōgakusha*-for-hire all too well. For all that, his response is dignified and restrained—he keeps his comments focused on the point that it would probably be premature to encourage too vigorous an opposition to the government from the people. This contribution sets the tenor of most of the remainder of his contributions as well. In Issue Five, Katō presents an excerpt from Bluntschli's *Allgemeines Staatsrecht*, a work which Katō first encountered in 1861 prior to having dealings with a Prussian envoy. In essence, it is revisiting earlier work but, as Katō himself is anxious to explain, the translation presented in the journal is based on a later edition of 1868 and was part of an ongoing program to translate the whole (this in fact was distracting him from taking a more active role in the society).

The excerpt itself is well chosen, particularly as Katō intended to challenge the drafters of the aforementioned petition for the immediate establishment of an elected assembly. Despite being a work in German, the passage actually lauds the English example explaining that the strength of the English model lies in the education and uprightness of its upper classes (particularly the aristocracy) whereas considerable amelioration of circumstances in Germany would need to be effected before a similar political structure could be adopted there. The bulk of the contributions for the remainder of 1874 are entitled "Church and State in America" and are in fact three translated excerpts from another work in German, *Kirche und Staat in den Vereinigten Staaten* (Berlin 1873) penned by a retired American, Joseph Parrish Thompson.[49] The content is of a rudimentary nature explaining the background to the legal separation of church and state in the US and explaining the necessity for religious toleration and the thorough separation of the state's financial affairs from those of any particular religion. There is also an interesting outline of the detail in the Fourteenth Amendment to the Constitution which details the penalties to be imposed on states that violate the religious freedom of their citizens as well as a discussion of how the government must always be ready to protect its citizens from the various forms of petty crime that masquerade in the name of religion (there is even a reference in this connection to the evils of Free Love). These contributions complement essays of a similar subject matter penned by Mori and Nishi, and as such are timely and cogent. Nevertheless they are not opinions or ideas originating from Katō himself.

By contrast, Katō's last three contributions are in fact his own works and it is arguable that they indicate a considerable amount regarding the limits of his intellectual horizons. The first one deals with the issue of excessive secrecy in government and ostensibly upbraids the contemporary rulers in Japan for not promoting openness in their discussion and implementation of policy thereby estranging the public. This is part of, in fact, a fairly common concern among the other contributors and Nishi raises precisely the same subject in the next issue with his essay,

"Secrets". Perhaps more significant is his double-barreled whine about the excessive deference shown to women in the West in the two-part "Abuses of the Equal Rights for Men and Women". While praising Mori and Fukuzawa for their efforts to improve their fellows, Katō bemoans the way that women in the West have doors opened for them, are addressed first by visitors and must be consulted as to whether one may smoke or not. Katō even highlights an instance in Tokyo where he was effectively told off by a Westerner for smoking in front of the women. The first essay elicited a fairly substantial wave of criticism, the gist of which was essentially that men, who are stronger, should show more concern to women, who are weaker. Katō wouldn't have a bar of it. He rejects such explanations arguing that, if deference to the weak were really the reason for such manners, then it would be applied to children and the incapacitated as well. His personal theory is that it is a case of men flattering women with merely amorous intent.

While a capable scholar of German institutions and thought, Katō was also neither particularly subtle nor particularly sophisticated in his ideas. He was definitely Old School so far as *Yōgaku* was concerned and one suspects that he regarded the likes of Mori and Fukuzawa with a fair degree of alarm. The fact is that Katō went on to become the first President of the Tokyo Imperial University and in many ways this elevation to a more ceremonial academic position rather than a "hands on" position of instruction would seem to be in keeping with his intellectual temperament and abilities.

Technocrat intellectuals

As is well known, the initial offer of the Society's presidency went to Fukuzawa who declined it. In some regards, this was perhaps appropriate as Mori, as key initiator of the Society arguably deserved the post in recognition of that fact.

Mori's output was not the most prolific, yet it was steadily maintained and of generally a high level. Mori "joined the charge" as it were when the *Meirokusha* members responded to Fukuzawa's essay on the role of scholars. His response was pointed and more or less suggested that when Fukuzawa depicted the people and the government as having mutually exclusive roles in *Bunmei Kaika*, he did not know what he was talking about. Mori's view of political institutions was based in an organic conception of society and he tended to regard social phenomena, including professional status, as part of a profoundly interrelated whole. In other words, people were members of Japanese society first, and were whatever they were after that. Some have taken this to denote that Mori could not conceive of "civil society" and therefore "misunderstood" Fukuzawa. The fact is that Mori understood the Western conception of civil society perfectly well but could not see the merit in maintaining the "government" versus "people" dichotomy as Fukuzawa had done as Japanese society needed much of its best talent in positions of administration. Mori was also one of the first among the Japanese intelligentsia to adopt Spencerian sociology enthusiastically, and one of the first to actually meet Spencer in person (this he did on his return voyage from his stint as charge d'affairs in Washington).

The degree to which Mori embraced social evolutionism is evidenced primarily by his next major contribution which was entitled "A First Discussion of Progress" (my translation). There is nothing particularly original or novel about his treatment of the social evolutionary conception of civilizational progress but perhaps the content is significant in that it sets out more neutrally (and indeed "scientifically") how one might discuss social development as a universal phenomenon. It was, in other words, a demonstration of what Mori himself believed to be the appropriate tenor of discourse for the subject. Compared with the discourse of Nishi or Nakamura, there is no attempt to invoke famous personages or precedents from ancient history. His main message is simply that human societies need to be grasped as dynamic and transformative entities which evolve on the basis of the gradual adaptation of institutions in tandem with the gradual moral and intellectual improvement of human character, the Spencerian view in a nutshell.

The two areas that Mori chose to focus on more intensely in the latter stages were two subjects that were close to his heart: the issue of religion and the issue of women's rights. The discussion of religion is of interest for the fact that, while it endorses the inviolability of the religious conscience, it nonetheless also directly sanctions the right of the state to proscribe a religion if it threatens political stability. Of greater significance, however, is Mori's discussion of the position of the concubine in family life within contemporary Japan. Mori devotes five essays to the subject and sets out to vehemently condemn the practice of men taking extra women under their roofs and even raising the illegitimate children side by side with the "legitimate" offspring. There has been considerable speculation about why Mori was so particularly incensed by such conduct (there is his involvement in a religious sect in the US prior to the Restoration which maintained particularly strong views on the nature of marriage) but, for want of more conclusive evidence, we shall have to settle for a conclusion drawn from his own marital arrangement, namely that he took the unprecedented step of marrying on the basis of a contract which gave his wife the prerogative of withdrawing from the marriage as and when she saw fit.[50] This was as close to realizing full legal equality as one can imagine but it is also interesting to note that as the debate over the equal rights of men and women heated up around Katō Hiroyuki's rather petulant statements on the status of Western women, Mori was quick to distance himself from any conclusion that men and women are equal in all regards, or that he had ever espoused such a view.[51]

Perhaps, the final contribution of note is Mori's address to the Society on the occasion of its first anniversary. In this speech, Mori is generally "up-beat" about the Society but he does make the rather pointed observation that it would be better if members would depart from excessively formal delivery and aim more for an easily understandable and discursive style. Given that Mori is reputed (according to Fukuzawa at least) to have had no confidence in the prospect of using Japanese to such ends, it is ironic that he chose the occasion of this anniversary speech to highlight the need to work harder toward fulfilling those aims. The clear implication is that considerable progress had been made and that Mori anticipated further improvement with a bit of friendly pressure.

Like many other contributors, Mori was to go on to have a significant career in the service of the government. In addition to serving once more as Japan's representative in London from 1879 to 1884, he went on to become the education minister in the first Itō cabinet of 1885. As part of that cabinet, he distinguished himself by working through a very broad array of institutional reforms which were to have a lasting legacy in Japan's educational culture. In this sense, he indeed epitomizes the pragmatic technocrat who had a substantial history of intellectual activity on the side.

Mitsukuri Rinshō, as a young and rising star of the *Yōgaku* fraternity, makes a number of competent contributions to the journal but they are, for the most part, translations of major Western texts. The two-essay sequence entitled "The Interrelation of the Freedom of People and the Climates of Regions"[52] is a translation from Montesquieu's *Spirit of the Laws,* and his next contribution, "Relying on Public Opinion Rather Than on Government to Advance Civilization"[53] is an abridgement from Buckle's *The History of Civilization in England.* Both these contributions indicate a strong positive regard for England as a model of open trade and liberal constitutionalism although the fact that he chose to translate Montesquieu reflects the increasingly strong specialization in French studies that would lead him to be involved in the compilation of

Meiji Japan's first Western-style legal codes. The two-essay sequence, "Liberty", draws on the Montesquieu material to discuss the evolution of liberal societies from the ancient world to more recent developments in France and the US. His key contention is that human societies go through alternating phases of tyranny and emancipation implying that Japan is going through precisely the latter of those phases. Rinshō's output is relatively sparse but it is competent and at least identifies more clearly the sources and the Western "models" that were in currency, whereas some of the Society's members were employing Western texts without overt referencing.

Sugi Kōji's initial contributions are likewise relatively brief and often second hand. He offers a translation of what was alleged to be Tsar Peter's "final instructions" along with a brief list of "symptoms" of national decline elucidated by Henry the Fourth's esteemed finance minister, Sully.[54] His essays, which outline the process toward the independence of the US and contrast the fortunes of the English-settled North America and the Spanish-settled South America, parallel the substance of Mitsukuri Rinshō's work on Montesquieu; however, in this case there are no clear references to original sources.[55] Of more interest is Sugi's overwhelming concern for the mischief created by unrestricted commercial activity, especially the fraudulent manipulations of "speculators". His favorite example is the case of John Law who succeeded in duping the French court of Louis XIV and a substantial proportion of Paris' upper classes out of their hard cash and valuables by issuing promissory notes on as yet unrealized (and unrealizable) profits from ventures overseas ("Speculators", "On Reforming Trade" and "Conjectures on an Imaginary Closed Country").[56] Sugi was one of the more ardent advocates of limited protectionism in stark contrast with some of the more optimistic advocates of free trade such as Tsuda Mamichi and Kanda Takahira (also known as Kōhei). The other point of interest is his rather exceptional attention to the rise of the propertied classes vis-à-vis the unpropertied, along with his assertion that all commercial profit involves some degree of injury—assertions that almost place him in the position of a proto Marxist. In his final installment of "Human Social Intercourse", he even made rather pointed remarks about the fact that taxes are levied to enrich society and not enrich those in government.[57] Oddly enough though, he couches his motivation as stemming from concerns to protect the "national body" (*kokutai*), a turn we might anticipate more toward the end of the Meiji Period rather than at the beginning.

Kanda Takahira presents a striking contrast to some of the other contributors in that he devoted his attention almost entirely to the one subject—the issue of reforming Japan's financial system. Even when he does go into the realm of debating the merits of a popularly elected assembly, it is integrated into a broader conception of reforming the way the Japanese people were to be taxed, the revenue accounted for and the expenditures justified.[58] He is arguably the most clear cut in his advocacy of the need for a popularly elected assembly but it is important to note that this is couched in strictly utilitarian terms and he actually followed up this early call for an assembly's establishment with a rather apocalyptic admonition that an elected assembly could probably only come about as the result of a political crisis in the relations between the people and the government and sovereign.[59]

Of more weighty merit is his series of four essays on the paper currency. Kanda was indeed a financial specialist and the methodical manner with which he progressively works through the issues is admirable. His basic contention is that the government was treading on thin ice by increasing the supply of paper currency while hard specie was increasingly being sucked out of the domestic economy through the procurement of military hardware, the maintenance of foreign missions and the employment of foreign specialists. He rather fearlessly depicts a scenario in detail where he envisages the government first engaging in draconian practices to coerce the domestic population to maintain strict convertibility between currency and specie while eventually being forced to find back door solutions to its own incapacity to come up with the hard cash to fund the procurements and employments it already has in place.[60] The final installment depicts Japan's current financial condition as being similar to a serious malady that requires an immediate reduction in excessive exertions and a cut back in social intercourse. Commendably, he also outlines in considerable detail the precise policies that need to be adopted to effect a recovery. Rather acerbically, he even admonishes his colleagues that progress (*Kaika*) without a sound financial basis is untenable.[61]

Kanda's second to last contribution is another important example of how the *Meirokusha* members were writing not in isolation but in a broader print-media context. Kanda goes through a list of comments and objections raised in other sources and, with refreshing humility about his capacity to satisfy all objections, argues in even greater detail about how he has arrived at the prescriptions that he has. His last contribution is an impassioned plea to establish a domestic iron industry which he rather convincingly advocates as indispensable in the long term, despite initial expense, due to the extraordinary array of construction projects (coastal defenses, railways, and so on) and procurements (warships, technical instruments, and so on) that the country was in need of fulfilling.

Overall, Kanda is a refreshingly detailed and practical contributor who in many ways epitomizes the kind of domestically produced specialist technocrat that Japan needed—and needed much more than cultural commentators.

Confucianist modernizers

Nishimura Shigeki's contribution to the journal can be divided into two phases. The earlier phase is where he stands out initially as a more esteemed representative of the *Yōgaku* fraternity but then sinks into relative silence emerging later on to voice pragmatic concerns regarding the difference between theory and practice. The latter phase can almost be described as philological in that Nishimura espouses a new mode of exposition with renewed vigor that centers on fairly exhaustive exploration of the origins of key phrases in English, their use in Western contexts and their implications in contemporary Japan.

Nishimura's first contribution in the first issue is precisely a level-headed and pragmatic rejoinder to Nishi Amane's proposal to adopt Roman letters. He enumerates three practical disadvantages of such a proposal not least of which is the cultivation of a people who would not be able to read their own histories. His next pronouncement in the third issue was a very broadly fashioned word of caution to the Japanese people to beware of losing the sturdy and industrious virtues that make a country great (such as in the earlier cases of ancient Greece and Rome) in their pursuit of civilization. There is a relatively long silence until issue Twenty-eight (February 1875) where Nishimura presents two papers outlining his thoughts on differing forms of government. Again, the tone is distinctly pragmatic as is reflected in his rejection of respective technical terms for autocratic government, constitutional government and republicanism in favor of "traditional government", "governments based on a mixture of tradition and reason" and "governments based on reason alone". Perhaps predictably, Nishimura pushes the middle option of "governments based on a mixture of tradition and reason" noting that while in theory "governments based on reason alone" must of necessity be superior, the fact remains that in practice they are not necessarily stable or conducive to the welfare of society as a whole. His ultimate justification is that, since the people are in a partial state of intellectual and moral elevation, it makes perfect sense to retain the traditional institutions they have been unconsciously following for many centuries.

The final assertion in this vein is a discussion of "free trade" which, again on essentially practical and experiential grounds, lambasts the effects of unbridled economic commerce between Japan and the Western powers. He points out the lamentable disadvantages in trade that Japan had from the outset and caustically points to the tradition of mercantilism in England which gave it the advantageous condition of being able to sally forth into an untrammeled world market populated by weaker economies. He recommends that Japan take a cue from America and introduce protective tariffs. More pointed, however, is his criticism of those within Japan who advocate continued unrestricted trade despite the clear evidence of harm. These he likens to physicians who believe that the best way to cure an ill patient is to do nothing.[62] Nishimura clearly has Tsuda's essay on free trade in mind when he is stating this but, even so, he indicates a degree of fair-mindedness by stating that Japan may well benefit from free trade in the future but only when a degree of parity has been established.

The move to the second phase of commentary commences with the first of a series of expositions on Western words where he discusses "civilization" (Issue 36, May 1875). It is a lucid exposition which nonetheless treads fairly familiar and commonly held notions based on the writings of Mill and Guizot; civilization is historically relative and ultimately dependent on the moral and intellectual elevation of the people at large through education if it is to have any practical meaning. His discussion of "liberty" and "freedom" is somewhat more sophisticated in that he expounds the origins of Western concepts of liberty in apposition to servitude in ancient Rome, tracing from there two sub-conceptions of natural liberty on an individual level and political liberty on the social level. His ideal as the contemporary expression of social liberty, interestingly enough, is England. After a brief diversion to discuss the necessity of prioritizing "public interest" over the "private interest" of certain members of the government and the people respectively (as always in the interest of social stability and common welfare), Nishimura returns to his series of expositions on Western words to discuss "rights". This too is quite thoroughly researched in terms of its cultural roots in the West (particularly in the context of its Teutonic and ultimately English usages) so that Nishimura comes up with no less than eight specific categories which range from natural and inalienable rights to rights which can be alienated willingly or unwillingly. Nishimura's final contribution is a discussion of social change which mirrors an earlier contribution on the same subject. In this case, Nishimura highlights the superficially contradictory nature of the coalescence of the *Sonnō Jōi* and civilizing movements, which nonetheless together hold the promise of providing the impetus for better things than either could achieve independently.

As ever, Nishimura rounds off with a customary caution that education of the people remains the key to fulfilling the promise of the civilizing movement. Nishimura did not have the opportunity of following to completion his series on Western terms as the journal was wound up within the next few months.

It has been remarked in both Braisted's introduction to his translation of the journal, along with Huish's review of the work in *Monumenta Nipponica*, that Sakatani Shiroshi, as one of the most prolific contributors, deserves much more attention than has been given to date. Braisted attributes this neglect to his often excessively ornate classical style, Huish to the fact that Sakatani has never matched the stereotype of the Westernizer and has therefore been discounted for convenience sake. Consequently, it would seem that considerable discussion is merited.[63]

On actually reviewing Sakatani's contributions, however, one is struck by his relative ignorance of Western affairs—he is by his own admission not a *Yōgakusha*—and even more by his unwillingness to substantially rework a worldview steeped in a classically orthodox form of Edo Neo-Confucianism (朱子学). The initial contributions are relatively neutral and do not make this orthodox position abundantly clear. He is certainly intrigued by the possibility of establishing a popularly elected assembly, though not immediately (see "Should We Not First Determine the Political Structure Before Introducing a Popularly Elected Assembly?"),[64] and he remains a staunch advocate of maintaining dialogue between the government and the people. Moreover, concerning all attempts at change and reform his watchword is (to use Braisted's translation) "judicious cultivation" (裁成輔相). Yet by the time we get to his two contributions on "Secular Ethical Teachings", it becomes apparent that his views on the merits of Confucian teachings in the service of good government are essentially classical ones; in the second essay he upbraids Western governments for not employing an orthodox "teaching" (*oshie*, 教え).[65]

Otherwise Sakatani's contributions range from the arcane to the repetitious, a fact that Huish also emphasizes.[66] One essay on cremation discusses the possibility of using cremated remains as fertilizer, as apparently had been done in the US ("Doubts On Cremation", Issue Eighteen, October 1874) and in later articles, we find him launching into discussions that pick up on themes or motifs raised by other contributors, often without adding much substantially in the way of debate or discussion (see "On Concubines" and the discussion in parallel with Nishi's "The Three Treasures").[67] His final contributions largely dissolve into a stream of moralistic expositions on the need for sincerity and humility—and they get increasingly longer and peripatetic. There has consequently not been any major loss incurred by omitting Sakatani except that his inclusion testifies to the genuine diversity of the participants (and perhaps even their extraordinary tolerance).

Entrepreneur scholars

By comparison to other contributors, Nakamura Masanao emerges as a constructive essayist who nonetheless lacks something of the intellectual clout of Nishi. In terms of career and outlook, Nakamura probably resembles Fukuzawa most of all but he does not have the same knack for systematization or popularization. Nakamura was also something of a slow starter—his first contribution does not appear until the tenth issue.

As already suggested earlier, Nakamura's "Outline of Western Culture" indicates a tendency for commentary on the West en masse that is shared with Fukuzawa Yukichi. Some aspects of the first issue of the 'Outline' parallel Nishi's discussion of the development of experimental method in the series on Knowledge. There is something not altogether well integrated about Nakamura's essay. It is naturally enough not incorrect in detail but rather presents a disjointed account of the origins of "liberal politics" and "pure ethics" that reflects an essentially English (and very distinctly Protestant) character in his outlook. He is certainly correct to alight on the invention of printing in 1441 as having enormous significance for the breaking down of exclusive scholasticism and the promotion of open scholarship and ultimately experimental method as expounded by Francis Bacon. His discussion of the significance of world exploration is also lucid and so we have in these two observations, the essence of an interpretation that would sit comfortably with the notions of pivotal developments in European history even today.

But as we see in the second essay (Issue Eleven, June 1874), the discussion of scientific revolution gets clouded up with references to a parallel metaphysical revolution enacted by Luther and followed up by Melancthon. The next installment introduces discussions of Machiavelli and Hume, the former characterized as a false teacher, the latter as a kind of savior of good morality. After yet another peripatetic diversion into a discussion of Jean Bodin and the Council of Basle (among other things) in Issue Fifteen (August 1874), Nakamura finally establishes a steady focus with a return to Francis Bacon in the sixteenth issue. The content of this fifth essay on Western culture is substantially better than any of the earlier ones. Curiously, at precisely the time that Nakamura seems to get into his stride, he also starts to introduce certain opinions under the pen name of "Mushosōshi" as if they were not his own. In any event, the change in style and focus possibly reflects a realization by Nakamura himself that a dilettante *Yōgaku* approach (which had more to do with name-dropping and making a display of knowledge) was no longer adequate.

At the close of this somewhat more substantial fifth essay, Nakamura also reprises a theme that was brought out in a slightly less integrated form in earlier issues; by referring to Bacon's conception of social change needing to occur like the seasons, Nakamura revisits the basic message of gradualism intrinsic to the earlier discussion of Jean Bodin in Issue Fifteen.

By this stage, we have a clear outline of Nakamura's conception of civilization and progress—civilization advances on the basis of the diffusion of a spiritually and intellectually emancipated pursuit of scientific knowledge which is mass-produced through the press; yet the promoters of such knowledge should also beware of meddling in government as well as seeking to promote social change in too drastic or sudden a manner. This is a position that does not differ substantially from that of Fukuzawa Yukichi at the same time and, for that matter, does not sit altogether uncomfortably with Confucian notions of morality and good government. A substantial part of the conclusion of the final essay is taken up by a decidedly classical turn where Nakamura highlights the achievement of the Emperor Jen Tsung of the Sung dynasty whose greatness was attested by the fact that no generals or ministers of state were able to "make a name for themselves" during his reign—in other words, his was a period of unparalleled good government.[68]

Indeed the remaining contributions of Nakamura seem to reflect a growing concern to accommodate such Confucian elements. In Issue Thirty-three (February 1875), "On Creating Good Mothers", though critical of the traditional Chinese view of women, Nakamura discusses the significance of mothers as a key influence, both on the physique and psychology of their children along with the attributes that make a good wife. The emphasis is placed on mothers as essentially affectionate and nurturing creatures rather than as possessors of intellect. To support this perspective, he quotes a mixture of Robert Browning, Robert Burns and *The Book of Changes* to make his point. We should not forget that the contemporary view of women in Victorian England did not part altogether from such sentiments but it is clear from his interpretation of Browning and Burns in relation to the Chinese text that it is the Chinese perspective which takes precedence.

The most strident commitment to Chinese culture emerges in Issue Thirty-five (April 1875), "China Should not be Despised". While very little of the discussion rises above the common-sense assertion that China was once great and will most likely be great again, it is nonetheless extremely significant that, apart from Sakatani, Nakamura, the star translator of *Self Help* and *On Liberty*, is quite singular in his support for Chinese traditional culture.

Nakamura makes his final contribution with the final installment of his "Outline of Western Culture" (Issue Thirty-nine, June 1875). In it he discusses the "Golden Age" of English letters that stretched from 1588 to 1640. This in many ways signifies his personal ideals in relation to Western learning; we should note that there are no references to an encyclopaedist or *philosophe* in sight, but rather the endorsement of the open and pragmatic exchange of knowledge throughout society based on an English precedent.

Fukuzawa Yukichi has already been discussed at some length at an earlier stage, but we must return to him to examine the contributions that he actually did make to the journal. It is not overstating matters to characterize Fukuzawa's relation to the journal as playfully obnoxious. The essay that gave such offence to so many in the *Meirokusha* (the essay on the role of scholars) was originally intended for the *Meiroku Journal* but was withdrawn to be published in *Gakumon no Susume* instead. A snub of sorts in itself. The content of the essay was frankly a blistering deprecation of all that the former Bakufu *Yōgaku* elite was engaged in at the time, and it is little wonder that it distracted the core members of the *Meirokusha* for an entire issue. When reading Fukuzawa's essay, it is hard not to feel that he was out to disparage his colleagues by depicting them as "compromised" by definition of their posts and then proceeding to dismiss them outright unless they followed the same path as himself (something they were clearly neither at liberty to do nor even inclined to do). Yet there is a certain playfulness in his style of engagement and also a devastatingly effective polemic that make his essays so (gallingly) powerful. This is borne out by his later contributions to the *Meiroku Journal* as well.

The essay in the twenty-first issue of November 1874 formally entitled "A Speech on the Peace Negotiations Relating to the Formosa Expedition" is, according to Fukuzawa himself, the speech (*enzetsu*) with which he enlightened the *Meirokusha* to the possibility of using Japanese to address a large gathering of people. This account is clearly contradicted by Nishimura Shigeki who insists later on that the custom of addressing people directly, or at least reading out one's essay aloud, was current from the inception of the Society.[69] Certainly, when one reads the essays of Nakamura and Tsuda, for example, there can be little doubt that they could be read aloud to good effect and indeed the content of some of their essays, which include references to the earlier utterances of critics, suggests that some kind of spontaneous and vocal interchange was common. Most significantly, the meetings were open to the public who, one imagines, could hardly be induced to attend so avidly if all they were to get was a ritualized rendition of something that could only be intelligible in printed form. Mori, characterized by Fukuzawa as quite singularly pessimistic about the possibility of using Japanese in this way, was in fact the one who exhorted his colleagues to strive for a more lucid and accessible style in his address as President of the Society after one year.[70]

As to the substance of the speech by Fukuzawa, it is something of an eye-opener for anyone who regarded him as a Western-style liberal. In international affairs, he is near to gloating over the humiliation of the Chinese, though this is also mixed with exultation at Japan's success in extracting an indemnity in the peace agreement. More significantly, however, he reminds his listeners that the ones to profit from the conflict without any personal loss whatsoever were Western merchants who sold weapons and goods to both the Chinese and the Japanese for the duration. Fukuzawa finishes with an exhortation to continue to work for the progress of the nation so that such profits should not accrue to others. He wholeheartedly endorses the prestige that military victory had ('rightly') bestowed on the national body (*kokutai*), but adds that the real battle is in fact Japan's intellectual war with the West. Here, Fukuzawa displays an attitude toward China that has been characterized as pertaining to a later stage of his intellectual development and not altogether typical of his outlook. Nevertheless the text of the speech speaks for itself. Of more interest is the clarity of political and strategic perception, which is certainly more typical of the Fukuzawa as depicted and admired by Maruyama Masao.[71] The essay is also longer than average, reflecting a more thorough approach. This is topped off with a lucidity of style that frankly makes most of the other *Meirokusha* contributors (particularly in their weaker contributions) look amateurish. The only figures who come close to Fukuzawa in matters of style are Tsuda, Mori and Nakamura (when in his best form).

The themes of this first contribution do not disappear but are taken up afresh in Fukuzawa's response to Nishi's arguments in favor of opening up the country for travel by foreigners. As suggested earlier, Nishi was perhaps unfortunate to come under such uncompromising criticism but he frankly set himself up for much of it by employing poorly chosen analogies and attempting to turn a practically complex matter of internal security into an issue of scientific investigation.

Fukuzawa had already raised the issue of foreigners traveling in the interior in a separate issue of his appropriately titled *Minkan Zasshi*.[72] He mentions this at the outset (to remind his colleagues no doubt that he had somewhere else to publish his opinions) and states that it was disagreement with the particulars of Nishi's arguments that prompted him to respond directly in the *Meiroku Journal*. What followed was a completely unrestrained demolition of Nishi's essay. Alighting on Nishi's facile discussion of how the Japanese did not know whether the pumpkin was good food or bad until they actually tried it at the behest of the British Consul, Parkes, Fukuzawa remarks, not without sarcasm, that it was not Parkes but Perry that introduced the pumpkin, and the only result of note was that it caused Japanese people diarrhea due to a difference in constitution. Next he turns to Nishi's also rather facile use of the deductive method. Nishi likened gauging the effect of foreign intercourse to the act of calculating the circumference of an entire circle from an arc segment. He uses this line of reasoning to argue that since good had come from opening the country thus far, more good could be expected to come from further opening the country. Fukuzawa, quite aptly, states that the logic could be applied to negative results of interaction as well. He enumerates the destruction already wrought on Japan due to Western trade, and says somewhat sardonically that, if we follow the argument based on deductive reasoning, we will therefore arrive at total destruction. Moving to the crux of his own argument, he asserts that Japan has not advanced sufficiently in a broad intellectual sense since the Restoration which, in terms that are truly remarkably bold for the times, he describes quite literally as the Bakufu shop with the old curtain frontage taken down and a new Imperial Household frontage put up. He characterizes the new leaders as differing from the Tempo leaders only in the number of their hairs. Using his own analogy this time, Fukuzawa likens the issue of foreigners' travel within Japan's interior to the issue of women and marriage, in the sense that there is a right time for a girl to marry and she is quite within the bounds of her rights to refuse to take a husband if she is twelve or thirteen years old.[73]

Having demolished that section of Nishi's argument, Fukuzawa moves to the "inductive method" wherein Nishi argued that if all the negatives could be accounted for in some way or another, the only thing remaining would be positives. Fukuzawa works through Nishi's list of the "seven injuries" and his "solutions" pointing out either the unworkability of the solution or the non-issue of the problem he mentions in the first place. Overall, the objection stems from Fukuzawa's doubts regarding the capacity of the government to regulate foreigners in the interior when at that time they could scarcely stop them from hunting. He also noted the frequency with which litigation between Japanese and foreigners almost invariably went the way of the foreigners so that an attempt to replicate litigation procedures throughout the country would simply mean that rather than the seven to eight losses in ten encountered at present, the country would experience losses on a greater scale—seventy to eighty in a hundred for example. Fukuzawa invites his readers to do the calculations and see which situation would be better. As for an example of a non-issue, Fukuzawa alights on Nishi's reference to foreigners' dogs. In a truly witty riposte at Nishi, Fukuzawa dryly remarks that "we need not be concerned with regulations to prevent foreigners from being accompanied by dogs. Whether they are accompanied by dogs or tigers is optional".[74] Quite rightly, Fukuzawa asserts that, in any event, rabbits would be a much greater threat than dogs.

After making "short work" of Nishi, Fukuzawa rejoins with some personal advertising—he recommends that his readers refer to an article on "Might is right" in the sixth issue of his *Minkan Zasshi*. He also reassures his readers that he is not opposed to the general direction of the "ship" at present, but that he feels that it is necessary to wait for the right conditions.

The manner with which Fukuzawa summarily dispatches Nishi is arguably awe-inspiring, but beyond that we can also see that at root he is an arch-pragmatist who, with regard to international and national affairs, is closely attuned to the dictates of power and practical conditions; and with regard to combating adversaries in print, he clearly has no mind for compromise or niceties. We should also note the pessimism with which he regards the condition of the greater masses of the Japanese people. In this regard, he differs not a great deal from Nishi, Katō or Nishimura. He employs the term "Gūmin" or "foolish multitudes" (愚民) without hesitation and his characterization of the intellectually impoverished condition of the Japanese people in the response to Nishi reflects this.[75]

Fukuzawa made just one further contribution to the journal and though it was ostensibly a contribution to the general debate in the journal on the relative rights of wives and concubines, it was also in another sense a rebuke to the various members of the *Meirokusha* who got themselves entangled in Katō's rather specious characterization of deference to women in the West as woman-worshipping. In an uncharacteristically brief contribution, Fukuzawa enjoins his colleagues to get out their *soroban* (abacus) and do some calculations regarding the roughly equal numbers of men and women (hence the title "The Equal Numbers of Men and Women").[76] While indicating some anxiety that the calculation may possibly be too advanced for some, he produces the conclusion that there is roughly one man for every woman. Here there is no need to worry about vexatious issues as veneration of women or helping women. A *soroban* is all you need. Fukuzawa predicts that once the logic that there are only so many women to go around sinks in, people who do take more than their fair share will have to do it secretly, indeed with a sense of shame which in turn leads to voluntary abstinence. And so, with a wry smile on his face, Fukuzawa wanders into the debate of the moment, tips the polemical furniture over and walks back out again.

Given the caustic nature of Fukuzawa's contributions to the journal, it is hardly surprising that he had less than cordial relations with *Meirokusha* members such as Nishi and Katō. Nonetheless, he remained in contact with many of them, including Tsuda, Nishimura and the Mitsukuris and even acted as witness at Mori's contract-based marriage. But of greatest import for the *Meiroku Journal*, and indeed this chapter, is the fact that Fukuzawa was not an indispensible contributor to the journal and what contributions he did make were not altogether in the spirit of good-humored debate. Little wonder perhaps then that when the time came for winding up the affairs of the Society, it was none other than Fukuzawa who drafted the memorandum outlining the several good reasons for so doing. Mori, Tsuda and Nishi were adamant regarding their desire to continue but, in any event, Fukuzawa managed to carry the vote at the last meeting. Nakamura, Nishimura and Katō were surprisingly absent, but later on indicated agreement with Fukuzawa's proposal.[77]

The final truly minor contributors are diverse in orientation and subject matter. Shimizu Usaburō raises two pet themes, one being the advocacy of the use of *hiragana* as a phonetic script, the other being am enthusiastic exposition on the state of play in modern chemistry. Shimizu, apart from being the Treasurer of the Society was in fact a very close friend of Tsuda and had quite substantial knowledge of the West and considerable linguistic skills.[78] Mitsukuri Shūhei made one contribution which was a solid if not particularly revolutionary advocacy of the importance of home education and in particular the need for good mothers to ensure the moral fiber of the household ("On Education").[79] Kashiwabara Takaaki was, curiously enough, the physician to the Tokugawas who had been dispatched to gather as much as he could about the new intellectual movement that the *Meirokusha* seemed to have such a significant role in.

His contributions are three rather long-winded rebuttals of Nishi's essentially laissez-faire attitude to religious reform—he advocated a more traditional Confucian view of governors providing a strong lead in moral affairs to the governed—and a slightly grumpy injunction against the new practice of using the Western institution of Sunday as an occasion for rest and pleasure-seeking; he could see no occasion for resting when the business of opening the country was at hand. Then there is Tsuda Sen's rather isolated contribution on seed propagation which stands out quite starkly by its prosaic and non-polemical content.

Re-evaluation

Having cursorily outlined the profiles and contributions of each member, it is perhaps permissible to venture the following broad observations. There is primarily a broad distinction between the *Yōgakusha* veterans and the later generation of Western-trained intellectuals, and some of the more strident and unmoved traditionalists in the group. This point requires some qualification in that there emerges in the writing of almost every contributor, an abiding concern to "touch base" with the pre-Restoration intellectual tradition of Chinese classics. Even in figures whose engagement with Western culture is relatively positive, we find a continuing willingness, if not a sense of necessity, to configure their positions in such terms. Nishi, despite his clear avowal of adherence to Comtian Positivism, quotes Chinese classics in some articles more than he quotes Western sources. Tsuda, as earlier mentioned, shows a like inclination as the journal enters into its second year of publication. And of course there is the notable case of Nakamura Masanao making an impassioned plea to maintain respect for Chinese intellectual traditions.

For the same token, we find that Nishimura Shigeki embarks on an open and well-balanced exposition of various Western political concepts while at the same time remaining profoundly skeptical of their workability in the Japanese context. Sakatani plays with elements of Western tradition but at root remains more or less an unreconstructed Neo-Confucianist.

The fundamental change from the first year of publication to the second is palpable; in one sense, it signifies a move away from rather stilted literati pontification to a more open and spontaneous form of polemic. Some of the most rewarding contributions come from this period: Nishimura's exposition on key Western terms, Fukuzawa's contribution toward the debate on foreigners being permitted in the interior and Kanda's excellent exploration of issues surrounding Japan's financial system.

However, the litmus in our evaluation of the *Meirokusha* is perhaps the degree to which discourse on civilization at the same time moved away from static, literary conceptions of "civilization" to dynamic, Positivistic conceptions of social progress, to include in some cases even self-conscious acts of social problem-solving and social engineering. The dynamic and positivistic conception of social progress was increasingly coming into coalescence with notions of gradual evolution and adaptation, and in many ways the shift in the second year matches a broader intellectual trend toward embracing the conception of social evolution as propagated through the sociology of Herbert Spencer (1820–1903).

Perhaps the most significant outcome of this infusion was that it enabled a number of leading intellectuals to shed their *Yōgakusha* "skin" and take up new intellectual positions in contemporary society more in keeping with their specializations and abilities. Howland very aptly emphasizes the dynamic and organic implications of Spencerian evolutionism and perhaps his best contribution is to highlight how the term for society in Japanese (*shakai*) was coined not by the likes of Fukuzawa or Nakamura but Ariga Nagao and Toyama Shōichi, two figures who were instrumental in establishing sociology at the nascent Tokyo University (post-Fenellosa). Of further note is the fact that they initially accompanied Mori Arinori to the US in 1871 and through his introductions devoted themselves to the study of Spencerian sociology at Michigan University. In this context, they signify a broader movement away from abstract and culturally specific notions of civilization to the more pragmatic and essentially sociological conception of social progress.

Anzai, in keeping with many other commentators on Fukuzawa, attributes a great deal to the popularity of *An Outline of Civilization* in reframing the outlook on civilization from a culturally specific one to a historically conditioned and relativized one.[80] It may well be true that the popularity of this work coincides with a decisive break from the early more static conceptions of civilization but there is the intriguing absence of the Spencerian oeuvre in the work in question. Indeed, Fukuzawa was working with material that was decidedly dated. This does tend to raise the problematic issue of just how much of the dynamism and historical relativism in his *Outline* stemmed from his earlier research or the infusion of new conceptions of civilization and society from his contact with members of the *Meirokusha*. It is clear that Fukuzawa did read Spencer, but that is after the *Outline* was finished. There is, of course, the fact that the greater part of the translations of Herbert Spencer were carried out by Yamaguchi Matsugorō, a graduate of Keiō, yet they did not appear until the 1880s. So it seems that Fukuzawa was certainly correct in his response to the implications of Spencerian sociology, but he was not himself at the core of its initial introduction. In an important sense, he was the one who popularized the idea without actually originating it himself. The place where Spencerian sociology "took off" was actually Tokyo Imperial University and it was a development that framed the thinking of the next generation of elites.[81]

The aforementioned transition in the nature of contributions to the *Meiroku Journal* reflect these broader intellectual trends to a substantial degree and, just as Huish has correctly emphasized, the *Meirokusha* has long needed to be treated more integrally as part of the broader social and intellectual milieu. Subsequent research will certainly need to address the broader *Kaika* movement which, as Okitsu Kaname's detailed study illustrates, had a substantially journalistic and at times even satirical flavor.[82] Huish seems to conclude that this contextualization requires us to diminish the degree to which we positively evaluate the *Meirokusha's* significance.[83] In that regard, I cannot agree. It is necessary to reassert the primacy of the fact that the members (with one or two obvious exceptions such as Sakatani) were some of the most knowledgeable, experienced and intellectually responsive exponents of the study of Western institutions and culture at the time; they were a distinct minority who, for perhaps precisely that reason, needed to "compare notes", debate intractably problematic issues and voice disquiet. They found it possible to overcome differences in points of view precisely because they shared this rather unusual circumstance (one might even say predicament).

It should not be assumed that the aim of the *Meirokusha* was to establish some kind of monopolistic hold on the discourse related to "progress", or to impose some kind of hegemony over the contemporary world of letters. The very robust culture of debate in the Society suggests a willingness to put more priority on debating the issues than promote the Society as an end in itself. Indeed the discussion on the opening up of the interior to foreigners indicates that they realized that the situation of there being only a few "specialists" on Western culture and institutions would not continue for long. Japan, or more specifically the broader Japanese populace, would come to be exposed increasingly to the West, not only to Westerners and their technological artifacts but also to the edifice of Western intellectual culture, a world of hitherto alien philosophy and morality. This infusion of Western science and culture was broadly accepted as an inevitable part of Japan's program of national reconstruction—and it would happen with or without the *Meirokusha*. Yet it was imperative that the dispersal of this culture should be constructive. This would require as many people as possible obtaining an accurate, comprehensive and, above all, critical knowledge of the West. Neither slavish West-worshipping nor bigoted rejection of foreign culture were options.

Accordingly, the *Meirokusha* became an important vehicle not just for promoting the dispersal of new information and discussion of Western institutions and culture (and demonstrating that it could be discussed comprehensively in Japanese, both textually and orally to boot), it also demonstrated that the West could be responded to critically and without jettisoning classical traditions indiscriminately. The various responses to the proposal to establish a parliament highlight precisely this sort of anxiety to avoid taking the West at face value, to examine where and how such institutions emerged in the first place, what made them feasible and how far they could realistically be established in Japan given the contemporary circumstances. This was not the enunciation of a state-endorsed policy by government apologists but the free and critical interchange of the views by informed commentators. It simply is no longer adequate to accept the characterization of the *Meirokusha* as being a coterie of lackeys incapable of comprehending the ideals of civil society promoted (apparently) by Fukuzawa Yukichi. Neither were they *philosophes* pontificating unilaterally about rationalism and liberty. As I have attempted to demonstrate, it was more typically Mori, Tsuda and Nishi who strived to understand and articulate the mechanics of modern social institutions in more Positivistic terms that would, by definition, hold forth the promise of open and rational debate at a more universal level.

Ultimately, Mori's aim in setting up the Society was cogent and pragmatic. And despite the fact that certain aspects did not go quite as foreseen, the Society provided a space for several important intellectual figures to transform their mode of communication and refine their approach to contemporary social issues. Reaching the public was clearly important but the merit of undergoing a rather intense two-year period of self-clarification was also of enormous benefit. Obviously some of the attempts at exposition of Western institutions and some of the speculations on what would be best for the Japanese circumstance were more cogent than others. Most, in any event, were to demonstrate an ability to move beyond "Western Studies" into the realm of applying their knowledge to practical issues.

It is at this juncture that a fundamental difference between the career trajectory of the likes of Fukuzawa Yukichi and Nakamura Masanao and the remaining *Meirokusha* members emerges. Fukuzawa went on to become the principal expositor of *Bunmei Kaika* to the masses. He was not necessarily the most experienced or even the most sophisticated but he was easily the most eloquent and successful. By contrast, other figures went on to make practical contributions toward the program of national reconstruction. In this regard, Mori can be appraised as a particularly spectacular example in education. Nishi went on to play an instrumental role in the reorganization of the military. In slightly less overt ways, Sugi Kōji went on to promote the use of statistical analysis in the public service while Kanda went on to become an important advisor and reformer in financial affairs.

Given the foregoing picture of the *Meirokusha's* activities, it should be adequately clear that a term like "Enlightenment" simply doesn't fit with what the members of the *Meirokusha* were endeavoring to achieve. Japan did not need a replica French salon replete with wits and *bon mots* (it already had a tradition of that to some extent anyhow). Their great collective contribution was actually to take *Yōgaku* and *Jitsugaku* and transform them into philosophy and social science in a more universal sense, not by merely translating Western concepts slavishly into Japanese but, much more importantly, by developing a critical cultural arena in the Japanese language wherein traditional Japanese concepts and priorities could be exposed and reworked in the light of Western scholarship.

The "Kaika" movement was a critical phase of intellectual clarification where a generation of non-Western intellectuals—persons of highly divergent backgrounds from journalists to technocrats—developed the conceptual tools and strategies for grappling with a profoundly dynamic and potentially unstable epoch of broad social change. Certainly, the clumsy and somewhat monolithic rubric of "civilization" would continue to be pursued in a more disparate way by some (to some considerable personal profit); meanwhile, a new wave of bureaucrats and technocrats who had become inculcated with a fresh cognition of the requirements of the new social order would move on to quietly assemble the institutional structure that the fledgling nation state required. It has hopefully been adequately demonstrated that the contribution of the *Meirokusha* to that process of clarification was substantial.

5
"The More Thorough Fulfilment of the Restoration"

The successful conclusion of the campaign against the rebel *shizoku* in the Seinan War emphatically ended the possibility of armed resistance to the government. By 1878, the last major armed insurrection against the new centralized government had been safely quelled and the Restoration leaders could look forward to moving on to, using Ōkubo Toshimichi's phrase, "the more thorough fulfilment of the Restoration."[1] From thereon in, other avenues of sedition and activism—either through the promotion of political organizations, the founding of an anti-government press or the carrying out of isolated acts of violence—would be the only remaining options.

Of equal significance was the fact that Satsuma, which up until the war had been the source of a considerable degree of dissent toward the central government, was finally forced to follow suit and join the rank and file. That this was accomplished by force of arms under the direction of a government that included Satsuma leaders signifies the degree to which the government had committed itself to a totally centralized form of government and, in having done so, alienated that segment of the *shizoku* population who either wanted to preserve the *shizoku* traditions practically unreconstructed or simply did not understand the administrative necessity of the seamlessly integrated nation state. Ōkubo, Kido and Itō were all well aware of what was at stake and pushed forward regardless of the potential for instability and even personal harm. Kido is said to have never recovered from the trauma of engaging his former comrades in war—and Ōkubo was to bear the mortal consequences of his government's decisions: he was assassinated by a group of *samurai* from Kanazawa on 14 May 1878. This left a smaller coterie of 1868 leaders, including Itō Hirobumi, Inoue Kaoru and Ōkuma Shigenobu, to pick up the pieces and attempt to give administrative and social substance to what was now still the sturdy but nonetheless relatively bare frame of government.[2]

There was a palpable difference in the nature of the political challenges that lay ahead; since widespread violent rebellion was no longer an option for the opponents of the government, the modes of resistance and agitation became much more subtle and complex. Moreover, the government was no longer the fledgling reform party that swept into control amid the turmoil and feverish anticipation of the *Sonnō Jōi* movement, but was itself now being held to account for the failure to revise the unequal treaties and the equally galling failure to keep Western influences—commercial, political and cultural—at bay.

Consequently, from 1879 the nation entered what could be described as a prolonged period of intense popular agitation against the government through the popular press and by means of organizing political associations and meetings with public speakers throughout the country. The government was to become increasingly aware that they were not the sole arbiters of the social agenda, as disaffected elements within the body politic, more often than not disaffected *samurai*, came to be galvanized through the popular (or populist) press.[3] Over time, it became evident that Itō Hirobumi needed to develop an ideological platform to underpin their policies—for sure enough, any glaring contradictions or inconsistencies in the raison d'être of state policy would be swiftly pounced upon and used to fan urban discontent in print. The most famous association active at this time was the *Aikokusha* (Society of Patriots) under Itagaki Taisuke which self-consciously adopted the radical democratic theory of Rousseau, an angle guaranteed to put Itō on the spot in front of Western observers who were anxious to see signs of Japan's political maturity[4]; alongside this was a counter-movement favoring the English model of constitutional monarchy that found an important advocate in Fukuzawa Yukichi who had a government-connected sponsor in the person of Ōkuma Shigenobu (who was later to establish the Constitutional Reform Party).[5] For Itō's part, he had no intention of committing himself to any Western model of representative government and, in any event, he could not claim to be well-versed enough in constitutional theory to argue substantially in favor of one model or another.[6]

Ōkuma, possibly sensing the void and an opportunity to "steal a march" over Itō, in 1881, boldly submitted a constitutional reform proposal to the Emperor that entailed, in essence, the immediate establishment of a parliamentary form of government modeled after the Westminster system. Itō was livid and the event sparked the major political purge that saw not only Ōkuma but also those associated with agitation in any form for the English model—including the former students of Fukuzawa Yukichi—removed from official posts. Itō realized that the time to take the initiative in constitutional matters was at hand—an edict was issued by the Emperor promising a constitution and representative government within ten years. Within time, however, it became apparent that the government would brook very little intensive political organizing, and ultimately drastic legislation was passed which made it illegal for specified agitators to remain within the capital.[7]

Eventually, Itō managed to acquit himself adequately in the arena of juridical conflict, yet the ultimate prize would be to establish unequivocal control over the one institution in Japanese society that was, for most intents and purposes, "inviolable"; the Imperial Household. A written constitution, in and of itself, would not safeguard the legitimacy of the government or be enough to achieve sufficient purchase within the electorate to maintain a consistent support for national policy. And a premature experiment in democracy was perhaps quite rightly regarded as a dangerous distraction from the more pressing matter of consistently promulgating and implementing national policies. The word of the Emperor was destined to become increasingly relevant to the arbitration of political influence and it was clearly with a view to ensuring that the Emperor's word would be held under tight institutional control that Itō instigated, in the first instance, a cabinet system of ministerial government along with the establishment of a Privy Council, an institution that would have as its main purpose the formalization of Itō's position as first confidant and advisor to the throne.[8] As will be discussed in more detail in the next chapter, Itō increasingly had to rely on the Privy Council but even then he was not able to enjoy an exclusive hold over affairs at the Imperial Court. The Ministry of the Imperial Household would slowly but surely become a separate institutional entity that attracted high-ranking and influential opponents to the government, ultimately leading to a bifurcation of sovereignty away from the very constitutional framework that was supposed to house it.[9]

Apart from the intensifying struggle in the public sphere domestically, there were also several diplomatic developments abroad that were to compound Itō's difficulties. From 1878 onward rather intense diplomatic maneuvering arose between Japan and China. In 1874, Sir Thomas Wade, Britain's representative at Peking, had facilitated a convention that recognized Ryūkyū Islanders as Japanese subjects but the Islands had not as yet been practically incorporated within the structure of the national government. The Japanese were aiming to revise the earlier Sino-Japanese Treaty of 1871, offering to incorporate a most-favored nation clause in return for which they indicated that they were prepared to cede some of the southern-most islands.[10]

Things were brought to a head in 1879 as the government aimed to capitalize on its good relations with the US to cajole the Chinese government into acquiescence. The visit of the former US President, General Ulysses S. Grant in 1879 established a basis for representatives of Japan's diplomatic corps to make personal approaches to Grant to act as a mediator between the two countries. Ultimately Grant's influence was limited, certainly so far as the Chinese were concerned. Nevertheless it emboldened the Japanese government to pursue its plans regardless of Chinese opposition; Japan formally announced the incorporation of the Ryūkyūs as the Prefecture of Okinawa in April of that year.[11]

This was the beginning of a period of sustained hostility between Japan and China, the focus shifting from Okinawa to Korea. The Chinese proved that they were able to cultivate ties with the Americans too, succeeding in brokering a new treaty between Korea and America in 1882 after Japanese cooperation had inexplicably failed to materialize for the US envoy, Commodore Shufeldt. Moreover, Chinese support for the reactionary and strongly anti-Japanese faction of the Taewonkun nearly led to full-scale war in July of 1882 when a Japanese military advisor was murdered and the Japanese Legation was burnt down by Taewonkun supporters. By the time the Japanese Minister returned with warships and troops, the Chinese had also sent considerable numbers of troops to the Korean capital. The stalemate was finally resolved in 1885 with the Treaty of Tientsin which stipulated the withdrawal of Chinese troops, the cessation of Japanese military training and an undertaking to keep each other informed of any intention to dispatch troops in future.[12]

Overall, it is hard not to be critical of the manner in which this diplomacy was conducted by both sides. Much of the substance of the dispute could have been sorted out through diplomatic channels if communication had been maintained in a professional manner. The Japanese were hampered by the continued reliance on a relatively small group of talented men who had the linguistic ability and tact to handle such delicate negotiations. Yoshida Kiyonari was entrusted with much of the liaison with the US while Mori Arinori was entrusted with handling the notoriously sage but prickly Chinese diplomat, Li Hung Chang. On the Chinese part, there was continuous prevarication and provocation in their communications, a fact that the former President Grant was himself to lament. On both sides, there was also the constant clamor from those critical of any compromise with foreign powers which made even the slightest appearance of "going soft" a marked domestic liability. This was indeed the essence of the government's predicament in diplomatic relations—the greater population expected immediate revisions to the unequal treaties but such a wholesale reworking of Japan's position in the world order was unlikely to be achieved without considerable compromise and flexibility—at least that was the case if immediate progress of any sort was to be had.[13]

Consequently, the great political upheaval of 1881 had implications not only so far as dealing with the advocates of representative government was concerned, but also in relation to the relative balance of power among the various conservative factions in government who had a constant eye on the disruptive potential of *shizoku* activists and the public clamor for a successful renegotiation of its place vis-à-vis the powers. In other words, Itō Hirobumi not only had to deal with the strident pro-reform clique that had formerly been within the oligarchic circle, but also with an articulate and often aggressive body of intellectuals and public figures who knew they had a rod, in the shape of failed treaty revisions, to beat the government with.

It is customary for the so-called "Freedom and People's Rights Movement" to gather attention in relation to developments both prior to and after the 1881 purge. The establishment of the Liberal Party under Itagaki Taisuke and the attempt to forge a national network of popular political associations seem to conform with the preconceived notion of the inevitability of agitation for popular representation in modernizing societies. Yet the Liberal Party was surprisingly short-lived, snuffed out as it was through internal bickering and political excesses that even Itagaki Taisuke himself had to disown. In the end, Yamagata Aritomo, who moved from the post of Minister of the Army to Minister of the Interior in December 1883, was able to stifle dissent of this kind with relative ease, ultimately even banning approximately three hundred political activists from the capital. Itagaki was packed off to Europe at the government's expense to observe the nations whose theories he so ardently subscribed to first hand. These forms of dissent were relatively easy to contain because they relied on a coinage that was at once idealistic and foreign. The greater awareness of the defects of Western societies was becoming more apparent among those who had been at the forefront of the Restoration reforms and it was expected that an adequate "reality check" for Itagaki would do a great deal to calm his enthusiasm.[14]

Some qualification of the use of the term Freedom and Peoples Rights is warranted for several reasons, although it must be acknowledged that it is now part of the common vocabulary of Meiji political history. The main difficulty with the title is that the Japanese phrase *Jiyū Minken Undō* (自由民権運動) rather unhelpfully blends together the activities of the Liberal Party under Itagaki Taisuke with other disparate agitations for representative government, including those of the non-Satsuma and Chōshū officers of state such as Ōkuma Shigenobu and the more generally disgruntled elites who had decidedly selective conceptions of constitutional reform—including downright illiberal conceptions of government—but were nonetheless apt to adopt the catchphrases of "justice" and "fair representation" all the same to chastise Itō Hirobumi's "despotic" regime.

Consequently, while we may well regard the outcome of the 1881 political turmoil as a significant turning point for the evolution of the "Freedom and Peoples Rights Movement", there was in fact an equally significant movement emerging in quarters within the military wing of the oligarchical circle that would appear to champion the same cause but, as will become more fully apparent in the next chapter, was actually more deeply tied to the aim of presenting a challenge to the line of "Westernizing" reform being promoted by Itō Hirobumi and his government.

There were two dimensions to the crisis as it emerged: on the one hand Ōkuma was developing a circle of patronage that included Fukuzawa Yukichi and other like-minded intellectuals, and he did not baulk at the use of the press to expose the rather shady aspects of some government land sales in Hokkaido that were due to proceed to the great personal benefit of Godai Tomoatsu. The reportage started with the *Tōkyō-Yokohama Mainichi* and spread to the *Yūbin Hōchi*, which ran a four-part series of stories. Very soon there was a veritable "feeding frenzy" as the mainstream papers competed to voice dismay.[15] At the same time, however, there was also the submission of a highly critical memorial by four Generals—Tani Tateki (1837–1911), Torio Koyata (1847–1905), Miura Gorō (1846–1926) and Soga Sukenori (1843–1935)—on 12 September 1881, which marked a new phase of conservative activism that was to have far-reaching implications for the future political configuration of the state. Known as the "Four General's Memorial", the paper was submitted to Arisugawanomiya, the Minister of the Left, and called for a constitutional form of government that retained a firm focus on moral rule centered on the Emperor. They were also out to protest the manner in which the superintendent of the settlement of Hokkaido, Kuroda Kiyotaka, had arranged for state assets to be sold off to Satsuma entrepreneurs such as Godai Tomoatsu on highly favorable terms.[16]

Superficially there is a degree of parallel in the nature of the Generals' criticisms and demands with those of Ōkuma Shigenobu who had already earned Itō Hirobumi's opprobrium for promoting the adoption of a British-style system of government and publicly opposing the Hokkaido deal. However, the Four Generals did not conceive of constitutional reform along British lines—their conception (as will be discussed in the ensuing section) was decidedly anti-Western and paternalistic. When the Hokkaido deal was called off and Ōkuma paid for his series of indiscretions with his dismissal on 11 October, there was something of a sigh of relief that emanated from the conservative camp and, ironically, Itō actually found himself restored to some extent in their estimation.[17]

It is worth noting a number of commonalities and distinctions among the "Four Generals." First, they were all relatively young at the time of the Restoration (Tani being the eldest at 31, the others being in their early to mid-twenties) which meant that their distinguished achievements in the Boshin War did not translate immediately into political influence. They were also relatively marginalized within the top circle despite their early connections. They remained faithful to the Restoration leadership throughout the turmoil of the mid-1870s and distinguished themselves yet again in suppressing the Seinan Rebellion of Saigō Takamori—Tani especially earning fame for doggedly holding the Kumamoto Fort against Saigō for over fifty days.

Yet there were signs of discontent and misgivings that began to develop in the aftermath of the Seinan War that were to grow into open opposition to Itō Hirobumi's leadership. The "Bunmei Kaika" movement was now recognized as an expensive failure, and yet the government seemed to blame the failure on the ignorance of the people rather than question the probity of adopting Western models in the first place. Moreover, it seemed that Itō, in his association with Ōkuma Shigenobu and other Anglophile progressives, had in mind an even more far-reaching program of reform which threatened to destroy the traditional substance of Japanese moral life.

On top of all this, it was clear that the circle of influence within government was slowly but surely shrinking to encompass a close-knit elite of the former Satsuma and Chōshū Clans. Tani and Miura were both from Chōshū, granted, but they were not affiliated with the leading faction of the clan that Itō Hirobumi had come to control. The others were from the former Tosa and Yanagikawa Clans,—important allies at the time of the Restoration militarily but increasingly marginalized thereafter.[18]

All the foregoing factors conspired to engender a profound disquiet among the more retrospective elements of the military elite about the nation's direction, and the focus of blame became increasingly directed toward the person of Itō Hirobumi himself. It was not always clearly articulated as an ideology; the ideal of the moral ruler in the modern context was rendered using a variety of terms and framed in reference to a variety of Japanese religious and philosophical traditions, from Buddhism and Shintō to Confucianism. Yet by the late 1880s it would have the clarity of a social movement and involve a network of political organizations—some merely consisting of loose "clubs", others being full-blown political parties.

Conservative activists: Tani Tateki and Torio Koyata

The "Four Generals" just alluded to were not the sole driving force behind the movement but they played an important role in giving it "bite" by virtue of being high-ranking officers of the army—unmistakable elites within the public service. They were not journalists, bureaucrats or career politicians, but indispensable personnel within that apparatus of the state dealing with the defense of the realm—an eminently significant position given the Japan's position in the world at the time. Most importantly, they regarded themselves primarily as servants of the Emperor more than employees of the government. Accordingly, they merit some discussion, although for the sake of brevity, I will focus on two here: Tani Tateki and Torio Koyata.

Tani was an exemplary soldier from the former Tosa domain who, as mentioned earlier, distinguished himself as the defender of Kumamoto castle against the besieging forces of Saigō Takamori during the Seinan War of 1877. Following his promotion, he was to get a closer view of the direction the nation was taking first hand, and it was beginning to alarm him. His outstanding military record led to his being appointed head of the army's Military Academy. Nonetheless, as his discontent with the government peaked in 1881, he engaged in the tactic that was to become the staple of military "hardball" with civilian institutions— he resigned. His resignation was ostensibly over a dispute regarding the scope of pension disbursements to the families of soldiers—they were limited to immediate family in line with the French system whereas he felt that this was inconsistent with Japanese familial ties. The fact of the matter is probably that he was chaffing under the yoke of the government and wanted to be openly critical from the outside.[19]

The ensuing public release of the Four Generals' memorandum had precisely the effect that was hoped for and indeed it seemed to allay the fears of conservatives as to the degree to which Itō Hirobumi would be permitted to proceed with radical reform. Eventually Tani would re-emerge as the Minister of Commerce and Agriculture in Itō's first "transcendental" cabinet. In the March of 1886, he set out for Europe to acquaint himself with European systems of government first hand. At the suggestion of Itō Hirobumi, he also visited Lorenz von Stein in Vienna to become versed in the historicist and socially organicist conception of constitutional development. Tani totally concurred with von Stein's prognostications about the need to accommodate the existing culture and traditions of a nation in a constitution, along with the concomitant caution required when attempting to adopt Western political institutions in the Japanese context. However, he took rather different lessons about which models Japan should refer to in its process of political redefinition. In his travel diary, he noted how the Egyptians had been virtually enslaved by the British and French as the result of over-ambitious reforms undertaken with huge (and practically un-repayable) loans from those powers. He noted too the despotism of Germany and its relatively fragile cohesiveness, preferring the relative independence and national integration of Switzerland—its body of militarily trained citizenry ready at any time to spring to the defense of the nation's borders. These lessons were indeed teased into a justification of the views he already had—a conviction that a morally benevolent ruler bound in unity with a morally and militarily educated populace was the safest foundation for Japan's future.[20]

Consequently, the reconciliation with Itō was relatively short-lived. After returning from Europe in June of 1887, an issue that became the immediate object of his ire was Inoue Kaoru's ill-fated proposal for revision of the "unequal treaties." It had become known that part of the proposed revision included the employment of foreign judges to sit in Japanese courts—something which amounted to extraterritoriality by another name. Tani again resigned in protest and thereafter sought to remonstrate with the government through a memorandum, "The Essentials of Government", that lambasted (among a number of things) the politics of personal connections, the frivolous influence of European culture and, of course, the nefarious treaty revisions. Interestingly, Tani became an instant *cause célèbre* among the more rowdy elements of the Freedom and Peoples Rights movement, leading even to a public rally of some three hundred agitators at Yasukuni Shrine where a banner describing Tani as "Shield and Bulwark of the Nation" was unfurled. It was certainly true that Tani had little sympathy for the radical aspirations of the Freedom and Peoples Rights movement—yet it must have been nonetheless gratifying to know that his supra-political approach was winning supporters even among his erstwhile foes.[21]

There was nothing exceptionally sophisticated in Tani's politics or his ideological outlook. Beyond the ideal of realizing a traditionalistic and paternalistic advocacy of a form of moral government centered on the Emperor and his vigorous insistence on reining in Westernizing influences, he had relatively little that was new to contribute intellectually, and he consistently distanced himself from party politics. He was, nonetheless, an instrumental figure in promoting the political concept of *Chūsei* (中正), the notion that public service consisted of loyally striving to maintain the good of the nation and the Imperial Household without recourse to the petty interests of personal gain or political party.[22] It was, in a practical political sense, dazzlingly naïve but it struck a chord among those who were either disgusted with the personalization of the executive and/or averse to any further accommodation of Western influences in domestic politics. In a propaganda sense, therefore, it was a masterstroke in that it moralized the political sphere and thereby encased the conservative political agenda in a supra-political discourse that implied, by definition, that opposition to that agenda was not so much political as *immoral*.

By contrast with Tani, a more direct political activism is evident in the activities of Torio Koyata, who ultimately became much more overtly involved in party-political organization. Unlike Tani, Torio was from Chōshū and therefore somewhat better connected. He began his career as an impoverished lower-ranking *samurai* who found a way out of obscurity and penury through dedication to the Restoration cause. After distinguishing himself on the field in the Boshin War, he was promoted to the rank of staff officer in the *Kemmutai* which was dispatched to quell the remaining resistance to the new government in Oū in 1869. However, en route, he became enmeshed in the political controversy surrounding the return of domain registers to the Emperor and actually went absent without leave to remain under cover at the house of Itō Hirobumi whom he chose to support. It was clearly a fortuitous decision, one that earned him an important future patron and ensured that even the misdemeanor of going absent without leave resulted in a symbolic punishment of confinement to quarters for 30 days.[23]

Torio clearly had an eye for the political implications of military organization and remained an ardent advocate of centralizing the military establishment under government control. He was also inclined to set down his forthright opinions in memoranda which he would fearlessly submit to superiors without qualm. One of the earliest examples was one submitted to Saigō Takamori in 1873 while the Iwakura Mission was still out of the country and Saigō was essentially the caretaker head of government. In it he describes how scholarship and martial training can be regarded as two wheels on a cart and how it would be impossible to reform both without the cart stopping altogether. His priority was firmly on military training (he suggested that two thirds of all tax revenue ought to be devoted to it!) and he insisted that it ought to take priority over the dilatory and largely disruptive reform of letters and learning that was happening in the name of *Bunmei Kaika*. Saigō welcomed Torio's opinion but felt constrained to wait until the Mission's return before proceeding to implement any of his suggestions.[24]

As has already been touched upon, the return of the Mission led to the curtailing of such a military-centered vision of reform and the quashing of all aspirations for embarking on a military expedition to Korea. Torio seemed to be talked round by his Chōshū superiors, particularly Kido Takayoshi; however, he did not altogether lose the notion of prioritizing military virtues along with a pronounced reticence with regard to Western cultural influences. In 1875, he produced a memorandum submitted to the *Genrōin* which was entitled "On the Origins of National Strength" (国勢因果論). In it, he appears to have come under some degree of influence from the nascent democratic movement in that he begins to advocate "popular rights". However, a close reading reveals that the core of his argument is to remonstrate with the government for pursuing Westernized notions of progress at the expense of the well being of the people. Moreover, he distinguishes between a "high" form of popular rights theory and a "low" form which he associates with the radical demands for a broadly enfranchised parliament—a clear swipe at the political program being propounded by the likes of former Councillors of State such as Itagaki Taisuke and his Liberal Party.[25]

In a further paper issued later in the same year and entitled "Popular Rights", he outlined more explicitly a notion of mutual rights and duties between the sovereign and the people which, in essence, reproduced the traditional Confucian notion of the Sovereign having a moral duty to maintain the welfare of the people who in turn must submit to his benevolent rule—in this, he makes it clear that he is not relying on Western concepts of popular rights but a paternalistic ideal of virtuous harmony between the ruler and the ruled.

Nonetheless, despite these reservations regarding Western conceptions of popular representation, he was in fact quite adamant about the need to expand representation and consultation at the executive level, primarily through expansion of the *Genrōin* (Chamber of Elders). Clearly, with the advent of the Seinan War, there was little room for discussion of such matters and from 1876 to 1878, Torio made no indication of disquiet or dissent with government policy. Following the cessation of hostilities, however, he made it clear that he expected an expansion of the deliberative apparatus of state and even claimed that Itō Hirobumi had personally undertaken to implement that aim. When no such action was forthcoming, he petitioned his superiors in the May of 1878 to be relieved of his duties within the military command and went "on holiday" in the Kansai region.

However, Torio's plans of protest did not go as anticipated. The Takehashi Incident, a mutiny where 260 soldiers rose up and assembled before the Akasaka Palace to demand better treatment and conditions following the conclusion of the Seinan War, led to a bloody suppression. Torio was recalled to the capital a number of times to assist in the "clean-up" but he refused to comply. In the end, as had been the case with other recalcitrants before him, it was a personal order from the Emperor that brought him back to his post.[26]

Torio redoubled his efforts to make his complaint known, this time writing directly to Itō himself, openly criticizing the manner in which the Satsuma and Chōshū domains had come to control "heaven and earth." Iwakura Tomomi attempted to mediate, indicating considerable agreement with Torio's proposals. Nevertheless nothing came of Torio's or Iwakura's efforts and, in 1880, the move to resign was more emphatic—and it was accepted. Torio spent the next six months working on a new memorial, this time to be submitted to none other than the Emperor himself. It was a bold missive that not only drew attention to the pitfalls of adopting mechanistic Western models (and the scurrilous printing of extra currency which had a disastrous effect on the fortunes of ordinary people), but even went so far as to lecture the Emperor on the proper scope of his office. In one sense, it is perhaps hard to understand how a person who regarded respect for the Emperor paramount, could venture to browbeat the very same personage. Yet it should be noted that Torio's view coalesced closely with the views of the Emperor's closest advisors and tutors at the time, and was indeed consistent with what they themselves were attempting to instill in the as yet politically uncertain and untried Mutsuhito.

A more public treatise produced by Torio in 1880, entitled *A Theory of Kingly Rule* (王法論), was to mark a decisive step in the doctrinal clarification and publicizing of the nascent movement for a more direct Imperial Rule (*Tenno Shinsei*, 天皇親政). Divided into ten chapters dealing thematically with the issues of rights and duties enunciated in the earlier treatise *Minkenron*, it worked out more thoroughly the notion of rule based on popular will—a will that was nonetheless expected to be cognizant of the sanctity and sovereignty of the ruler. It was thoroughly Confucian in its political organicism and, in another sense, markedly utopian in that it worked on the premise of an as yet unrealized ideal ruler and an ideal populace.[27]

The treatise also contained the conceptual vagueness that was to become a characteristic element within later conservative debates on the constitution—insisting on the special sanctity of Emperor as ruler while retaining an "out clause" for ministerial responsibility should things go wrong. There seems little reason to doubt that Torio believed that an expanded deliberative assembly, one that incorporated all the notables of the land, not just the elites of Satsuma and Chōshū, would provide the Imperial government with the mechanism to mediate this duality. Yet it was conceptually muddled and constitutionally unworkable—not that that in fact mattered to the advocates of Emperor-centered rule. Their focus was on stemming the tide of facile emulation of the West and the realization of a "moral" form of government. Theirs was indeed a profound sense of moral panic akin to that felt strongly at the beginning of the country's opening 30 years earlier. If they could succeed in rousing their fellows to the same degree of alarm then there was some sense of having achieved something "positive."

In the contemporary context of "popular rights" agitation, *shizoku* discontent and seething anti-foreign sentiment, the fact is that this new ideological movement proved to resonate profoundly with the disaffected of various stripes. Indeed Torio's treatise was an important harbinger of the future possibility of marrying the retrospective aims of Emperor-centered rule with radical activism.

In any event, it is no surprise that Torio leapt into the breach with Tani Tateki and the other two Generals to reproach the government publicly in the aforementioned jointly issued memorandum of 1881. As a result, each one of them reaped the favor of that cadre of influential figures within the Imperial Household such as Motoda Eifu and Nishimura Shigeki who could see to it that a career detour could be arranged if need be. In the case of Tani Tateki, he became (in 1884) the Chancellor of the Peers College (Gakushūin), a tertiary educational institution set up primarily to cater to the Imperial family and the aristocracy. Torio was dispatched to Europe at the public expense in 1885 as an officer appended to the *Genrōin*. As for the other two generals, Miura was sent to Europe to study military institutions with Ōyama Gake in 1884 and

Soga Sukenori became by turns a special attaché to the Imperial Household, the President of Nippon Rail and later on an attaché to the Privy Council. All four Generals entered the House of Peers following the promulgation of the Meiji Constitution in either the capacity of appointed officers or by virtue of becoming members of the aristocracy. Miura was even appointed as special envoy to Korea in 1885, although his reputation became somewhat tarnished through association with the assassination of a member of the Korean aristocracy.[28]

The real clout of these military elites was to be felt even more strongly in the late 1880s following their various stints of touring in Europe and the furor that arose over Inoue's proposed treaty revisions. This drove them back to the familiar turf of anti-government activism and, more significantly, the organization of political associations. Ironically, it was the very spectre of factionalized and divisive party politics that alarmed them most and drew the likes of Torio Koyata and other like-minded conservatives to set about establishing a broad political coalition that would compete with the political parties aligned with radical "Freedom and Peoples Rights". These developments will be examined in more detail once we have reviewed some of the other key players in the development of 1880s conservatism in other institutional contexts.[29]

Conservative activism: The court faction

The other main challenge to Itō Hirobumi from within the uppermost circles of the Meiji establishment was to come from the Imperial Household, particularly the cadre of special advisors to the Meiji Emperor who, from the late 1870s onward, came to have considerable success in redirecting and grooming the young Emperor for fulfilment of the more august role that they conceived as being more appropriate. As Itō Yukio's recent biography of the Meiji Emperor lucidly details, there was an initial phase from the Restoration to the late 70s where the Emperor evolved from being the puppet of the new regime to being an important player and power-broker in his own right. He was, after all, only 16 when he ascended the Chrysanthemum Throne – far too young to be regarded as much more than an important talisman in the turbulent business of Restoration reform. As has already been alluded to, the cultivation of the Emperor as warrior through a rather strict regimen of training in horse-riding, target practice and parade ground drills was implemented largely at the behest of Saigō Takamori. Yet as the star of Saigō began to wane following the return of the Iwakura Mission, and the Imperial Household began to reassert its influence, it became apparent that the Emperor himself was becoming aware of the need for training in areas other than martial arts. It was within this context that the first Imperial Tutors, or *Jiho* (侍補), were appointed to give instruction in matters deemed appropriate for the Sovereign of the realm.[30]

The initial *Jiho* were appointed on 29 August 1877, as part of a more general shake-up of government following the conclusion of the Seinan War. Apart from Motoda Eifu (1818–91), about whom there will be much more to say in the ensuing pages, there were four others appointed: Yoshii Tomozane (1828–91), a Satsuma *samurai* who was a disaffected former supporter of Saigō Takamori; Takasaki Seifu (1836–1912), another Satsuma clansman of *samurai* lineage whose father was forced to perform *seppuku* during the period of clan infighting prior to the Restoration—his specialization was poetry composition; Hijikata Hisamoto (1833–1918), a Tosa clansman who had strong connections to the aristocracy prior to the Restoration, particularly Sanjō Sanetomi, and acted as an undersecretary to a succession of ministers of state, particularly those related to Internal Affairs, the *Dajōkan* and later on the Imperial Household; and Tokudaiji Sanenori (1840–1919), a member of the Imperial family whose role it was to oversee the program of training.[31]

With the exception of Tokudaiji, all these persons, including the Satsuma members, had some sort of grievance against the existing government and/or a special interest in seeing the Imperial Household strengthened and promoted above the Satsuma–Chōshū government as it then existed. A significant addition was made in the February of 1879—the inclusion of Sasaki Takayuki (1830–1910), a former officer within the Council of State who hailed from Tosa (along with Hijikata) and quickly distinguished himself as one of the most single-minded activists in the promotion of conservative political associations, including the eventual establishment of the *Chūseito* in 1881 with the collaboration of his fellow clansman Tani Tateki.[32]

The quietly determined intention of Motoda, Takasaki and Sasaki was to cultivate the young Emperor with a view to establish a more direct form of Imperial rule (天皇親政). Following the assassination of Ōkubo Toshimichi on 14 May 1878, the *Jiho* group attempted to capitalize on the turmoil to promote the Imperial authority (and by extension themselves) within the structure of government. However, Tokudaiji, who regarded the direct engagement of the Emperor in politics as a dangerous move soon quashed their plans. Itō Hirobumi, once fully aware of the group's intentions, formally abolished the position of *Jiho* on 13 October 1878.[33]

Consequently, the much-vaulted reinforcement of the Restoration reforms along the original lines determined among the 1868 clique centered around Ōkubo Toshimichi came crashing to something of a halt. More alarming than this was the slow realization that there was a growing cadre of antagonists who were beginning to subtly wrest the Imperial Household out of government control and indeed use it to subvert government policy. The greatest danger so far as the public domain was concerned was the fact that these antagonistic parties could portray themselves as representing the spirit of the *real* Restoration—they held out the promise that the Emperor would actually rule and the treaties would be revised without delay.

Even after the office of *Jiho* was formally abolished, this did not mean that the influence of the *Tenno Shinsei* faction was neutralized. The Emperor still received "instruction" from a variety of relevant experts and he himself began to see merit in developing political influence within the government.

A major turning point was an Imperial tour of the provinces to the north in Hokuetsu, south along the coast to Fukui and thence back to Tokyo via Kyoto and Shiga. During this late summer tour, the Emperor was able to witness the effects of the post-Restoration educational reforms first hand, and it appears that he was appalled by the break-down in social order and traditional propriety among the common people, particularly as witnessed in the classroom. Motoda naturally concurred with this view, indeed would have positively encouraged it, and duly set about writing a memorandum to Itō Hirobumi remonstrating with him about the collapse of moral education and advocating the introduction of a curriculum of Confucian-based moral instruction termed *Shūshin* (修身). The document, framed as an outline of the Emperor's personal opinion, was actually made up of two sections that had been penned by Motoda himself—one dealing with the fundamental rationale of education (教育大旨), the other dealing with the matter of juvenile education more specifically (小学条目二件).[34]

The main complaint was that the offspring of businessmen and farmers were having their heads filled with "empty theories" from the West that had no practical merit and, if anything, were positively detrimental. In lieu of such meddling in Western theories, the memorandum demanded a return to a more practical focus while education would be grounded in the promotion of the traditional virtues of benevolence, obligation, loyalty to the throne and loyalty to one's parents (仁義忠孝). Since Itō was specifically asked to comment, he drafted a reply, *Kyōikugi* (教育議), which basically agreed with the essence of the observation that the standard of moral conduct had slid over the past ten years, yet he rejected the view that it was due to "Westernizing" reforms. It was the inevitable result of a major social transformation which had to be carried through regardless of short-term ill effects.[35]

Motoda, not at all satisfied with this reply, issued a further remon-strance to the same effect, the *Kyōikugi Fugi* (教育議付議). In the end, Itō undertook to look into ways in which moral instruction could be gainfully implemented in the classroom and in the Revised Educational Ordinance of 1880, moral education went from being at the bottom of the list of curriculum content to being at the top.[36]

It is at this point that Nishimura Shigeki became particularly active in the capacity of an occasional tutor to the Emperor and an increasingly prominent official within the Education Ministry, becoming the head of the new textbook compilation bureau in 1880. In his lectures to the Emperor, Nishimura had aimed to give a comprehensive overview of both Western and native schools of thought yet his ultimate objective was the promotion of traditional Japanese morality through *Shūshin*. In 1874, Nishimura had established an association to promote moral education, the *Tōkyō Shūshin Gakusha* (東京修身学社). This developed into a network of regional branches and thereafter grew into a national association later renamed the *Nihon Kōdōkai* (日本弘道会) in 1884, an organization that was to go on to have a substantial national member-ship and considerable political influence. And of particular significance in connection with the foregoing dispute over moral education, it is noteworthy that it was Nishimura who was entrusted with the task of supervising the textbook for moral education (小学修身訓).[37]

Gradualist conservatism under siege

Given the extraordinary rise in activism not only from within the popular rights movement but also from within the Emperor-aligned establishment, it is not hard to comprehend that Itō Hirobumi felt hemmed in and surrounded by hostile forces in 1880 (and in many regards he literally was). The "revolt" by Ōkuma in 1881 was after all one more instance of political opportunism sprouting in the wake of Ōkubo Toshimichi's demise but it came from within the circle that was supposed to be on his side. Accordingly, Itō could understandably feel entitled to act swiftly and ruthlessly in dealing with it.

As had been the case following the sort of political resolution that was achieved through the abolition of the domains in 1871, Itō struck out on a bold move to take the initiative by absenting himself and undertaking an investigative tour—this time in Europe. Given that so much attention has been heaped on the liberal democratic movement, it is understandable that the presumption prevails that it was the sense of threat from the more radical parliamentary reform advocates such as Itagaki Taisuke and Ōkuma Shigenobu that drove him overseas to develop a more fully wrought intellectual response. That was certainly true to a certain extent, but the objections that Itō made to the radical parliamentary reformers hardly needed a tour of Europe to be clarified. On the contrary, it was the need to come up with something to convince his conservative colleagues, allies and foes alike, that an alternative to the crude direct rule advocated by them existed and that it was likely to have greater credibility and be more durable.

When Itō set out for Europe in the March of 1882, he had a form of "insurance" prior to his departure—a special proclamation made by the Emperor, at Itō's behest, which enjoined soldiers to serve loyally and maintain discipline. In the month immediately following Itō's departure, Ōkuma established the *Rikken Kaishintō* (*Constitutional Reform Party*). Thereafter, Itō's de facto "caretaker", Yamagata Aritomo, was forced to deal with a surge in agitation through the popular press that led in April of 1883 to heavy-handed circumscription of the press through new legislation.[38]

However, from the August of 1882, Itō had finally found a cogent scholar and commentator on constitutional issues in Europe who also had an eye for practical administration—Lorenz von Stein. Von Stein, far from being a member of the Prussian jurisprudential school, was in fact an outcast and in exile in Vienna. Consequently, Itō was embarking on an extended program of "education" through a series of lectures and consultations delivered by von Stein and a record of those initial encounters still exists. The essence of von Stein's approach was a certain social organicism which was increasingly becoming an intrinsic element in Germanic social thought through the broad influence of Haeckel and Bluntschli. Most importantly, von Stein advocated the most extreme caution in experimenting in Western representative institutions and constitutional arrangements given that they were themselves relatively new in European experience and only arrived at after an extremely drawn-out period of gestation. It was with a sense of triumph that Itō could write back to Yamagata to announce that he had found the ideal ammunition to fend off the radicals and, one mustn't forget, win over the traditionalists who would not have a bar of any institutional arrangements that were not the practical equivalents of institutions that had not functioned in Japanese society since the period of the Ancient Court.[39]

From the February of 1883, Itō traveled to London where he stayed for two months. During this time, he consolidated his lecture notes and apparently consulted another great contemporary social thinker, Herbert Spencer.[40] Spencer's social evolutionism was of a more thoroughly positivistic nature and lacked perhaps the historicism of his

Germanic counterparts, yet he offered more or less identical comments on the proposed constitutional reforms for Japan—Japan must not attempt to move too far from its existing social and political configuration as any excessively radical departure would be bound to fail through the lack of requisite experience and social development. After a brief visit to Russia, he departed from Napoli for Japan on 26 June.

While Itō was in transit, the government was struck by the loss of Iwakura Tomomi who had been unwell for some time. In one sense, it meant that a key advocate of Emperor-centered government was now out of picture, yet it remains true that Iwakura and Itō had worked well together since the inception of the Restoration, and the death of Iwakura meant the loss of an important avenue of influence within the aristocracy.

As already alluded to, Yamagata had felt it necessary in Itō's absence to clamp down on the popular press. Yet, if anything, the general tenor of public order was heading in an unfavorable direction with the radical wing of Itagaki's Liberal Party getting embroiled in violent acts of political agitation, the most famous being the Chichibu Incident of October 1884 where an alliance of Liberal Party activists and discontented peasants rose in Saitama demanding a decrease in taxation and clashed with the local police. It was quelled by the military in ten days. In a more arcane vein, there was also a plot by radical Liberals to engage in an armed robbery to finance an insurgency—the Nagoya Incident. This was foiled and three of those accused were executed while another 23 were given indefinite sentences of imprisonment.[41]

At the same time, issues related to Korean–Japanese relations were also resurfacing, this time with intensified conflict over a broader area. The "Jingo" Incident as mentioned earlier, drew the Japanese government into direct conflict with China over Korean self-determination. This had the rather curious effect of drawing popular rights activism into avenues of anti-Chinese sentiment and the promotion of Korean "independence", naturally with a very strong input from Japan. In the November of 1885, Ōi Kentaro was arrested as part of a 123-man contingent that was planning to cross over to Korea and fight against the Chinese. This would have been an enormous embarrassment to the government given its diplomatic resolution of the conflict with China earlier in the year.[42]

Itō regains the initiative

Despite the protracted phase of unrest, the government under Itō Hirobumi's leadership was by 1885 able to move back into a proactive mode and consolidate its position with relative independence from the pressure of popular agitations and high-level sabotage from within other quarters of government. In the December of 1885, the *Dajōkan*, essentially the relic of earlier attempts to accommodate the institutional precedents of the Ancient Court, was abolished and in its place a new system of Cabinet-based government was established with Itō as the first Prime Minister. The appointments to other portfolios reflected a new solidity in Itō's position—Tani Tateki was brought back into the fold through the offer and acceptance of the post of Commerce and Agriculture Minister. Mori Arinori was appointed the first Minister of Education in the new system, and this was despite concerted lobbying on the part of Motoda Eifu directly to the Emperor himself to have the appointment quashed. Most importantly, the fact that the Emperor chose to endorse Itō Hirobumi's choice rather than follow the advice of his former "tutors" indicated a deepening level of trust between the Emperor and his Prime Minister.[43]

The foregoing resolution indicated the burgeoning confidence of the young Emperor and an ostensible preparedness to take more decisive positions with regard to crucial appointments. The first sign that the Emperor was inclined to flex his power independently came earlier in 1885 following the protracted negotiations with China to resolve the Korean issue. The Emperor had made it clear that he did not favor a military conflict and, although it does not conclusively indicate direct political influence, the outcome that ensued was in line with the Emperor's wishes and there can be little likelihood that the Chiefs of Staff in the military, given their usual predilection to put the Emperor above the ministers of state, would not have been inclined to ignore the Imperial will if it were made clear to them.

In the aftermath of the 1881 purge, the Emperor had in fact exhibited an increasingly strong inclination to express an independent line and even at times withdraw cooperation. In fact, it was due to precisely such assertiveness that the Emperor began to absent himself early from the Council of State meetings that he had been attending regularly since 1879, often talking with court ministers about matters of personal interest before retiring prematurely. These were acts of political disruption that frustrated Itō to the point of him offering his resignation. Fortunately, by late 1885, their relationship and mutual trust had been restored—but it was with a more subtle reconfiguration of their relationship.

Itō now had more stable control over the broader political arena and was finally free to devote his attention to the weighty matters of the Imperial Constitution and the promulgation of the legal ordinances that codified the status of the Imperial Household. With the assistance of Inoue Kowashi, who increasingly came to have a key influence in such matters, Itō was able to expedite the new legal code covering the aristocracy with relative speed—effectively emasculating the broader aristocracy as a political class while defining the Imperial Household in terms that would be more conducive to Constitutional Monarchy.[44]

The Meiji state and the academy

At this juncture it would be pertinent to address in brief how the leading intellectuals of the earlier *Bunmei Kaika* phase were faring during the post–Seinan War period. As was broadly outlined at the end of the chapter on the *Kaika* movement, the various Charter Members went their several ways, and did so very much according to their idiosyncratic skills and interests. However, it was not to be the end of their association altogether. An important reprise of the *Meirokusha* was conducted from 1879 onward when the government set up the *Tōkyō Gakushikaiin* (東京学士会院).

The *Tōkyō Gakushikaiin* (hereafter "the Tokyo Academy") was initiated by Tanaka Fujimaro when he was undersecretary to Saigō Tsugumichi, the Minister of Education, at the end of 1878. In December of that year, he invited seven of the former *Meirokusha* members—Nishi Amane, Katō Hiroyuki, Kanda Takahira, Tsuda Mamichi, Nakamura Masanao, Fukuzawa Yukichi, Mitsukuri Shuhei—to his private residence and broached the idea of establishing a broadly inclusive association of leading scholars to participate in the deliberation of the nation's educational policy. It was to have its own constitution and an elected President while being placed administratively within the jurisdiction of the Ministry of Education. According to Katō Hiroyuki's recollection of the occasion, the proposal was assented to with all round enthusiasm and Fukuzawa Yukichi, in marked contrast to his earlier reticence at the founding of the *Meirokusha*, accepted the offer of the Presidency (he received three votes to Mitsukuri's two with one each for Kanda and Katō). The first official gathering was held on 15 January of the following year at the Ministry's *Shūbunkan* building and Fukuzawa attending the meetings thereafter without a single lapse.[45]

The Tokyo Academy was to have its membership limited to 40 persons and at the regular meetings on the fifteenth of each month (with some occasional extraordinary sessions), the number of participants was slowly expanded through the election of two new persons at each meeting. At the seventh meeting held on 15 April, a new regulation was

adopted to accommodate the possibility of members making presentations and Fukuzawa immediately obliged by delivering a paper entitled
"On Education." At the eleventh session, there was a change of President
with Fukuzawa being replaced by Nishi Amane (with six votes). In any
event, Fukuzawa continued to attend and participate assiduously.

Some particular emphasis needs to be put on Fukuzawa's enthusiasm
for the Tokyo Academy as there is the rather controversial issue that arises
in relation to the fact that he later on tendered the explosive proposal
that the Tokyo Academy relinquish its government-paid honorarium, in
effect disrupting proceedings for some months as the debate over this
proposal raged. It warrants emphasis here that Fukuzawa was enthusiastic about the Tokyo Academy's aims at the outset, and the nature of his
contributions indicate a degree of engagement that was rather lacking in
the *Meirokusha*. His initial contribution, "A Proposal for Determining the
Examination of Exceptional Students for Exemption from Conscription
at Private High Schools" comes third after Fukuba Bisei's paper proposing
the publication of a textbook for Japanese grammar and Mori Arinori's
contribution of a paper on physical education.[46]

As the membership of the Tokyo Academy expanded substantially,
a journal was produced to publicize the presentations. As is evidenced
by the table of contents for each issue, the list of contributions to the
journal came to include those of persons somewhat removed from the
"former-*Meirokusha*" orbit. On the one hand, there were new specialists
in science such as the noted botanist, Itō Keisuke, who became a particularly prolific contributor, as well as an increased presence of figures
who were hostile to the original Tanaka Fujimaro line and intent on
reforming education toward more traditionalistic and conservative aims.
The early appearance of Fukuba Bisei is especially noteworthy given that
he was a fervent advocate of State Shintō. There is also the increasing
prominence of conservatives such as Nishimura Shigeki, not surprising
in itself given his earlier *Meirokusha* associations, but significant at this
time given that he was increasingly collaborating with Motoda Eifu.

The foregoing emergence of a conservative clique within the Academy
was part of a broader movement that led to the eventual ousting of
Tanaka Fujimaro from the position of Education Minister in the March
of 1880 and the promulgation of a new Revised Education Ordnance
later that year. This certainly indicated a fundamental redefining of
the context within which the Tokyo Academy had to operate. On
15 January 1880, Nishimura Shigeki tabled a proposal for improving
the performance of the Tokyo Academy by calling for a higher level
of output from the members. In one sense, this was a call for more

effort to invigorate the Tokyo Academy and give it the public role that was anticipated at its inception.[47] On the other hand, it indicated the ascendant influence of the conservative elements and it is to this that Ōkubo Toshiaki, in his writing on Fukuzawa and the Tokyo Academy, attaches the greatest importance when discussing Fukuzawa's motives for his "bombshell" proposal regarding the honorarium being given to the Tokyo Academy members.

Fukuzawa submitted his proposal at the twenty-second meeting of the Tokyo Academy on 15 September 1880. The details of the honorarium payments themselves do not require extensive discussion here—the matter of greatest purport in the petition was Fukuzawa's contention that receipt of payments from the Ministry of Education by state servants amounted to a form of "double-dipping" and ought to cease. Katō Hiroyuki, who had been stung personally by Fukuzawa's earlier broadside at the government-employed scholars of the *Meirokusha* in 1873, reacted immediately and with the greatest vehemence stating plainly that Fukuzawa's petition amounted to a proposal to disband the Tokyo Academy. Nishimura Shigeki attempted to mediate with a proposal that the Tokyo Academy should carry on as usual and consider the matter of whether to disband or not, purely on the basis of assessing the Tokyo Academy's performance.[48]

There were few supporters of Fukuzawa—a prominent exception was the qualified agreement of Nakamura Masanao who suggested the payments be accumulated and redisbursed after a number of years according to the wishes of each member. The remainder divided up into either supporters of Katō's assessment that the proposal was to debate whether to disband the Tokyo Academy or not (including Kanda Takahira and Fukuzawa's protégé, Kohata Tokujirō) or supporters of Nishimura's sage gradualism (including Mitsukuri Shūhei). Overall, the majority were probably possessed by a sense of bafflement that Fukuzawa had chosen to submit such an inflammatory petition after having been so active in the Tokyo Academy. Mitsukuri Rinshō and Fukuba Bisei were the only ones who expressed the opinion that the Tokyo Academy should not be debating such a matter in the first place.

Nishi as President adjourned the debate until the following meeting on 15 October. The springboard for continued discussion turned out to be a letter submitted to Nishi by Mitsukuri Shūhei who was unable to attend. In it, he stated that "although Fukuzawa's suggestion regarding the honorarium payments is logical and of some interest, it is nonetheless a little exaggerated and disruptive." He went on to suggest a compromise that involved reducing the amount of the payments and expanding the membership. To this, both Sakatani Shiroshi and Fukuba Bisei added their own views which amounted to a rejection of both the proposal to disband the Tokyo Academy and the unreasonableness of Fukuzawa's petition.

In the midst of this continuing discussion, Fukuzawa Yukichi once more stood to present his own view. With characteristic clarity, he asserted that his original aim was simply to point out the inappropriateness of public servants receiving income from two public sources and that he could not comprehend so trivial a debate about how much was being received and whether it befitted the work being done. This sparked another flurry of response which ended with Mitsukuri Rinshō suggesting that indeed the focus of discussion had drifted away from the original intent of the petition and would require a fresh round of debate. Immediately following this suggestion, Shigeno Yasutsugu, a noted scholar of classical Chinese, gave vent to his frustrations and more or less dismissed the issue of honorariums as something that pertained purely to the decision of each individual and should not be deliberated on in such a fashion.

With Shigeno's eminently sensible observation, Nishi clearly felt that the way was clear to bring the issue to a close. He proposed that the matter of whether the Tokyo Academy be disbanded or not be dropped and discussion limited to whether Fukuzawa's petition could be debated in relation to improving the administration of the Tokyo Academy. The members were invited to bring written comments on how the regulations of the Tokyo Academy might be amended to accommodate such revisions and consider setting up a committee to oversee the matter.

At the ensuing meeting held on 15 November, a detailed proposal was tabled by Hosokawa Junjirō (a Tosa scholar of Western studies) and discussion continued afresh, albeit without Fukuzawa. Given that so many difficulties had been raised with regard to the feasibility of opening this administrative "can of worms", and given that Fukuzawa had so few supporters in the matter, the decision had obviously been made to quit the Tokyo Academy. Fukuzawa's request to be removed from the membership of the Tokyo Academy, accompanied by the resignation of his disciple Kohata Tokujirō, was tabled at the meeting of 15 December, and reluctantly formally accepted in February of the following year.

Clearly there is a degree of validity in Ōkubo Toshiaki's assessment that it was the deviation from the original direction of the Tokyo Academy combined with frustration at the inveterate fastidiousness and, at times, downright silliness of some of the more senior members such as Katō Hiroyuki and Nishi Amane. Yet Fukuzawa was no stranger to the foibles of these people and one would have expected him to be twice wary of becoming involved at all in this re-run of the *Meirokusha* if indeed it were such an issue.

Other explanations of his conduct toward the end of his involvement in the Tokyo Academy tend to take his petition (as well as his Autobiography) completely uncritically, ascribing his attack on public servants receiving honorariums as an example of the highest liberal and civic aspirations. Establishing exactly what motivates historical figures at a particular juncture in their careers must always be difficult; however, one would expect that explanations based on the assumption of the very noblest intentions are bound to be unreliable. More prosaic, albeit convincing explanations are available based on a reasonable assessment of the long-term trends and general context of that person's conduct, and in Fukuzawa's case this also holds true.

First, if there had been any particular reservation about mixing public and private offices, Fukuzawa must surely have had these concerns at the outset and been wary of becoming involved in it. The fact is that he relished the opportunity to participate and did not display any reservations until much later on. Moreover, from 1878 he had been elected as a Prefectural Diet member and was thereby already in breach of his averred ideals from the outset. And while it is certainly the case that he resigned from the Prefectural Assembly in the January of 1880, it is noteworthy that this coincided with the establishment of the *Kōjunsha* (交詢社), a gentlemen's club that was to have a national network and to have considerable number of contemporary entrepreneurs and businessmen enrolled in it. It is hard to conceive that he could have succeeded in this undertaking without the connections he developed as a member of the Prefectural Assembly or without the prestige he enjoyed as first President of the Tokyo Academy.[49]

Second, the wording of his petition was so bound to offend and create divisions that it is hard to escape the conclusion that he fully intended to cause a rupture between himself and the Academy, thereby justifying a quick exit. Fukuzawa was in no hurry to disabuse Katō of his initial assessment that the petition was in effect calling for the disbanding of the Academy, and Katō, based on his earlier experience of dealing with Fukuzawa, was probably fully accurate in his appraisal of Fukuzawa's intentions and therefore intent on making it an utterly adversarial "all or nothing" affair.

It is also possible that Fukuzawa was seeking patronage and funding for his Keiō Gijuku which had come upon lean times due to increased competition from other educational institutions. Just as becoming a member of the Prefectural Assembly would enhance his standing and connections in the local municipality, joining the Academy would undoubtedly have been all to the good in terms of cultivating influence in government circles. The fact that Nishimura and Motoda came to possess greater influence than himself in the Academy may have disappointed him in some regard, but it is interesting to note that Fukuzawa was able to secure a substantial financial endowment from the Imperial Household just prior to his leaving the Academy.

Perhaps most significant to our understanding of Fukuzawa's motivation at the time of his resignation is the fact that his bailing out of the Academy did not signify a move away from courting persons in government circles but quite the reverse. He came to collaborate more closely with Ōkuma Shigenobu and Itō Hirobumi and was on the verge of taking charge of a government-aligned newspaper when the political upheaval of October 1881 wrecked this plan completely. If there were much doubt about the degree to which Fukuzawa had become deeply enmeshed with the political leadership prior to the falling out in October, there is the thoroughness with which Itō felt the need to distance himself from Fukuzawa by purging Keiō graduates from government service.[50]

As for the remainder of the Tokyo Academy members, they muddled on with the revision of the Academy's regulations despite the fact that Fukuzawa was not even there pursuing the matter. Over time, however, the character of the Academy became more ossified as the older generation of scholars came to predominate and the nature of contributions became more staid. Those who had some more gainful contribution to make in government administration, such as Kanda Takahira in finance or Itō Keisuke in science, went on with their lives and left the *Yōgakusha* veterans to it. That is not to say that the veterans ceased to be influential or active in Japanese society. Katō Hiroyuki went on to become the President of Tokyo University and Nishi Amane was prominent in the drafting of the Imperial Rescript to Soldiers and Sailors of 1882. Mori Arinori, after being dispatched to England as Japan's diplomatic representative from 1879, wrote back suggesting that the notion of an Academy was itself moribund and on the decline in Europe. Perhaps not unexpectedly, upon his return to Japan in 1884 and his appointment to the post of Minister of Education in Itō's cabinet in 1885, he effectively sidelined the Academy and it became more the club of academic elites rather than a deliberative body focusing on education policy.[51]

As for Fukuzawa Yukichi, the fortunes of the *Keiō Gijuku* (later Keiō University) were restored and he embarked on a more mainstream publishing venture through the *Jiji Shimpō* newspaper, reflective in many ways of the fact that the days of "pot-boiler" works on Western civilization had had their day and that the urban public were now eager for responses to issues of the moment on a daily basis. His output of this period indeed reflects that he had become attuned to the popular mood with works on national sovereignty (*Kokkenron*) and the need for Japan to relinquish its ties with Asia (*Datsuaron*). It was the result of what Banno Junji aptly highlights as a "decisive moment" in the fate of the movement for representative government in Japan.[52] The political arena was now larger, more complex and unpredictable—a reality that was to come crashing in on Itō's otherwise orderly conception of gradual reform.

6
The Imperial Household, the Popular Press and the Contestation of Public Space

Mass communication and political activism

Fukuzawa was in one sense highly astute in tuning into the new trend in Japanese social and cultural development as there emerged, especially from the early 1880s onward, a distinctly new force in the public arena. This development was different from earlier intellectual activism in that it involved a decidedly younger cohort of intellectuals and it was distinguished yet again by the degree to which the popular press had come into a new phase of maturity, reflecting no doubt the emergence of a more educated, more informed and increasingly urbane reading public.

In relation to the movement for "Freedom and Peoples Rights", Tokutomi Sohō (1863–1957) emerges as one of the most articulate and prolific political commentators of his generation. Born in 1863 to non-*samurai* parents in Kumamoto, he was only five years old at the time of the Restoration and barely into his twenties when he made some of his most important contributions to the debate on popular rights and representation. He had studied at Dōshisha University under Niijima Jō but withdrew from the school prior to graduating due to a falling out with the university's administration. In 1881, he established a private academy, the *Ōe Gijuku*, back in his home region and began making contributions to the local newspapers. He is particularly remembered, however, for his articulation of equal rights through the idiosyncratic term of *Heiminshugi* (平民主義, literally "commoner-ism") which he promoted through substantial treatises, most notably *The Future Japan* (1886), and *Kokumin no Tomo* ("The Nation's Friend") a journal produced under the auspices of the *Minyūsha* which he established in Tokyo from 1887. The *Kokumin Shimbun* was established in 1890 and eclipsed the earlier publication which was wound up in 1898. His later slow but undeniable shift toward the politics of the establishment is less well-documented in English but he was undoubtedly one of the most durable and astute pamphleteers and political commentators of his time.[1]

In contrast to the *Minyūsha*, the *Seikyōsha* emerged as a rival conservative group which became heavily engaged in journal and newspaper publishing at more or less the same time. In 1888, Miyake Setsurei, along with Shiga Shigetaka (18 60–1945) and Sugiura Jūgō (1855–1924), formed the *Seikyōsha* (literally the "Political Education Society") and published a society journal, *Nihonjin*. From 1889, he joined forces with Kuga Katsunan contributing to Kuga's *Nihon* ("Japan"). Brief outlines of the biographical details for each of these persons is required before making any observations about the changes in political direction that their emergence signified.[2]

Miyake Setsurei (1860–1945), the son of a doctor in Kanazawa, was a graduate of the Faculty of Letters, majoring in philosophy at Tokyo University in 1883. While at Tokyo University, he was profoundly influenced by Ernest Fenollosa, who was, somewhat paradoxically given his specialization in visual arts, entrusted with teaching the curriculum for philosophy. The brand of contemporary social philosophy that Fenollosa propagated was more or less unreconstructed social evolutionism as propounded in the voluminous Synthetic Philosophy of Herbert Spencer. To this was added a hefty infusion of Germanic philosophy, particularly Hegelian philosophy of history (as was indeed current in American philosophical circles at the time).[3]

Shiga Shigetaka born in what is now Aichi Prefecture, graduated from the state-run Agricultural College in Sapporo in 1884. Following his graduation, he toured Australia and the South Pacific extensively and produced *Nanyō Jiji* ("Conditions in the South Pacific") in 1887 on his return before joining the *Seikyōsha* as a founding member.[4]

Sugiura Jūgō hailed from Shiga Prefecture and was distinguished as one of the nation's leading students in science, being selected by the government to travel to Britain in 1876 to study chemistry and physics, thereafter returning to Japan in 1880 and, after a brief stint as superintendent of the Science Faculty museum at Tokyo University, was offered the post of Principal of Tokyo University's Preparatory School in 1882. He quit this position in 1885 to take up editorial writing for the Yomiuri newspaper and from there moved into collaboration with the *Seikyōsha* members.[5]

Kuga Katsunan had a slightly distinct background to the other members, being from one of the clans originally most intransigent in their opposition to the Restoration—the Tsugaru domain, now known as Iwate Prefecture. Like Miyake, he was the son of a doctor but he did not complete his education at either the Miyagi Normal School or the Justice Ministry's Law School due to a falling out with the principals of both institutions (in the former case the principal was from Satsuma). While at the Law School, he became acquainted with the future Prime Minister Hara Kei who came from the same prefecture and they both returned to their home region after suspension from the school in 1879.

After a stint at the Aomori Newspaper and several visits to Hokkaido, he returned to Tokyo in 1881 where his talent for French was recognized and he was appointed to the secretariat of the (then) Dajōkan. This post he quit in 1887 following the furor over Inoue Kaoru's controversial treaty revisions and this led him into publishing a newspaper at his own initiative, the *Tōyō Dempō* (Oriental Telegraph), which was later renamed *Nihon* a year later. Though not a founding member of the *Seikyōsha*, he had a natural affinity with its members and his newspaper attracted an increasing number of *Seikyōsha* contributions from 1889 onward (from 1890, Miyake Setsurei became more directly involved among the editorial staff).[6]

There is one more figure who ought to be given special attention in relation to the *Seikyōsha* even though he was not a prominent contributor after its establishment in 1888—Komura Jūtarō (1855–1911).

Komura hailed from Miyazaki (formerly the Obi Clan), after attending the *Kaiseigakko* in Nagasaki as a scholarship student. Eventually, he was dispatched to the US to study at Harvard Law School, graduating in 1880. After a series of relatively elevated yet unsatisfying positions within the legal system in Osaka, he joined the Foreign Ministry in 1884 under the patronage of Mutsu Munemitsu (1844–1947). While in Tokyo, he founded the *Kenkonsha* (乾坤社) with Sugiura Jūgō in 1885, a group that was effectively a forerunner to the *Seikyōsha*.

After rising to head the translation bureau at the Foreign Ministry in 1888, he also bitterly opposed the treaty revisions being promoted by Inoue Kaoru which had the predictable consequence of earning him disfavor within the Ministry. He nonetheless later rose to prominence under Mutsu when he was sent to the Japanese Legation in Beijing in 1893 and later became Japan's envoy to Korea in 1895. After two stints as Japan's representative, in the US (1898) and Russia (1900), he was instrumental in moving to thwart Russia's attempts to win over Great Britain securing favor for Japan instead. He oversaw the diplomatic initiatives prior to the Russo-Japanese War (1904) and was the chief negotiator at the Treaty of Portsmouth deliberations following the end of that conflict (1905).[7]

The first thing to emphasize about this group is that, apart from their relative youth, they were all part of a new cohort of educational elite who had come through the post-Restoration education system (partial as that might be in the case of Kuga Katsunan). Of special interest is the fact that Komura and Sugiura were both *kōshinsei* (貢進生), recipients of special places allocated to the most gifted students of their domains prior to the Restoration, who then went on to be nominated as part of the first wave of government-sponsored students to England and the US in the 1870s. They were, academically speaking, the best of the best.[8]

In connection with this, the second point to emphasize is that they were not enamored with the West that they came into contact with. In many regards, they were better versed and better educated than any of their predecessors in the specializations that they had taken up—especially so in the case of Komura and Sugiura who studied at elite Western institutions, yet it did not make them West-worshippers but quite the reverse. When Komura and Sugiura were contemplating their course of action as members of the *Kenkonsha* (prior to the establishment of the *Seikyôsha*), they agreed that the factionalism of Western political parties was something to be avoided at all costs—democracy in the Western form, so far as they had seen, could only exacerbate existing divisions in Japan. The avenue of the popular newspaper seemed the best means of presenting an alternative to Western-style party politics. And, as Sugiura was to quip rather pointedly regarding the proposed journal's content, "[i]t won't do if it's just a collection of translated Western texts."[9]

The third point of note regarding this group is that despite their eminent abilities, they nonetheless "suffered" to various degrees from being poorly connected to the Satsuma and Chōshū oligarchy which made career prospects in government service tenuous. Komura succeeded due to the patronage of Mutsu Munemitsu who, despite being imprisoned for five years following the Seinan War, managed to rehabilitate himself and attain considerable distinction by dint of sheer ability. Komura was in that sense very much in the mould of his mentor.

The final point of note is their redefinition of the concepts of "progress" and "civilization" as it had been presented previously. In various forms of critiques, they lamented the superficial Westernization that was being pursued by the government arguing instead for progress based on a cultural and intellectual movement that was more genuinely Japanese. The term that they gave to this ideal was *kokusuishugi*, literally "national essentialism", and by it they meant the aim of preserving the essence of Japanese culture and identity while pursuing broad national reconstruction. As a by-product of this movement, the term *Kaika* came back into circulation with a renewed vigor but it was clearly not *Kaika* as it had been presented and promoted by the preceding generation of *Yōgakusha*.

There was not necessarily any clear agreement on the nature of *kokusuishugi* in terms of policy objectives or practical measures—it was an expression of protest against rampant Westernization on the one hand and a call to redefine the direction of the country on the other; it was necessarily open-ended because, as yet, the essence of the new Japan was yet to be defined.

Perhaps the clearest practical outline of the dimensions of *Seikyō sha* outlook was contained in successive articles appearing in the second and third issues of *Nihonjin* written by Shiga Shigetaka, respectively, entitled "A Clarification of the Beliefs Embraced in the Nihonjin Journal" and "On the Necessity to Choose 'Preservation of the National Essence' to Protect Japan's Future" (「『日本人』が懐抱する処の旨義を告白す」 and 「日本前途の国是は「国粋保存旨義」に選定せざるべからず」).[10] In Shiga's own terms, he defines *Kokusui* as "nationality" in English, though not in the sense of citizenship but in the sense of national character or national characteristics. He suggests that although this national essence is intangible due to its pertaining to Japanese spirituality and culture, it finds expression in concrete institutions such as educational institutions, political organizations, aesthetic pursuits and so forth. The matter of greatest interest, however, is the manner in which he compares Japanese "civilization" with Western "civilization." Using a string of numbers 1 to 10 to denote the Western level of attainment, he states quite frankly that Japan only reaches from 1 to 4. Employing an evolutionary paradigm, clearly structured according to Herbert Spencer's organic models of biological and social development, he asserts that what the government is trying to do is simply tack on "9" and "10" without having gone through the necessary preliminary stages, the exclusion of which meaning that whatever is established is of necessity disjunctive and premature. In another vein, he suggests that all that the government is pursuing is the mere mimicry of the West rather than true national development that would make Japan genuinely civilized.[11]

The aspect of this outline that makes the *Seikyōsha* mission particularly distinctive is the fact that the term they collectively employ, *kokusuishugi*, was not as such a translation of a Western word, neither was it taken from a classical Chinese precedent. It was a term coined from scratch because there was no other term to use—indeed this was arguably the first time that a non-Western society stood on the cusp of modernization while grasping clearly for the first time that there might in fact be an alternative to the cultural baggage that, up until that point, had seemed to be a non-negotiable part of the Western "civilization" package. We should also note here that *kaika* and *bunmeika* are used almost interchangeably to denote a process of "civilization"—that is, civilization in a neutral sense without specific cultural preconceptions. This was arguably a conception of civilization in Japan that for the first time clearly rejected the assumption that the Western Enlightenment would fill the gaps. The same cannot be said for even Fukuzawa Yukichi who as recently as 1885 had argued in his newspaper, *Jiji Shimpō*, that Japan should "leave Asia and join the Western hemisphere." Indeed, the *Seikyōsha* were quite consciously reacting against such statements.

Not all the *Seikyōsha* members or their immediate circle of like-minded collaborators left the substance of Japanese "national essence" open-ended. One of the other prominent contributors to *Nihonjin* who attempted to give concrete expression to "kokusuishugi" was Kikuchi Kumatarō, a physicist by training. He was more forthright in stating that the Imperial Household, and the sentiment of attachment that the Japanese people had toward that institution, were a central element in the national psyche. This gave ammunition to critiques of the *Seikyōsha* who were wont to label it as merely reactionary and traditionalist, including Tokutomi Sohō who referred to the members as the "new conservative party." This led Shiga Shigetaka in time to drop the term "kokusui hozon" (国粋保存: conservation of the national essence) and opt for a less political sounding "kokusui kenshō" (国粋顕彰: honoring the national essence). Kuga Katsunan, for his part, preferred to use the terms "kokuminshugi" (国民主義: variously translated as "ethnic nationalism" or "nationalism") or "nihonshugi" (日本主義: Japanism).[12]

The largely negative connotations associated with the "conservative" label were particularly unfortunate. A great part of what the *Seikyōsha* was aiming to promote, especially in the initial stages, was sensible, dignified and arguably more rigorous intellectually than the more facile imitators of Western liberalism. The degree to which various individuals identified with conservatism as a political alternative to both the "Freedom and Peoples' Rights" movement was also more pronounced than may be imagined. Kuga Katsunan was one of the first to introduce the classical conservatism of Edmund Burke to the Japanese readership in *Kinji Seiron Kō* (『近時政論考』, *Thoughts on Recent Political Theories*). In the founding number of *Nihonjin*, Shiga Shigetaka also explicitly repudiated the connection between conservatism and extremism, arguing that "[w]e must be reformers without being revolutionaries, we must be improvers rather than iconoclasts."[13] In this sense, there was a clear parallelism between the conservatism of the *Seikyōsha* and the "Gradualism" of the Itō government (cf. *zenshin no shugi*; 漸進の主義).

Unfortunately, however, even though there genuinely was a distinction to be made between the aims of the *Seikyōsha* and the activism of outright traditionalists, the attempt to deflect such associations was largely ineffectual as in practice it was increasingly difficult to maintain such a distinction. As the date for promulgating the new Constitution drew nearer and the practical prospect of participation in a parliamentary process of deliberation became a distinct political reality, the scramble for political mobilization intensified and political organizations mushroomed from all quarters of the political arena.

Mass media: A new kind of political crisis

The issue that was to become one of the most powerful and politically unpredictable forces in popular political mobilization was certainly the issue of the "unequal treaties." Tied to it were the issues of Japan's relations with Korea and China, increasingly premised on the assumption that Japan was somehow entitled to act by force to protect its "interests" in East Asia, along with perceptions of Japan's "rightful" place among the Western powers. As already alluded to, the *Jingo* rebellion of 1882 in Seoul had set off a vehement drive for increased armed intervention on the continent, with China's dispatching of troops leading to popular agitations for retaliation. As an example of how volatile and at times paradoxical the "Freedom and Peoples Rights" movement could become, there was the instance of a mass disturbance in Tokyo in early 1885. On 18 January, a massed gathering occurred at Uenoyama amassing some three thousand persons, a considerable proportion of them including students and *sōshi* (former *samurai* who had taken to political agitation with a vengeance). After the congress called on the government to send a retaliatory expeditionary force to China, the mob marched through Ginza, stopping in front of Fukuzawa Yukichi's pro-war *Jiji Shinpō* to cheer and then proceeding to the offices of the anti-war (but ostensibly pro-freedom and popular rights) *Chōya Shimbun* which they proceeded to pelt with stones before dispersing.[14]

That was the broad tenor of political activism in the capital in 1885 and although a relative calm might have been re-established and a degree of administrative stability achieved through Itō's initiative to restructure the executive, the potential for public opinion to ignite around the familiar issues of discontent was never far away. The following year, one incident occurred which set off a train of furious recrimination and inflicted serious damage on Itō's government—the Normanton Incident.

On 24 October 1886, a British steamer sank off the coast of Wakayama with the loss of 23 Japanese and 12 Indian lives; all the European passengers and crew survived in lifeboats. The English captain and crew were arraigned on charges of negligence before the British Consul but were found not guilty. This coincided with the revelation that the Foreign

Minister was negotiating a settlement with the European Powers that would permit the establishment of "local jurisdiction" but would at the same time recognize foreign judges; essentially a watered-down form of extraterritoriality. The repercussions of this in terms of the public perception of the injustice of the Treaties and the untrustworthiness of the government were enormous. Indeed, it is hard to comprehend how Inoue Kaoru could ever have thought that treaty revisions that left the substance of extraterritoriality in place had any merit.[15]

While some of the standard pro-government newspapers remained cautious about picking up on the story, others ran it with an extraordinary intensity. For example, the *Yomiuri Shimbun* posted first the names of those who drowned and then followed up with almost daily reports and commentary for the remainder of the year.[16] This was a focused media campaign very much akin to the sort of focused barraging of content that we are familiar with even today. In the midst of Inoue Kaoru's correspondence with Itō Hirobumi, there is a brief and slightly desperate sounding note that refers to a visit he had received in one day from the representatives of five of the major newspapers.[17]

By the year's end, the story had lost some of its heat in the media, sporadically re-emerging again thereafter as details of the Captain's acquittal and the ongoing recriminations and appeals followed. One particular point of interest in this case, however, is the manner in which the Incident was popularized through other media as well. There was a song penned, and the famous French caricaturist, Georges Bigot, depicted the British pompously posing in their life rafts holding the British naval ensign, while the Japanese passengers were being left to drown.[18] Moreover, there was a Kabuki play written by Furukawa Shinsui for the Shintomi-Za based on the Incident entitled *Sanpu Gokō Utsusu Gentō* (三府五港写幻燈) which refers to the three major urban areas, Kyôto, Osaka and Tokyo, along with the five ports that were opened up through the Restoration. The play was a *zangirimono*, a piece performed in Western costume and performed with some consideration of western notions of drama. The Shintomi-Za was in fact an established playhouse that had enjoyed the patronage of high-ranking government Ministers and become something of a flagship for experimentation in Western theatrical forms.[19] This marked the final *zangirimono* that they performed. Finally, some striking *nishiki-e* prints were also produced depicting both scenes from the play and the sinking of the ship.[20]

It is within this context that in October of 1886 there was a massed gathering of former Liberal Party affiliates in Tokyo. Hoshi Tōru, a veteran activist within the party, expressed the aim of forging a new grand alliance of opposition parties against the Satsuma- and Chōshū-controlled government, one that would discard petty differences and aim to realize a great common aim (hence the name of the ensuing movement; *Daidō Danketsu Undō*; 大同団結運動). Gotō Shōjirō, one of the veteran agitators for representative government since the upheaval over invading Korea in 1873, became the movement's charismatic leader, embarking on speaking tours of the provinces to galvanize national support for the new momentum that appeared to be building.[21]

Following hot on the heels of this development was the emergence the following year of the *Sandaijiken Kempaku* Movement (三大事件建白運動) which drew more directly on the fury engendered by the Normanton Incident and the Inoue treaty revisions, and included a call for less taxation, freedom of speech as well as the cessation of negotiations based on the current treaty revision proposals. This movement overlapped considerably with the former movement but had a distinct character in that it involved figures who were decidedly more conservative and ambivalent about party politics—especially so given that it came to be represented by Tani Tateki who resigned from Itō's first cabinet and various associates of the *Kenkonsha* such as Sugiura and Komura. In parallel with this there was also Tani's old partner in mischief, Torio Koyata's *Hoshutō Chūseiha* which began to develop a national following. The *Seikyōsha* members involved in *Nihonjin*, particularly Miyake Setsurei, drew closer to the *Daidō Danketsu* movement having reason to believe that the cause being espoused by Gotō Shōjirō was in many ways identical to their own. After all, there was a pronounced anti-Westernization streak in the *Daidō Danketsu* platform that grew if anything stronger as time went on. Kuga Katsunan and his publication drew closer to Tani Tateki and the *Kenkonsha*.[22]

For the government's part, it issued new, even stricter security ordinances toward the end of 1887 that provided for political undesirables to be banished from the capital and the forced cessation of publication for newspapers and journals that fell foul of the authorities. For Itō, it was an *annus horribilis*, a year that he actually felt constituted "one of the most serious challenges to internal stability and foreign affairs since the Restoration." He took the unprecedented step of issuing a memorandum to all provincial officials as Prime Minister, outlining the severity of the recent unrest and the need to communicate the need for restraint in the face of the difficult initiatives that were being undertaken in domestic and foreign affairs.[23] However, with the resignation of Tani and the continuing furor over the treaty revisions, Itō himself also came under intense pressure to resign from the Imperial Household post that he continued to hold in tandem with his post as Prime Minister. He actually privately proposed resigning from the position to the Emperor, but there was no agreement on who should succeed. Itō wanted Kuroda to take over but there was strong lobbying against Kuroda by Motoda Eifu based on reservations about Kuroda's character. In the end, Itō was left with little option but to relinquish the Imperial Household portfolio which was taken up by Hijikata Hisamoto, the former *Jiho* to the Emperor who was a close affiliate of Motoda.[24]

Consequently, even though Itō was forced to resign from the post of Minister to the Imperial Household, it was clear that the Emperor regarded Itō as the only member of government capable of handling the matter of drafting the Imperial Constitution along with the simultaneous promulgation of the equally weighty legal ordinances covering all aspects of the Imperial institution, the *Kōshitsu Tenban* (皇室典範). The vehicle established to enable Itō to conduct this business by another route was the *Sūmitsuin*, the Privy Council which was convocated on 30 April 1888, and was to include the team that had been engaged in drafting the Constitution with Itō (Itō Miyoji, Kaneko Kentarō and Inoue Kowashi), the Ministers of the Cabinet and several officials of the Court and other related branches of government.

The Meiji constitution and the crisis of conservatism

It remains commonplace to assert that Itō was basing the Constitution on a Prussian model; however, such a characterization has serious flaws. A consideration of the contemporary legal situation in Germany as a whole at the same time indicates that Germany itself was not fully integrated legally (a fully integrated legal code did not come into effect until 1900) and, despite having the 1871 Constitution as the basis for founding the Second Reich under Kaisei Wilhelm the First, there was in fact considerable diversity in the manner in which each constituent principality or state was run and how persons were brought into their various elected bodies. As Kaneko Kentarō was at pains to stress in *The Promulgation of the Constitution and its Reception in the West* (憲法の制定と欧米人の評価, 1937), it was inconceivable that the position of the Emperor of Japan was akin to the Kaiser given that he had been elected the head of the North German Confederation. Moreover, he emphasized the degree of disparity between Japan's ethnically and administratively unified composition vis-à-vis the situation in Germany which was highly heterogeneous.[25]

The final draft of the Meiji Constitution was deliberated upon in considerable detail from 18 June until 23 July 1888. A detailed record of the deliberations was kept and although there were instances of pedantry, for example Torio Koyata's insistence that the phrase for "determining the law" should be standardized throughout the document,[26] there were other cases where intriguing points were made out of seeming trivialities, for example Mori Arinori's insistence that "Great" (大) be appended to Japan in the Constitution just as it had been in the *Kōshitsu Tenpan*. Itō's argument that "Japan" by itself had a better ring to it on an international level held no sway and the amendment was passed.

The debates were often lively, and at times even acrimonious. In the initial stages, Mori Arinori was exceptionally outspoken (and perhaps rather inappropriately so given his position as Education Minister). Yet his contributions were some of the most germane attracting the unlikely support of even Motoda Eifu himself.[27] The most contentious issue was the matter of clarifying the degree to which all legislation required parliamentary approval—in the final draft, the term "approval" (承諾) was substituted with the term "assent" after discussion had been adjourned on several occasions. The other matter that generated the greatest conflict was the definition of "Rights and Obligations" within the Constitution.[28] Mori argued that it was politically imprudent to overstate the rights of subjects toward their sovereign; Itō countered that defining such rights was an indispensable element in any constitution. In the end, Itō, as Chairman, actually banned Mori from making any comments at the deliberations.

Nevertheless Mori was not the only "difficult" participant in the meetings. Sano Tsunetami (1823–1902), who had been a former Finance Minister prior to the 1881 purge and had founded the Japan branch of the Red Cross in 1885, proved to be a lively contributor in the capacity of a consulting committee member. Also, the Justice Minister, Yamada Akiyoshi (1844–92), was a more critical contributor, often referring to specialist examples from Western legal institutions (and it is of interest that Itō tended to rebuff certain "issues" raised by German precedents as essentially irrelevant to the drafting of a Japanese constitution). Moreover, Torio Koyata (one of the Four Generals who remonstrated with the government in 1881), emerged as an antagonist in the latter part of the deliberations following Mori's being silenced.[29]

The protracted debate over the term "approval" (承諾) indicated a split that had emerged between two competing conservative notions of how to push ahead with a Constitution but not yield too far in terms of how far the newly convened parliament would be permitted to restrain the hand of the Emperor and his Ministers. Theoretically, all legislation would have to pass a parliamentary vote before becoming law, the sole exception being the matter of the annual budget which could be "carried over" in the event of a parliamentary deadlock. At the time of drafting the constitution, it was far from likely that even with the limited qualifications of suffrage and the increasing clout of conservative political parties that such a deadlock could be averted. Consequently, the issue of how solid the constraint of parliamentary assent would be was indeed very significant.[30]

If we were to venture to identify the single great defect of the Meiji Constitution, it would have to be that no "safety mechanism" for resolving a stalemate was effectively incorporated. Even in the German case, there was the precedent of the *Bundesrat*—a 25-member upper council that was composed of representatives of the constituent states who were appointed by their respective potentates and not democratically elected—which had the power to override the Reichstag with vetoes and other prerogatives.[31] If Itō were attempting to emulate the German example, then this was surely the aspect that should have appeared most salutary. There were other alternatives, such as the one Mori seemed to be hinting at before being silenced—the incorporation of a right of executive prerogative that could only be overridden by a two-third majority as was current in the US. In any event, no such mechanism was clear and it was more or less a foregone conclusion that there would be a deadlock. When asked directly how such a deadlock would be resolved, Itō's response suggests that he expected the parliament's regard for the Emperor to outweigh party political interests.

Quite apart from this issue, however, there was also another more subtle problem that was in the making and would eventually be extremely detrimental to the effective working of the government. As already alluded to, the emergence of the Imperial Household and indeed the Emperor himself as a distinct political force in the 1880s foreshadowed the development of a quite separate locus of power within the executive. With Itō's being forced out of the post of Minister to the Imperial Household in 1887, the institutional break-up was underway. The establishment of the *Sūmitsuin* did not rein in or subjugate the *Kunaishō*—it simply shifted the front for contesting executive influence to a body removed away from where the contest ought to have been. Once the Constitution and the Imperial Ordinances had been deliberated over, its immediate utility was at an end (Itō resigned as Chair of the *Sūmitsuin* following the promulgation of the Constitution in February 1889). In the interim, Kuroda Kiyotaka, who was appointed Prime Minister at the same time as Itō set up the *Sūmitsuin*, sat as the caretaker while Itō oversaw the last preparatory details, including the finalizing of the electoral laws for both houses.[32]

At the same time as these developments were occurring in the corridors of state, there was an additional factor that was coming into Japan's political configuration that was to have long-term significance.

Reference has already been made to the rise of certain non-Satsuma/
Chōshū elements within the government and the national administration who were engaging in the subtle redefinition of the body politic
toward the person of the Emperor, something which had perhaps its
most tangible expression in the relative independence of the Imperial
Household just discussed. On another more populist level, however,
there was also burgeoning national associations whose aim was the
redefinition of national consciousness toward the Emperor; this was
anything but a genteel mode of political engagement entailing as it did
means that were more overtly violent and intimidatory.

Reaction and political intimidation

The degree to which Japan's political culture was experiencing a profound transformation became evident during the months of agitation following the presentation of the Constitution to Prime Minister
Kuroda on 11 February 1889. This date was also the day that Mori
Arinori, the Education Minister, was assassinated by Nishino Fumitarō,
a young fanatic who managed to meet Mori at his residence just before
he was to depart for the presentation ceremony at the palace. Mori was
assassinated on the grounds of having allegedly committed an act of
"disrespect" at the Ise Shrine—apparently, he parted the curtain of the
inner sanctum with his walking stick. The pretext for his murder was
one thing—it remains debatable how accurate reports of the incident at
Ise were, but, in any event, there were clearly those who regarded Mori
as one of the most "dangerous" Westernizers in the government and
at least one of them was prepared to take the most drastic of steps to
negate him. More significant is the fact that the public were clearly far
more sympathetic with the assassin who was dispatched on the spot by
Mori's bodyguard.[33] And things were to get worse.

When it became apparent in the April of 1889 that Ōkuma Shigenobu
(the replacement for Inoue Kaoru as Foreign Minister in Kuroda's cabinet) had been engaging in a new round of one-on-one negotiations with
various powers and had offered provisions which would permit mixed
residence and foreign judges, there was an eruption of anti-government
sentiment that was just as vociferous as the earlier furor over Inoue Kaoru's
proposed revisions in 1887. Interestingly, the details came back to Japan
via an article in the British press which was re-circulated back to Japan
in the issue of *Nihon* (Kuga Katsunan's newspaper) for 31 May to 6 June.
Unlike the previous movement, however, the former *Jiyūtō*-aligned and
Kaishintō-aligned *Daidō Danketsu* was now broken into two factions, the

Daidō Kurabu and the *Daidō Kyōwakai*, and the main impetus was coming from the *Hoshutō Chūseiha*, the *Seikyōsha* and its affiliates, along with relatively recently formed reactionary political associations that were based in Kyūshu, the likes of the *Shimeikai* (紫溟会) from Kumamoto and the *Genyōsha* (玄洋社) which was based in Fukuoka.[34]

The *Shimeikai* was established in 1882 by Sassa Tomfusa (1854–1906), a former supporter of Saigō Takamori who had been incarcerated following the Seinan War of 1878 but had returned to his home domain of Kumamoto to band together with like-minded colleagues to establish an educational institution to promote Emperor-centered rule. The *Shimeikai* was a more clearly politically motivated association which entered the public media with the journal *Shimei Zasshi* from 1882 onward with Sassa as the chief editor (this became the *Kyūshu Nichi-nichi Shimbun* from 1888 onward).

The *Genyōsha* (sometimes referred to as in English as the Black Ocean Society) was established in 1881 by Toyama Mitsuru (1855–1944), someone who had also spent time in prison for armed rebellion, in this case the Hagi Rebellion of 1876. Its members were active within the "Freedom and Peoples' Rights" movement but the association was more practically subversive in its political objectives. Apart from promoting a more virulent notion of nationalism (using the term "kokkashugi"/ 国家主義 with a rather different nuance to the post-war period), the *Genyōsha* was involved in promoting anti-Western solidarity in the greater Asian region through Pan-Asianism.

Both the foregoing groups had influential clan-based connections in the government—the *Shimeikai* having Kumamoto's Motoda Eifu as a most prominent and powerful patron in the Imperial Household and Inoue Kowashi, also from Kumamoto, who was an early collaborator in the group's educational activities. The *Genyōsha* could count on influential military figures such as Miura Gorō, one of the "Four Generals" that reprimanded the government in 1881 who from the November of 1888 became the head of the Imperial academy, *Gakushūin*, along with the cooperation of other groups that felt that violent political activism was conscionable.[35]

The "Alliance of Five Groups" (the two "Daido" groups, the *Hoshuto Chūseiha*, the *Seikyōsha* group and the Kyushu associations) held a national congress in Tokyo from 26 to 28 August, marking the high point in their capacity to galvanize public antipathy toward the government and signifying the increasing dominance of the conservative elements in popular political agitation. At this point, Ōkuma Shigenobu had precious few supporters, even within the government, and it was clear that another backdown was imminent. Even so, the curtailing of treaty revisions was to be far more dramatic than the previous case—on 18 October, a member of the *Genyōsha*, Kurushima Tsuneki, attempted to assassinate Ōkuma with a bomb while he was en route home from government offices in an open carriage. Ōkuma was fortunate to escape with his life, although he lost a leg as the result of his injuries.[36]

Following the postponement of treaty revisions, the momentum certainly went out of the opposition movement as a whole. Particularly the "Nihon Kurabu"—the *Seikyōsha* affiliates, the related *Kenkonsha* members, and those associated with Kuga Katsunan's *Nihon*—used the subscriptions they had collected as part of their anti-revision campaign to hold a banquet before returning to the business of the popular press. The *Shimeikai*, the *Genyōsha* and the *Hoshutō Chūseiha*-aligned senior-statesmen remained steadfastly focused on political activism; Sassa Tomofusa stood for the Kumamoto *Kokkentō* and entered the lower house of parliament in 1890. Tani Tateki became a Minister in the first Yamagata cabinet while Torio Koyata and Miura Gorō, like many other conservative traditionalists, ended up sitting in the upper House of Peers due to having been bestowed with aristocratic rank.[37]

Conservatism and national education

Much has been made of Mori Arinori's evident conservatism while Minister of Education to buttress the characterization of his legacy as essentially the founder of post-1890 "statism." However, a closer look at his policies and initiatives reveal that although he did indeed advocate a vigorous patriot-ism and brought much of the disparate network of educational institu-tions into a centrally integrated system, he had no intention of endorsing the enshrinement of the Imperial Household as the fount of national virtue as conceived by his detractors at Court and in other sections of the Ministry. Prior to his assassination, he had contributed to the drafting of a new "common sense" textbook for ethical instruction (cf. *Rinrisho*; 倫理書) which displayed the unmistakable influence of Herbert Spencer's ethi-cal philosophy—an essentially sectarian and positivist discourse that was in no way conducive to the later Confucian "turn."[38]

Nevertheless given the aforementioned surge in the political influ-ence of the Imperial Way-oriented political organizations and anti-government "educational" associations, it is not hard to fathom how the Imperial Rescript on Education came into existence and did so rather quickly once the assassination of Mori Arinori left a vacuum of influence that could be quickly seized upon. From February of 1889, there was concerted lobbying from Nishimura Shigeki (now attached to the Imperial Household) to have a new academy established under the jurisdiction of the Imperial Ministry that would deliberate over and implement curricular changes to moral education—the Meirin'in (明倫院). He also continued to promote the views of the *Nihon Kōdōkai* through the organization's journal (despite a brief interruption through government proscription which was in fact circumvented by giving the journal a different title).[39]

In the meantime, Motoda Eifu set to work on gaining the Emperor's support for redefining the direction of education in the country in such a way as would embody the ideals expressed in Motoda's earlier polemic with Itō Hirobumi in 1881. Following the attempted assassination of Ōkuma, activity to coordinate the various anti-treaty revision conservatives, including Tani, Torio and Sassa Tomofusa , was intensified with all these persons being given the opportunity, via Motoda, to either directly present their opinions to the Emperor in person or to make written representations.[40] It was hardly surprising then that Kuroda tendered his resignation from the prime ministership to be replaced by Yamagata Aritomo in December of 1889. Motoda was naturally not altogether happy with the retention of the services of Inoue and Aoki Shuzō in the Foreign Ministry but he had the immeasurable "consolation" of seeing Itō resign from all cabinet posts and his protégé Kuroda taken out of play. With the appointment of Yamagata, the way was clear for undertaking to draft and promulgate a Rescript on Education that would complement the earlier Rescript to Soldiers and Sailors (4 January 1882), a document which had been issued when Yamagata had been Army Minister in 1882.[41]

In the February of 1890, there was a meeting of the top provincial officials who were given the opportunity to express their views on the matter of moral education. This led to a directive being issued by the Emperor to both the Prime Minister Yamagata Aritomo and the replacement Education Minister Enamoto Takeaki (later replaced in May by Yoshikawa Akimasa) to expedite the drafting of a document that would lay down a basic direction for the populace, something which Motoda had argued had been lacking since the inception of the Restoration.

Initially, the drafting of the Rescript was entrusted to Nakamura Masanao, perhaps a perplexing choice given his background in Western Studies, but not altogether surprising if one considers that he was the author of several articles in the *Meiroku Journal* that defended Chinese classical scholarship. In any event, the drafting was soon taken over by Inoue Kowashi and Motoda Eifu who, as has already been noted, came from the same domain and had more in common in their outlook on education as might first appear.[42] Apart from some quibbling about retaining a reference to the need for citizens to uphold the law (and by extension support the government) the text of the Rescript was completed without great delay. On 30 October 1890, the final document was formally presented to Yamagata and Yoshikawa.

The content of the Rescript is well-covered in the general literature on Meiji history and there is little necessity to go into the detail of the text except to note that it defines the grand object of education as the promotion of the virtue of loyalty to the Emperor first and also the fostering of proper moral relations with parents and other members of society. In essence, it was a manifesto of political paternalism based more or less on unreconstructed classical Confucianism.

This, of course, did not mean that Motoda wanted to replicate a Chinese Court, far from it. The Imperial lineage and the concomitant Shintō tradition were what set the *kokutai* apart as a unique historical and, indeed, moral entity. We should note that while Motoda was working at ensuring the realization of the Rescript on Education, he was also furiously lobbying with former *Jiho* colleagues within the *Sūmitsuin* and the Court to have the *Jingikan*, the ceremonial branch of the ancient court, re-established as a separate institution within the Imperial Ministry. There had been an attempt to replicate this institution at the commencement of the Restoration some twenty years earlier but this was quickly relegated to a position below the *Dajōkan* and then restructured out of all recognizable form into the *Kyōbusho*, the forerunner of the Education Ministry. In due course, Shintō was to be classified as the "national teaching" (国教) and distinct from "religion" as such—yet by the 1880s, it was being administratively handled within the Ministry of Internal Affairs along with the administration of temples. Motoda had hoped to build on the ideal confluence of personnel in government and the Court administration to bring pressure on the cabinet to approve such a move. By October of 1890, it was actually given tacit approval but by December the idea was being decisively shelved—the argument offered was that redefining the national religion as Shintō would damage Western perceptions of Japan by creating the image of a trenchantly "pagan" nation.[43]

In any event, the successful promulgation of the Rescript on Education was a decisive success for the traditionalist conservative movement that had relied on influence at Court and within the Education Ministry to see it through. Certainly, Motoda was not entirely satisfied with things as a whole, as has already been noted, but it is possible to say that by late 1890, Japan had come all the way back to substantially revisiting the original aims of Restoration; the reassertion of Imperial sovereignty through an Imperial Constitution and the substantial re-establishment of

Imperial Rule in government, albeit partially and at times without clear constitutional foundation, through the increasingly influential Imperial Ministry and its auxiliary networks within the Ministries of the Army, Navy, Internal Affairs and Education.

At the same time as this transition was to become more pronounced in government, there was also clear evidence that there was a more fundamental transition that had been occurring at the intersection of Japan's urban political culture and academia. The late 1880s saw the emergence of two currents of thought that were in one sense incompatible yet in some cases surprisingly symbiotic. The enthusiasm for German specialists in administrative studies has been referred to, and occurred for the sensible reason that, at that point in time at least, the German-speaking academy in Europe was producing the most cogent theoretical and practical commentaries on such issues. The intensive period of study with Lorenz von Stein sparked off a veritable "grand Tour" mentality with an extraordinary array of leading political officers and intellectuals making their "pilgrimage" to Vienna, among them Tani Tateki, Yamagata Aritomo and Mutsu Munemitsu (1844–1947), the patron of Komura Jutarō in the Foreign Ministry.[44]

In parallel with this phenomenon, there was at Tokyo University a burgeoning interest in Germanic philosophy and it can be broadly described as having two strands: one being Idealist philosophy as presented in Hegel's phenomenology and the contemporary work of Herman Cohen (1842–1918), the other being a stultifying Positivism which was increasingly being applied to the social sciences.

It is not the aim at this stage to provide a comprehensive outline of this new trend and its substantial influence, but so far as it remains relevant to the issue of the development of a new political and cultural configuration in support of an Emperor-centered polity, there are some particularly instructive examples that can be highlighted. One of the best examples of how this Germanic influence was being adapted in practice is provided by Inoue Tetsujirō (1855–1944) of Fukuoka, a graduate of Tokyo University, and noted as the author of *Rinri Shinsetsu* (*A New Theory of Ethics*, 1883) and the first Japanese dictionary of philosophical terms. After publishing *Rinri Shinsetsu*, which was a broadly introductory text that reflected an typically strong Spencerian evolutionary bent (and one that was not to altogether disappear either), he traveled to study in Germany from 1884 to 1890 becoming particularly enamored of Idealist philosophy. After returning to Japan, he became the first Japanese professor of philosophy at Tokyo University and thereafter was instrumental in securing the services of Raphael von Koeber from Heidelberg University to teach there from 1893.[45]

Inoue applied Western philosophical approaches to Confucianism producing a series of introductory texts on the main branches of that tradition in Japan: *Yōmeigaku, Kogaku* and *Shūshigaku*. Of greatest relevance here, however, is the "Commentary on the Rescript on Education" (*Chokugo Engi*, 1891) which was commissioned by the Ministry of Education. In this work, he was attempting to give a more thorough philosophical basis to the Rescript, although it is arguable that it was a rather lamentable hotchpotch of social evolutionism and moral determinism. Nevertheless it is an important example of how the shell of Western philosophical method was being employed to consolidate an ethical system that was at the self-same time conceived as being fused into something that was immanent and inviolable.[46]

In 1893, Inoue also published a highly influential series of articles entitled "The Conflict between Education and Religion" in which he condemned Christianity as being inimical to the Japanese *Kokutai*, and characterized believers in Christianity as being less than proper subjects of the realm. It was the beginning of what was to become a life-long aim of devoting himself to the promotion of national morality.

As an important coeval of Inoue Tetsujirō, some mention should also be made of Inoue Enryō (1858–1919) who was born into a Buddhist temple (Shinshu Otani Sect) in Niigata and studied at Tokyo Imperial University. After graduating from there, he wrote treatises from 1886 onward criticizing Christianity and promoting a hybrid Buddhist philosophy incorporating aspects of German Idealist philosophy and theories of energy. In 1887, he became a founding member of the *Seikyōsha* but, rather than devoting himself exclusively to *Seikyōsha* publishing activities, he turned his energies to the establishment of an academy, the *Tetsugakkan* (later Toyo University) which eventually produced a philosophical journal *Tōyō Tetsugaku* from 1894 onward.[47]

One of the distinguishing features of the *kokusuishugi* movement was in fact its profound connection to Japanese religious and artistic traditions, with the movement's leaders, including both Miyake Setsurei and Kuga Katsunan, making a point of publishing poems and devotional pieces alongside the political commentary. The same could also be said for the *Hoshutō Chūsei-ha* in that Tani Tateki and Torio Koyata were both fervent practitioners and active in promoting awareness of Japan's Buddhist traditions. Komura Jutarō of the *Konkensha* was also an avid devotee of Zen Buddhism.[48]

Yet perhaps the most significant aspect of the writing of the likes of Inoue Tetsujirō and Inoue Enryō was the fact that, although they were ostensibly employing Western philosophical motifs and terminology, the centre of gravity, as it were, was no longer with Western learning but with Japanese intellectual traditions, the Western discourse forming more of a veneer than the substance of what was being handled. It is hard to conclude that at this point there was a particularly plausible symbiosis established between the Germanic philosophical tradition— that was arguably to be established some thirty to forty years later by the Kyōto School, including those on the school's periphery such as Watsuji Tetsurō.

Controlling memory: Reaction and academia

As a particularly significant illustration of how the new Imperial Way movement was coming to make an impact on academia, we should also briefly note the circumstances around the dismissal of Kume Kunitake (the chronicler of the Iwakura Mission discussed in Chapter 3), from his post as a Professor of History at Tokyo Imperial University in 1892.

"Modern" historiography had been introduced to Tokyo University through Ludwig Riess, a young German professor from Berlin University. Riess was a disciple of Leopold von Ranke, and so he brought with him a rather thorough Positivism which he hoped to impart to his colleagues in Japan. The style of discourse was not altogether riveting by most accounts but it reinforced an approach to Japanese history that was relatively objective and fearless.[49]

Shigeno Yasutsugu and Kume Kunitake were quick to apply the rigorous standards for historical verification to a number of classical works, including the *Taiheiki*, a history of Emperor Go-Daigō's struggle against the Ashikaga in the fourteenth century. The *Taiheiki* was a "politically sensitive" text in that it had become a touchstone for accounts of loyalty to the Emperor as displayed by his General. Shigeno was bold enough to suggest that one of the central heroes of the work was fictitious, Kume was forthright in dismissing the work as having little historical value.[50]

Kume and Shigeno attracted students despite the controversy and initiated a highly respectable tradition of scholarship—ironically, however, they were not to enjoy the fruits of their academic labor undisturbed. The articles on the *Taiheiki* had by now garnered attention of the unfavorable sort and they needed to be circumspect.

The article that finally got Kume dismissed was a discussion of Shintō religion which suggested that it was a primitive belief. It was published in the *Shigakkai Zasshi* in 1891, and was largely neglected until an ardent admirer of Kume, Taguchi Ukichi, had the article reproduced in its entirety in his own publication, *Shikai*, in January of 1892. This immediately drew intense hostility from the more fanatical supporters of direct Imperial Rule. Both Kume and Taguchi were subjected to various forms of intimidation but it was Kume who had the misfortune to be visited by four uninvited guests who came to remonstrate with Kume about the article. They would not leave until they secured a promise that he would retract the article. Triumphantly, they announced their success in their own publication and criticized him still further for his lack of respect for the Throne. Kume undertook to retract the article as he had promised, but he was summarily dismissed anyhow on 4 March.[51]

The foregoing events exemplify the ground shift that had occurred in the 1880s—public statements found an audience much more quickly than had been the case in the past, and groups whose wont was to use direct intimidation to bring about political conformity could organize and publicize with greater ease. One might have expected that Kume would have received a greater amount of respect given his background and academic position; these were, unfortunately, not adequate protections in this case.

1890: The uneasy settlement

In early 1886, Itō Hirobumi could hardly have imagined that the program of constitutional and parliamentary reform which seemed to be finally coming into shape and getting capable of orderly resolution would encounter unprecedented popular discontent, and that even his place as Prime Minister would be in question. However, unexpected and largely uncontrollable events wrought a fundamental alteration in the balance of political forces within the broader polity: the shipwreck of the Normanton, the defections of Tani Tateki and Gotō Shōjirō, along with the rupture in the executive caused by yet another impetuous Minister, in this case Inoue Kaoru with his highly inflammatory "secret" agreements on treaty revision. He also could not have imagined that the promulgation of the Constitution in February of 1889 would be accompanied by the loss of Mori Arinori through assassination or that Ōkuma Shigenobu would be rehabilitated within the executive and ultimately nearly meet the same fate as Mori as well.

On one level, the crises that hit the government may well seem to be the consequence of unusual misfortune, but on a deeper level it is also clear that the ground was shifting underneath Itō's administration. The dimensions of public space that encompassed the arena of political contestation were being transformed and the government was increasingly under pressure to keep pace with the changes. As the preceding overview of intellectual developments in the 1880s has demonstrated, there was a growing ambivalence and hostility toward Western political ideals and Western conceptions of representative government among the new wave of elites, many of whom were coming through the Imperial University (though not exclusively so). In tandem with this, there was a growing section of the urban public in general whose antipathy for the government's program of "Westernization", combined with an enthusiasm for military expeditions in the broader Asian region, was burgeoning. This is not to say that there were no genuine liberals or democrats among the politically active population, but they were not as significant within the contemporary political configuration as the development of a constitution, a radical press, a parliament and the introduction of elections may suggest.

The essence of how Japanese political culture was being transformed in the late 1880s is exemplified by the make up of the broad coalition that sprang up in the wake of Tani Tateki's resignation from the Itō cabinet in 1887. The *Daidō Danketsu*, and the ensuing "Alliance of Five Groups" which arose to oppose the Ōkuma treaty revisions, indicate the gradual marginalization of the erstwhile leaders of popular discontent, the Liberal Party and the Constitutional Reform Party, and their being supplanted by conservative forces as exemplified by the *Hoshutō Chūsei-ha* (formalist) and the *Seikyōsha* (relatively progressive), along with the overtly traditionalist and aggressive Kyūshū associations including the *Genyōsha*.

Consequently, a situation where politics was profoundly polarized was well established by the time of the Meiji Constitution and the first parliamentary elections. It may well be tempting to characterize the phase immediately following the promulgation of the constitution as signifying the beginning of the "birth pangs" of democracy—an "immature" phase that was unavoidably turbulent and often unseemly but would nonetheless usher in a more sustained "mature" democratic culture in the future. This characterization assumes that "democracy" was indeed what was being forged in these early stages. The foregoing has hopefully peeled away such misconceptions and revealed the complexity of Japan's modern political revolution, one that, at this stage of Japan's political development at least, revolved more around the poles of traditionalism, competing notions of conservatism and an emergent ideological movement focused on the Imperial Household rather than on the conventional dichotomy of liberal democrats versus statists.

7
Conclusion: Conservatism, Traditionalism and Restoration

This work commenced with the assertion that there is a need to comprehend the Meiji Restoration not so much as an instantaneous event but as a far-spanning movement that had profound roots in the social conditions and intellectual discourse of the late Edo Period. The extent to which early tendencies toward the reconstitution of Imperial rule would have been worked out given the absence of foreign incursions in the early nineteenth century is significant, and largely unanswerable. However, given the spur of foreign encroachments and the palpable inadequacy of the Edo system of government to meet those challenges, the emergence of the Imperial Household as the fulcrum enabling national transformation was emphatic and unequivocal. The Imperial Household possessed what the Shogunate did not: the capacity for charismatic inspiration, a religious dimension that would enable incongruent forces and disparate elements to be recast into a new whole as if they had always been destined to be so conjoined.

By the early 1860s, the capacity of the Imperial throne to empower aspirants to national authority was amply evident and led at times to an unbecoming scramble to grasp control over the Court, as evidenced by the premature attempt of the Chōshū clan to secure the palace in Kyōto with its forces in 1863. Nevertheless this was a forerunner of the later developments which entailed the seizing of an option that was open to the clans who had the military wherewithal to do so. Theoretically the Shogunate should have had the preponderant advantage but, as has been illustrated in the opening chapters, the Shogunate was beset by the constraints of its own raison d'être—it was an authority premised on the expulsion of foreign invaders, yet in practice needed to deal with them in order to refurbish the nation's defenses. The Western clans, especially Satsuma but also Chōshū, had evident advantages in terms of their relative proximity to the sole locus of international trade, Nagasaki (and in the case of Satsuma, there was the "back door" of the Ryūkyū Islands).

The relatively free hand of the Western clans also meant that when they dispatched their sharpest students to the countries of the West, particularly England and the US, they created the opportunity for the cultivation of a rather unique echelon of personnel. By dint of their exceptionally direct exposure to Western society, as exemplified by their relative expertise in foreign languages as compared with Bakufu students, these people would facilitate the more complete re-conceptualization of the nation and indeed a "modern" Japanese culture.

An important aspect of this process that has remained under-emphasized is that the experience thus gained while overseas did not lead to the conversion of this group en masse to a cohort of Westernizers. As has been highlighted in several cases, the experience of the West had a decidedly cautionary impact on many Japanese students. Even Mori Arinori, who is often noted for his proposal to adopt English as an official language, was to return from the US in 1873 fully cognizant of the evils of Congressional party politics and "the misuse of freedom". If anything, the experience of Western society, first hand, engendered a more cautious response rather than unbridled enthusiasm for imitation.

The fruits of the experience of such figures, however, could unfortunately not be easily imparted to the uninitiated. For those who regarded any contact with the "Barbarians" as self-defiling, personnel such as Mori Arinori were little better than foreigners themselves. The "Revere the Emperor, Expel the Barbarians" sentiment was the overriding factor influencing the majority of the *samurai* class who threw their support behind the Satsuma and Chōshū led Restoration in 1868. As the praxis of national reconstruction played out, they found themselves increasingly alienated and disillusioned. This was a political "time-bomb" that the new model government constantly struggled to defuse.

The Iwakura Mission was an audacious attempt to initiate a broader spectrum of top-ranking officials and consolidate a common understanding of the challenges facing the nation as well as the most effective means of successfully refurbishing the national defenses and economy. It was also to provide confirmation of the need for exercising enormous caution as well as rock solid determination in implementing reforms. From the governmental perspective, the ensuing *Kaika* movement was an extension of the intellectual aims of the Iwakura Mission on the domestic front, an attempt to initiate the broader populace and promote constructive contributions to the debate regarding future developments. Both the Iwakura Mission and the government-endorsed program of "improvement" had a degree of success; however, there was a fissure that emerged between the segment of the leadership group in the Mission and the remainder that was left behind to "hold the fort". The participation of the nation's leading scholars of the West in the *Meirokusha* also made an important contribution to the expansion of public space and public discourse, but it was always a largely urban phenomenon and did not succeed in substantially defusing the hostility toward "Westernization" that remained deeply entrenched among the more reactionary elite and the broader population.

Ultimately, there was never any guarantee that increased exposure to Western learning would produce constructive results. As knowledge of Western liberalism and representative government became accessible through translation, there was the possibility of cultivating a naïve imitation of Western radicalism. The forerunners who had witnessed the praxis as well as the theory of Western political institutions could issue cautions and admonitions regarding the premature adoption of Western forms of representative government but they would appear as little more than self-interested excuses. In either case, the strata of personnel within the government who had such experiences and were attempting to steer a middle course between the two conflicting interests were doomed to disappoint both the reactionary and the radical elements in the polity.

Eventually the mistrust of the *samurai* class would erupt into full-blown rebellion, the Seinan War of 1877 being the most powerful and conclusive instance. The victory of the government in this decisive conflict meant that the focus of national policy could move from consolidating the military authority of the state and look toward more thorough treatment of the national infrastructure, including the matter of resolving the relation of the Imperial Household to the organs of government. This also marked the beginning of the clarification of a more self-conscious program of conservative reform, commencing with Ōkubo Toshimichi's musings on the most appropriate form of government for Japan and ultimately providing the sobriquet of "gradualism" for Itō Hirobumi.

However, the political arena was not the exclusive province of the Satsuma and Chōshū oligarchy, and alternatives to their conception of progressive conservatism would be challenged from several quarters. Apart from the home-grown radicalism that sprang up under the influence of Western liberalism, there were elements within the administrative elite who would attempt to pull policy further toward a formalistic conception of Imperial sovereignty based on the retrospective premises of the Restoration. Moreover, the defeat of the *shizoku* on the battlefield also led, ironically, to the gradual infusion of such anti-government and xenophobic elements into the movement for the expansion of "popular representation". It is here that one of the most fundamental oversights in Meiji historiography has emerged—Freedom and Popular Rights by the 1880s was increasingly contaminated by forces that were highly illiberal and anti-democratic.

The appearance of popular movements and nationwide political organizations from the late 70s onward makes it tempting to conclude that popular representation is the inevitable accoutrement of any truly modern nation. However, that conclusion is premature. As seminal works such as Benedict Anderson's *Imagined Communities* and Ernest Gellner's *Nations and Nationalism* have elucidated in their disparate ways, the sine qua non of the modern nation state is simply a highly integrated mass culture and an educational apparatus that enables (ideally) all citizens to be acculturated therein.[1] There is no inherent requirement that the new political configuration be either liberal or "universalist"—indeed it is perfectly possible to establish a quasi-oligarchical political structure along with an anti-individualist ethos within the compass of the national community.

The problem is that "traditionalism" of any authentic sort becomes very difficult to accommodate within the new mass-cultural environment, especially so given that the absolute maintenance of traditions, political or otherwise, is predicated on the retention of institutions that become largely infeasible in the face of the imperatives of industrialization. The traditional arts are an important exception, but their removal from the original social and historical context has always necessitated that thoroughly traditional modes of presentation and dissemination have become largely untenable—there is a "hot house" aspect to their preservation which, if anything, accentuates the general point.

Applying these observations to the Japanese situation in the 1880s, it is apparent that while a certain faction of the Imperial Way were unreconstructed traditionalists, they were in fact a minority and were, apart from the exception of perhaps Motoda Eifu, not at the centre of the changes concerned. As has already been stressed, the likes of Yamagata Aritomo and Nishimura Shigeki were not traditionalists pure and simple. They understood the inevitability of new institutional structures for national administration and the infeasibility of reintroducing past Imperial institutions without any form of qualification or constraint.

Their interest was, by contrast, more firmly focused on the creation of a national ethos that would embody the moral essence of the Imperial tradition of Japan and impart it without exception to every citizen. It was to be a very *modern* solution to a modern problem.[2]

The aspect that distinguishes the Japanese "solution" from many other solutions to the "modern" question of political integration in the nineteenth century was the manner in which the political and moral were maintained in a profound coalescence with each other. As stated at the outset, the forced opening of the country was not merely a disaster in terms of the rather rude surprise of discovering the technical superiority of Western military hardware; it was moral horror that accompanied that realization and gave the crisis an edge that was hard for contemporary Western observers to appreciate (after all, the perception was that the Japanese were being offered a morally superior alternative to Japanese traditionalism)—and this seems largely neglected even in contemporary commentary. The starting point was a condition of relative political stasis, a configuration that was inviolable and the maintenance of which was in and of itself an inherently "good" act. It was a legalism (or formalism) that had the propensity to slide into a fetishism about the innate moral goodness of political institutions. The grand resolution propounded in the Imperial Rescript on Education was in effect, therefore, a coming full circle to instate a moral outlook that resonated profoundly with the pre-Restoration moral outlook of *Shushigaku*, yet was invested in the new and largely hybrid construct of the modern Imperial Household.

As Inoue Tetsujirō stated in the *Chokugo Engi*, the morality propounded in the Imperial Rescript was not mere unreflective traditionalism—traditions, after all, were not able to survive the current of social change that was sweeping the nation. The morality of loyalty and respect as set out in the Rescript had a clear social utility and, more importantly, would ultimately enable the Japanese to bond together through their own cultural heritage rather than partake of the heady and divisive influence of the West. Inoue was criticized by the *kokusui* intellectuals, including Miyake Setsurei, for making such utilitarian arguments but his outlook was consistent with what was the fact of the matter so far as building a new national consciousness was concerned. Tradition by itself simply would not hold.

The year 1890 therefore constitutes a watershed where tradition in the obsolete sense was finally transformed and integrated into a modern ideological package, one that would seem to take care of the problem of melding the nation with the state and potentially do so more effectively than any of the more liberal or rationalist options on offer. The illiberal option was not taken to in its entirety in one fell swoop or in some exclusive sense by the broad public, but the events of that year and thereafter illustrate that it was now part of the core of the political configuration and could easily expand into a more full expression of ultra-nationalism, ultimately fascism. To quote Collingwood's incisive analysis of the allure of fascism, the strength of such illiberal ideologies, despite inherent contradictions and even patently stupid assertions at times, is that they work on the basis of encouraging people to "think with their blood"—rationalism as such is denigrated as "weakness" and those who attempt to counter the more emotive political creed are easily discredited for their lack of passion and dedication to the nation. This is increasingly what becomes more evident from the 1890s onward.

The Japanese polity had ultimately arrived at a resolution, a kind of equilibrium where a relative balance between the leading reformers among the Satsuma and Chōshū Ministers of State and the nativist conservatives within both the state bureaucracy and the Ministry of the Imperial Household. It entailed a more complete accommodation of the institution of the Imperial throne but at enormous political cost.

Notes

1 Introduction

1. *Japan in Transition: From Tokugawa to Meiji*, Marius B. Jansen and Gilbert Rozman (eds), Princeton University Press, 1986.
2. T. M. Huber, *The Revolutionary Origins of Modern Japan*, Stanford University Press, 1981, and G. M. Wilson, *Patriots and Redeemers in Japan: Motives in the Meiji Restoration*, University of Chicago Press, 1992.
3. Nagai Michio and Miguel Urrutia, *Meiji Ishin: Restoration and Revolution*, United Nations University, 1985.
4. Andrew Gordon, *A Modern History of Japan: From Tokugawa Times to the Present*, Oxford University Press, 2002.
5. It should be acknowledged that Jansen has come close to providing such an integrated narrative with *The Making of Modern Japan* (Harvard University Press, 2000), although it remains an extremely generalized overview that does not substantially revise conventional characterizations of the Meiji period. To this we might also add *The Emergence of Meiji Japan*, edited by the same author (Cambridge University Press, 1995) but this is essentially a republished selection of chapters from Vol. 5 of *The Cambridge History of Japan* (originally published in 1989) and in need of further updating in certain regards. There is also W. G. Beasley's *The Rise of Modern Japan: Economic, Political and Social Change Since 1850* (St. Martin's Press, 1995), which benefits from giving greater attention to the build-up to the Restoration but remains a rework of earlier scholarship.
6. Richard Sims, *Japanese Political History Since the Meiji Renovation, 1868–2000*, Hurst, 2000.
7. Carol Gluck, *Japan's Modern Myths: Ideology in the Late Meiji Period*, Princeton University Press, 1985.
8. Tokutomi Sohō, "Ishin Kakumei-shi no Hanmen", in *Kokumin no Tomo*, No. 207, 3 November 1893. Regarding the conservate turn in Tokutomi Soho's outlook, refer to my chapter "Tokutomi Sohō and the Problem of the Nation-state in an Imperialist World" in Dick Stegewerns' *Nationalism and Internationalism in Imperial Japan: Autonomy, Asian Brotherhood or World Citizenship?* RoutledgeCurzon, 2003.
9. Meiji Bunka Kenkyukai (ed.), *Jiyū Minken Hen*, vols. 5–6 of *Meiji Bunka Zenshū*, Nihon Hyoronsha, 1992–3.
10. Gotō Yasushi, "Jiyū to Minken no Shisō" in *Iwanami Kōza Nihon Rekishi (Kindai 3)*, Iwanami Shoten, 1962, pp. 167–183.
11. Robin Collingwood, *The Idea of History*, Clarendon Press, 1946, pp. 282–302.
12. One of the earliest discussions of this perspective is Thomas C. Smith, *The Agrarian Origins of Modern Japan*, Stanford University Press, 1959. More recently, there is the excellent collection of essays in seven volumes edited by Michael Smitka, *Japanese Economic History 1600–1960*. The volume of most relevance here is *Japanese Economy in the Tokugawa Era, 1600–1868*, Garland Publishing, 1998.

13. Sakamoto Koremaru, *Meiji Ishin to Kokugakusha*, Daimeido, 1993.
14. Asukai Masamichi, *Nihon Kindai Seishinshi no Kenkyū*, Kyoto University Press, 2002, pp. 326–32.
15. Karl Mannheim, *Conservatism: A contribution to the Sociology of Knowledge*, Kettler et al. (eds), Routledge and Kegan Paul, 1986, p. 76.
16. Barrington Moore's discussion of the paradoxical outcomes of revolutionary movements remains highly relevant; Barrington Moore, *The Social Origins of Dictatorship and Democracy: Lord and Peasant in the Making of the Modern World*, Beacon Press, 1966, pp. 433–52.
17. Helen Hardacre, *Shinto and the State, 1868–1988*, Princeton University Press, 1989, pp. 21–34.
18. Alistair Swale, *The Political Thought of Mori Arinori: A Study in Meiji Conservatism*, Japan Library, 2000.
19. One of the best overviews of this as intellectual history remains that of Matsumoto Sannosuke in *Nihon Seiji Shisōshi Gairon*, Keiso Shobo, 1982, pp. 48–89.
20. More specifically, under the name of "Yoshida Torajiro" in Robert Louis Stevenson, *Familiar Studies of Men and Books*, Scribner, 1905, pp. 148–64.
21. Katō Hiroyuki is generally regarded an early advocate of Western conceptions of natural rights who essentially repudiated them in 1882 with *Jinken Shinsetsu* (人権新説). In this volume, additional attention will be given to his less than liberal stewardship of Tokyo Imperial University.
22. Isabella Bird, *Unbeaten Tracks in Japan*, John Murray, 1880, vol. II, pp. 236–46.
23. A classic on this subject, which merits "rediscovery" is Fukuchi Shigetaka, *Shizoku to Shizoku Ishiki*, Shunshusha, 1956.
24. This aspect of Japan's political history is almost uncovered in detail in either English or Japanese; an important Japanese exception is Takii Kazuhiro, *Doitsu Kokkagaku to Meiji Kokusei, Shutain Kokkagaku no Kiseki*, Minerva Shobo, 1999.
25. See Nakanome Tōru, *Seikyōsha no Kenkyū*, Shibunkaku, 1993.

2 Japan Within the World System: Urbanization, Political Stasis and Western Economic Expansion

1. Townsend Harris, *The Complete Journal of Townsend Harris*, as reprinted in Tokyo Daigaku Shiryo Hensansho (ed.), *Meiji Shiryō Senshū 1*, vol. 1 (hereafter *Shiryō Senshū 1*), Tokyo University Press, 1970, pp. 34–5.
2. Yoshida Shōin, letter to Kitayama Yasuyo as reprinted in *Shiryō Senshū 1*, pp. 87–9.
3. Donald Keene, *The Japanese Discovery of Europe, 1720–1830*, Stanford University Press, 1969, pp. 59–90.
4. Okada Takehiko, "Neo-Confucian Thinkers in Nineteenth Century Japan" in P. Nosco (ed.), *Confucianism and Tokugawa Culture*, Princeton University Press, 1984, pp. 215–50. Regarding political stasis within the Tokugawa system, see Conrad Totman, *Early Modern Japan*, University of California Press, 1993, pp. 316–47.
5. Totman, *ibid.*, pp. 472–82.
6. Paul E. Eckel, "Challenges to Dutch Monopoly Of Japanese Trade During the Wars of Napoleon", *The Far Eastern Quarterly*, vol. 1, no. 2, pp. 173–9.

7. Totman, *op. cit.*, pp. 511–18.
8. See "Sankin Kōsansei Henkaku Kankei Shiryō 1 & 2", in *Shiryo Senshu 1*, pp. 132–4.
9. Regarding Gutzlaff in China, see Edgar Holt, *The Opium Wars in China*, Putnam, 1964, pp. 107–9. Regarding the *Morrison*, W. G. Beasley, *Great Britain and the Opening of Japan*, Luzac, 1951, pp. 21–8.
10. Totman, *op. cit.*, pp. 532–3.
11. Beasley, *op. cit.*, 1951, pp. 66–9.
12. W. G. Beasley, *The Rise of Modern Japan: Economic, Political and Social Change Since 1850*, St Martin's Press, 1995, pp. 28–32.
13. Kutsuzawa Nobutaka in *Yōgakuji Hajime*, Bunka Shobo Hyakubunsha, 1993, pp. 14–15.
14. Mukai Akira, in *Yōgakuji Hajime*, Bunka Shobo Hyakubunsha, 1993, pp. 231–2.
15. Kutsuzawa Nobutaka, *op. cit.*, p. 14.
16. Mori Mutsuhiko, "Ahen Sensō Jōhō to shite no Tō Fūsetsusho", in Houya Tōru (ed.), *Bakumatsu Ishin to Jōhō*, Yoshikawa Kobunkan, 2001, pp. 13–26. Also, see the report of Tokawa Yasukiyo as reprinted in Iwashita Tetsunori, *Bakumatsu Nihon no Jōhō Katsudō*, Yusankaku, 2008, pp. 353–5, for an example of how the Chinese account became incorporated into Japanese reportage.
17. Mukai Akira, *op. cit.*, pp. 233–4, p. 241.
18. Mukai Akira, *ibid.*, p. 235.
19. B. T. Wakabayashi in Timothy Brook and Bob Wakabayahi (eds), *Opium Regimes: China, Britain, and Japan, 1839–1952*, University of California Press, 2000, p. 61.
20. Beasley, *op. cit.*, 1951, p. 90.
21. Miyachi Masato, "Bakumatsu no Jōhōshūshū to Fūsetsusho", in Houya Toru (ed.), *Bakumatsu Ishin to Jōhō*, Yoshikawa Kobunkan, 2001, pp. 219–22.
22. Mukai Akira, in *Yōgakuji Hajime*, Bunka Shobo Hyakubunsha, 1993, p. 241.
23. Mukai Akira, *ibid.*, pp. 237–8.
24. Beasley, *op. cit.*, 1995, pp. 31–2.
25. Matsumoto Kenichi, *Kaikoku· Ishin 1853–1871*, Chuo Koronsha, 1998, pp. 121–9.
26. There is an extremely useful selection of Black Ships related *kawara-ban* with a lucid introduction in Tanaka Akira (ed.), *Kaikoku*, Nihon Kindai Shiso Taikei, vol. I, Chikuma Shobo, 1991, pp. 193–203.
27. Beasley, *op. cit.*, 1951, pp. 113–44.
28. J. Y. Wong, *Deadly Dreams: Opium, Imperialism and the Arrow War (1856–1860) in China*, Cambridge University Press, 1998, pp. 43–68.
29. Hotta Masayoshi, correspondence on behalf of the government to Emperor Kōmei, *Shiryō Senshū 1*, pp. 39–40. The Emperor's response can be found on pp. 41–3.
30. Beasley, *op. cit.*, 1951, pp. 188–90.
31. Matsumoto Kenichi, *op. cit.*, pp. 148–58, and pp. 178–86.
32. Matsumoto Sannosuke in *Nihon Seiji Shisōshi Gairon*, Keiso Shobo, 1982, pp. 48–89.
33. Matsumoto Kenichi, *op. cit.*, pp. 38–52.
34. Matsumoto Kenichi, *ibid.*, pp. 228–33.
35. Matsumoto Kenichi, *ibid.*, pp. 260–3. For the original text of *Kokuze Sanron*, see Yokoi Shōnan, *Shōnan Kikō*, Minyusha, 1898, pp. 44–101.

36. Thomas M. Huber, *The Revolutionary Origins of Modern Japan*, Stanford University Press, 1981, pp. 42–59 and pp. 71–7.
37. Tokutomi Sohō, *Yoshida Shōin*, reprinted in *Tokutomi Sohō Shū*, Chikuma Shobo, 1974, pp. 224–5.
38. Huber, *op. cit.*, pp. 59–68. Huber seems to suggest that there was an element of tactical posturing involved in this position; however, this does not seem to be a necessary conclusion and arguably Yoshida's political tactics indicate that indeed the Mencian position was significant in a more intrinsic sense. For a more recent discussion of the intellectual influences on Yoshida, see Kojima Tsuyoshi, *Kindai Nihon no Yōmeigaku*, Kodansha, 2006, pp. 57–62.
39. Matsumoto Kenichi, *op. cit.*, pp. 118–21.
40. Kasahara Hidehiko, *Ōkubo Toshimichi: Bakumatsu Ishin no Kosei*, Yoshikawa Kobunkan, 2005, pp. 6–11.
41. Kasahara, *op. cit.*, pp. 12–16.
42. Ōkubo Toshimichi, *Ōkubo Toshimichi Nikki* (hereafter *Nikki*), vol. 1, pp. 1–19.
43. Ōkubo Toshimichi, *Nikki*, p. 34.
44. For Fukuzawa's lively and highly critical account of how the Mission sequestered themselves as much as possible in close proximity to each other with provisions stacked in the corridors for cooking and other domestic necessities, see his autobiography, *Fukuō Jiden*, Jiji Shinpo Sha, 1899, p, 202–11. Beasley, *op. cit.*, 1995, pp. 72–94.
45. See the diary of Muragaki Norimasa, as reprinted in *Shiryō Senshū 1*, pp. 107–9.
46. Beasley, *op. cit.*, 1995, pp. 56–67. Beasley tends to associate this reticence to make public statements upon their return with indifference; however, as Numata Jiro discusses in the commentary on the collection of Bakufu memoirs published by Iwanami, the leaders would return to find themselves in the midst of an extremely intense wave of anti-Western agitation, Ii Naosuke having only recently been assassinated; see Numata Jirō, "Bakumatsu Kengai Shisetsu ni Tsuite" in *Seiyō Kenbun Shū*, Iwanami Shoten, 1974, p. 607.
47. Numata, *ibid.*, pp. 604–5.
48. Beasley, *op. cit.*, 1995, p. 71.
49. Beasley, *ibid.*, 1995, pp. 72–3. Again, Numata introduces a more positive view of the Mission's composition and general competence. He also emphasizes that it was in fact the Japanese who proposed the ratification to the Americans and not the other way around. Numata, *op. cit.*, pp. 603–4 and p. 608.
50. Matsumura Masaie, *Bakumatsu Shisetsudan no Igirisu Ōkanki—Vikutorian Inpakuto*, Kashiwa Shobo, 2008, pp. 11–18.
51. See Miyanaga Takashi, *Bakumatsu Ken'ō Shisetsudan*, Kodansha, 2006, pp. 133–5. Beasley, 1995, pp. 79–84.
52. Beasley, *op. cit.*, 1995, p. 88.
53. One of the best and most recent discussions of the question of the competence of the various translators appended to the mission can be found in Miyanaga, *ibid.*, pp. 313–21, where he compares the English letters of both Matsuki Kōan and Fukuzawa Yukichi. There is also substantial discussion of the friendship between Fukuzawa and the Frenchman Leon de Rosny whose correspondence seems to have been heavily peppered with Dutch phrases; Numata, *op. cit.*, pp. 173–6.
54. Kōmei's Edict, *Shiryō Senshū 1*, pp. 118–120. Shogun's compliance, *idem.*, pp. 139–41. Kōmei's back-down, *idem.*, p. 173. A record of Shimazu

Hisamitsu's meeting with members of the nobility and Bakufu officials indicates a willingness to go along with the plan, albeit with reservations; see "Shimazu Hisamitsu Kokuji Shūsen Kankei Shiryō", *idem.*, pp. 148–50.

55. Matsumoto, *op. cit.*, pp. 190–200, pp. 233–40.
56. Kasahara, *op. cit.*, pp. 44–8.
57. Matsumoto, *op. cit.*, pp. 240–53.
58. Ōkubo Toshimichi, memorial to Konoe Tadahiro, October 1866, *Shiryō Senshū 1*, pp. 263–4.
59. Ishizuki Minoru, *Kindai Nihon no Kaigai Ryūgakushi*, Minerva Shobo, 1972, pp. 32–48.
60. Andrew Cobbing, *The Satsuma Students in Britain: Japan's Early Search for the "Essence of the West"*, Japan Library, 2000, pp. 56–60.
61. Ishizuki, *op. cit.*, pp. 16–18.
62. Ishizuki, *ibid.*, pp. 28–37.
63. Ishizuki, *ibid.*, pp. 60–8.
64. Beasley, *op. cit.*, 1995, pp. 126–9.
65. Beasley, *ibid.*, 1995, pp. 114–7.
66. Alistair Swale, *The Political Thought of Mori Arinori: A Study in Meiji Conservatism*, Japan Library, 2000, pp. 64–9, pp. 205–9.
67. N. Nakai and J. L. McClain, "Commercial Change and Urban Growth in Early Modern Japan" in Michael Smitka (ed.), *Japanese Economic History 1600–1960: The Japanese Economy in the Tokugawa Era, 1600–1868*, Garland, pp. 191–207.
68. Alistair Swale, "America: The First Stage in the Quest for 'Enlightenment'", in Ian Nish (ed.), *The Iwakura Mission in America and Europe: A New Assessment*, Curzon Press, 1998.
69. Matsumoto Kenichi, *op. cit.*, pp. 109–11.

3   The Meiji Coup d'État

1. Kasahara Hidehiko, *Ōkubo Toshimichi, Meiji Ishin no Kosei*, Yoshikawa Kobunkan, 2005, pp. 50–2.
2. Ōkubo Toshimichi, *Ōkubo Toshimichi Nikki* (hereafter *Nikki*), vol. 1, Nihon Shiseki Kyokai, 1927, p. 398.
3. Tokyo Daigaku Shuppankai, *Meiji Ishinshi Shiryō Senshū*, vol. 1 (hereafter *Shiryō Senshū 1*), Tokyo University, 1970, pp. 303–7.
4. Ōkubo Toshimichi, *Ōkubo Toshimichi Monjō* (hereafter *Monjō*), vol. 1, p. 35; Ōkubo, *Nikki*, pp. 391–6.
5. Ōkubo, *Nikki*, pp. 399–400.
6. Matsuo Masahito (ed.), *Meiji Ishin to Bunmei Kaika*, Yoshikawa Kobunkan, 2004, pp. 8–13.
7. Ōkubo, *Monjō*, pp. 72–82.
8. Ōkubo, *Monjō*, pp. 98–100.
9. Ōkubo, *Monjō*, pp. 154–8. Ōkubo even records that Iwakura was at one point in tears! See *Nikki*, p. 428; Matsuo, *op. cit.*, pp. 13–15.
10. Matsuo, *ibid.*, pp. 15–21.
11. Hugh Cortazzi, *Mitford's Japan: Memories and Recollections 1866–1906*, Japan Library, 2002. Also noted with alarm in Ōkubo's diary, *Nikki*, pp. 441–3.
12. Cortazzi, *ibid.*, pp. 61–122.

13. Cortazzi, *op. cit.*, pp. 108–22.
14. Ōkubo, *Monjō*, pp. 191–2.
15. Ōkubo, *Nikki*, p. 424. Matsuo, *op. cit.*, pp. 15–16.
16. Matsuo, *ibid.*, pp. 21–5.
17. Albert Craig, "The Central Government" in Jansen and Rozman (eds), *Japan in Transition from Tokugawa to Meiji*, Princeton University Press, 1985, pp. 54–5.
18. Author's translation as per the original in Tokyo Daigaku Shuppankai, *Meiji Ishinshi Shiryō Senshū*, vol. 2 (hereafter *Shiryō Senshū 2*), Tokyo University Press, 1972, pp. 67–9.
19. Matsumoto Kenichi, *Kaikoku Ishin: 1853–1871*, Chuo Koronsha, 1998, pp. 319–28.
20. Refer to *Seitaisho*, as reprinted in *Shiryō Senshū 2*, pp. 109–21, particularly p. 111.
21. Ōkubo, *Nikki*, p. 467 and p. 489, regarding Western transport and Western meal in Edo; p. 494 regarding the Emperor's visit to Edo to review warships.
22. Ōkubo, *Nikki*, pp. 10–1 regarding the assassination of Shōnan; pp. 22–4 and pp. 44–5 regarding administrative initiatives.
23. Craig, *op. cit.*, pp. 56–7. Ōkubo, *Nikki*, pp. 144–5.
24. Matsuo, *op. cit.*, pp. 32–7.
25. Craig, *op. cit.*, pp. 52–3.
26. Matsuo, *op. cit.*, pp. 25–32.
27. Matsuo, *ibid.*, pp. 50–6.
28. Craig, *op. cit.*, pp. 53–7.
29. Matsuo, *op. cit.*, pp. 37–41.
30. A. D. Swale, *The Political Thought of Mori Arinori: A Study in Meiji Conservatism*, Japan Library, 2000, pp. 48–68. Ivan Parker Hall, *Mori Arinori*, Harvard University Press, 1973, pp. 132–42.
31. M. B. Jansen and G. Rozman (eds), 1985, pp. 76–7. Susan Hanley, *Everyday Things in Premodern Japan*, University of California Press, 1997, p. 167.
32. Helen Hardacre, *Shinto and the State, 1868–1988*, Princeton University Press, 1989, pp. 21–41.
33. Takii Kazuhiro, *Bunmeishi no Naka no Meiji Kempō*, 2003, pp. 20–1.
34. Hall, I.P., *Mori Arinori*, Harvard University Press, 1973, pp. 178–9.
35. Swale, A. "America: The First Stage in the Quest for 'Enlightenment'", in *The Iwakura Mission in America and Europe: A New Assessment*, Ian Nish (ed.), Curzon Press, 1998, pp. 21–22.
36. Kume Kunitake, *The Iwakura Embassy, 1871–73: A True Account of the Ambassador Extraordinary & Plenipotentiary's Journey of Observation Through the United States of America and Europe* (editors-in-chief, Graham Healey, Chushichi Tsuzuki), Japan Documents, 2003, vol. I, pp. 52–7, pp. 210–2, pp. 328–32.
37. Kume, *ibid.*, vol. II, pp. 11–25.
38. Kume, *ibid.*, vol. III, p. 373; vol. IV, pp. 58–64, pp. 373–4.
39. Kume, *ibid.*, vol. III, pp. 273–5.
40. A. Swale, *op. cit.*, 2000, pp. 504.
41. Kōsaka Masaaki, *Meiji Shisō Shi*, vol. VII of *Kōsaka Masaaki Chosaku Shū*, Risosha, 1969.
42. Hanley, *op. cit.*, pp. 155–75.

43. Art Directors' Club of Tokyo (eds), *Nihon no Kōkoku Bijutsu—Meiji, Taishō, Shōwa*, vol. III, *Pakkeeji*, Bijutsu Shuppansha, 1968, pp. 75–91.
44. Itō Yukio, *Meiji Tennō: Mura Kumo wo fuku Kaze ni haresomete*, Minerva Shobo, 2006, pp. 180–4.
45. Kōsaka, *op. cit.*, pp. 70–3.
46. See Kōsaka, *ibid.*, pp. 86–93; Asukai, *op.cit.*, 1985, pp. 4–8.
47. Nakanome Tōru, in Yamamuro Shinichi and Nakanome Toru (eds), *Meiroku Zasshi*, Iwanami Shoten, 1999, pp. 433–7.
48. Fukuzawa used the phrase as early as 1866, see Asukai, *op. cit.*, 1985, pp. 1–4.
49. Ernest Gellner, *Nations and Nationalism*, Blackwell, 1983, pp. 110–14.
50. In his classic work on the *shizoku*, Fukuchi Shigetaka methodically enumerates the areas where the *shizoku* continued to exert a most profound influence over Japanese society; see, Fukuchi Shigetaka, *Shizoku to Shizoku Ishiki: Kindai Nihon wo Okoseru Mono· Horobosu Mono*, Shujunsha, 1956.
51. Asukai, *op. cit.*, 2002, pp. 229–53.
52. Ōkubo, *Nikki*, pp. 203–7. Also see Iwata Masakazu, *Ōkubo Toshimichi: The Bismarck of Japan*, University of California Press, 1964, p. 162.
53. See "Itagaki Taisuke Nado Kenpakusho" in *Shiryō Senshū 2*, pp. 325–30.
54. He also notes that the popular movements among the former peasantry failed to coalesce with these *shizoku* movements for precisely this reason. Ultimately, the samurai ethos was such that *shizoku* struggled to even maintain a coordinated movement among themselves and it was ultimately this which spelled their doom even in the armed revolt that broke out in 1877. See Fukuchi, *op. cit.*, pp. 101–23.
55. Kasahara, *op. cit.*, pp. 182–3. Iwata, 1964, pp. 180–3.
56. Ōkubo, *Nikki*, p. 257; Ōkubo writes with uncharacteristic candour, "Etō's testimony was so evasive that I couldn't stop laughing".
57. Kasahara, *op. cit.*, pp. 137–44.
58. Kasahara *ibid.*, 156–8.
59. Ōkubo Toshimichi, *Ōkubo Tōshimichi Monjō*, Nihon Shiseki Kyokai, 1962, vol. V, p. 183.
60. Ōkubo Toshimichi, *ibid.*, pp. 188–9.
61. Yamamuro Shinichi, *Hōsei Kanryō no Jidai: Kokka no Seikei to Chi no Rekitei*, Bokutakusha, 1988, pp. 178–94.
62. Kasahara, *op. cit.*, pp. 163–4.
63. Kasahara, *ibid.*, pp. 155–7.
64. A. Swale, *op. cit.*, 2000, pp. 59–60.
65. See Oda Yasunori, *Ishin Kaika to Toshi Ōsaka*, Seibundo, 2001, pp. 242–54.
66. Asukai, *op. cit.*, 1985; and Hanley, *op. cit.*, 1997.

4   Mass Media and the Development of Civil Culture

1. Sasaki Takashi, *Media to Kenryoku*, Chuo Koronsha, 1999, pp. 27–39.
2. Fukuzawa Yukichi, "Shimbunshi" in Matsumoto Sannosuke and Yamamuro Shinichi (eds), *Genron to Media*, Iwanami Shoten, 1990, pp. 3–4.
3. Yamamoto Takctoshi, *Kindai Nihon no Shinbun Dokushaso*, Hosei University Press, 2006, p. 60; J. Black, *Young Japan: Yokohama and Yedo, 1858–1879*, Oxford University Press, 1868, pp. 370–2.

4. Momose Hibiki, *Bunmei Kaika: Ushinawareta Fūzoku*, Yoshikawa Kobunkan, 2008, pp. 113–19.

5. For the text of the original ordinances, see Tokyo Daigaku Shiryo Hensankyoku, *Meiji Ishinshi Shiryō Senshū*, vol. 2 (hereafter *Shiryō Senshū 2*), Tokyo University Press, 1972, pp. 358–64. Also Momose, *ibid.*, pp. 58–103 (includes full reproductions of the *Ishiki Kaii Jōrei* as well).

6. Nakanome Toru in Matsuo Masato (ed.), *Meiji Ishin to Bunmei Kaika*, Yoshikawa Kobunkan, 2004, p. 221.

7. And occasionally somewhat longer; see Nakanome in Matsuo, *ibid.*, pp. 215–17 re time frame.

8. D. Howland, *Translating the West*, University of Hawaii Press, 2002, pp. 38–40.

9. R. Porter, *Enlightenment: Britain and the Creation of the Modern World*, Macmillan, 2000, pp. 1–23.

10. Nishiyama Matsunosuke, *Edo Culture: Daily Life and Diversions in Urban Japan*, University of Hawaii Press, 1997, pp. 64–75.

11. David Huish, "Aims and Achievements of the *Meirokusha*—Fact and Fiction", *Monumenta Nipponica*, vol. 32, no. 4, p. 514.

12. Howland, *ibid.*, pp. 31–8. Takano Shigeo and Hinata Toshihiko (eds), *Meiroku Zasshi Goi Sō Sakuin*, 1998, pp. 26–7 and p. 84.

13. Meiji Bunka Kenkyukai (eds), *Meiji Bunka Zenshū*, Nihon Hyoronsha, 1993.

14. Ōnishi Hajime, "Keimo Jidai no Seishin wo Ronzu", in *Kokumin no Tomo* (October 1898, no. 362) reprinted in *Ōnishi Hakase Zenshū*, vol. VI, Keiseisha Shoten, 1907, pp. 624–37.

15. See Natsume Soseki, "Gendai Nihon no Kaika" in Fukuda Tsuneari (ed.), *Han-Kindai no Shisō*, Chikuma Shobo, 1968, pp. 53–72.

16. Kosaka Masaaki, *Meiji Shisō Shi* (Kōsaka Masaaki Chosaku Shū, vol. VII), Risosha, 1969, vol. VII, p. 110; Ōkubo Toshiaki (ed.) "Introduction" in *Nishi Amane Zenshū*, Nihon Hyoron Sha, 1945, p. 48.

17. Maruyama Masao in Matsuzawa Hiroaki (ed.), *Fukizawa Yukichi no Tetsugaku: Hoka Rokuhen*, Iwanami Shoten, 2001; and Matsumoto Sannosuke, *Nihon Seiji Shisōshi Gairon*, Keiso Shobo, 1982.

18. Huish, *op. cit.*, pp. 510.

19. Nakanome Tōru, in Yamamuro Shinichi & Nakanome Tōru (eds), *Meiroku Zasshi*, Iwanami Shoten, 1999, pp. 446–9.

20. The persistence of this view is perhaps largely attributable to the influence of the colossus of post-war political thought, Maruyama Masao. Quite apart from his early sortie into an exposition on the origins of Japanese fascism, there were two essays on Fukuzawa that actually won him higher acclaim at the time: "Fukuzawa Yukichi ni okeru 'jitsugaku' no tenkai: Fukuzawa Yukichi no Testsugaku Kenkyū Josetsu", and "Fukuzawa Yukichi no Testsugaku: Toku ni sono Jiji Hihan to no Kanren", both in Maruyama, 1995, vol. III, pp. 107–32 and pp. 163–206, respectively. See also, Maruyama Masao, *"Bunmeiron no Gairyaku" wo Yomu*, Iwanami Shoten, 1986.

21. There is an excellent commentary on the changing perceptions of *Bunmei Kaika* (and indeed Fukuzawa Yukichi as well) in an article by Koyanagi Kensuke which provides a glimpse into the increasingly politicized nature of evaluating the Meiji period in relation to the *Kokutai* (国体): *Meiji Bunka*, vol. 16, no. 1, pp. 1–6; reprinted in *Meiji Bunka Kenkyū*, vol. 7, Meiji Bunka Kenkyukai (ed.), Kobunko, 1942.

22. Yoshino Sakuzō, *Kaikoku to Meiji Bunka* (Yoshino Sakuzō Senshū, vol. XI), Iwanami Shoten, 1995, pp. 100–5. Yoshino also had a decidedly detached view of the achievements of the era of Freedom and Peoples Rights; it was the era of largely *ersatz* liberalism, the "real thing" was yet to be fulfilled in the Taisho era.
23. Ishii Kendō, *Meiji Jibutsu Jigen*, Kyonando, 1908.
24. Yamashita Shigekazu, *Supensaa to Nihon Kindai*, Ochanomizu Shobo, 1983, p. 19. In this connection, we might note a special expanded edition of *Taiyō* produced by the Hakubunkan in 1909 (Meiji Shi Dai Nana Hen, *Taiyō*, vol. 15, no. 3), where Fukuzawa is discussed in remarkably no-nonsense terms as an arch-pragmatist; an intellectual vulgarian of sorts who nonetheless was a necessary creature of the times (!).
25. The overall thrust of the articles on the Meiji period are consistent with Yoshida, Ishii and Osatake. The article by Miyatake Tobone entitled "Bunmei Kaika no Sendōtachi" refers to neither Fukuzawa nor *keimō*, only *bunmei kaika* and attributes the earliest driving force behind popularization of the term to the popular press. See *Meiji Bunka*, vol. 7, no. 11, pp. 1–2, reprinted in *Meiji Bunka Kenkyū*, vol. 6, Meiji Bunka Kenkyukai (ed), Kobunko, 1942.
26. Yamashita, *op. cit.*, pp. 182–95.
27. Yamashita, *ibid.*, pp. 121–60; also see Howland, *op. cit.*, pp. 171–82.
28. Huish, *op. cit.*, p. 514.
29. Howland, *op. cit.*, p. 40.
30. A. Swale, "America: The First Stage in the Quest for Enlightenment" in I. Nish, *The Iwakura Mission in America and Europe: A New Assessment*, Japan Library, 1998, pp. 14–17.
31. Anzai Toshimitsu provides an extremely thorough examination of the Spencerian legacy in relation to Fukuzawa in *Fukuzawa Yukichi to Seiō Shisō*, Nagoya University Press, 1995, pp. 159–227.
32. Manabe, "Meiji Keimōki no Nishimura Shigeki" in *Nihon Rekishi*, no. 617, Yoshikawa Kobunkan, 1999, pp. 56–8.
33. Takahashi Masao, *Nishimura Shigeki*, Yoshikawa Kobunkan, 1987, pp. 9–11.
34. William Braisted, *Meiroku Zasshi: Journal of the Japanese Enlightenment* (hereafter *MZ* when quoting the essays of *Meirokusha* members), University of Tokyo Press, 1976, pp. xvii–xxxiii; W. G. Beasley, *Japan Encounters the Barbarian: Japanese Travellers in America and Europe*, 1995, pp. 209–12.
35. Beasley, *ibid.*, pp. 181–2.
36. Beasley, *ibid.*, pp. 127–8.
37. Asukai Masamichi. *Bunmei Kaika*, Iwanami Shoten, 1985, pp. 116–25.
38. See Braisted's translation, *MZ*, pp. 1–24; all essay titles are as per Braisted unless stated otherwise.
39. Nishi Amane, Issue Two, *MZ*, pp. 25–9.
40. Nishi Amane, *MZ*, pp. 40–3.
41. See Koizumi Takashi, *Nishi Amane to Ōbei Shisō to no Deai*, Sanrei Shobo, 1989, pp. 65–99.
42. Thomas R. T. Havens, *Nishi Amane and Modern Japanese Thought*, Princeton University Press, 1970, pp. 92–113.
43. Also see Takano et al., *op. cit.*, pp. 7–8.
44. Tsuda Mamichi, "In Opposition to Protective Tariffs", Issue Five (undated), *MZ*, pp. 56–9; "On Desiring Freedom of the Press", Issue Six (undated), *MZ*,

pp. 72–3; "On Torture", Part One, Issue Seven, May 1874, *MZ*, pp. 94–6 and "On Torture", Part Two, Issue Ten, June 1874, *MZ*, pp. 127–31.

45. Tsuda Mamichi, "On Official Insignia", Issue Eight, May 1874, *MZ*, pp. 102–4.
46. Tsuda Mamichi, "On the Plurality of the Origins of Things", Issue Eight, May 1874, *MZ*, pp. 111–14; also see Ōkubo Toshiaki (ed.), *Tsuda Mamichi; Kenkyū to Denki*, Misuzu Shobo, 1997: re Tsuda's materialism, pp. 88–94; re Tsuda and Spencerianism, pp. 95–101.
47. Tsuda Mamichi, Issue Eighteen, October 1874, *MZ*, pp. 226–7.
48. Tsuda Mamichi, "On the Death Penalty", Issue Forty-one, August 1875, *MZ*, pp. 498–500; "Travel by Foreigners Within the Country", Issue Twenty-four, December 1874, *MZ*, pp. 298–301; "On the Trade Balance", Issue Twenty-six, January 1875, *MZ*, pp. 324–7; "The Distinction Between Husbands and Wives", Issue Twenty-two, December 1874, *MZ*, pp. 277–9 and "On Destroying Prostitution", Issue Forty-two, October 1875, *MZ*, pp. 517–18.
49. Braisted, *op. cit.*, pp. 70–1.
50. See Hayashi Takeji, *Mori Arinori: Higeki he no Josō*, Chikuma Shobo, 1986, pp. 75–83.
51. See Mori's footnote to an article of Sakatani in Issue Thirty-two, *MZ*, p. 399.
52. Mitsukuri Rinshō, Issue Four (undated), *MZ*, pp. 45–7 and Issue Five (undated), *MZ*, pp. 65–7.
53. Mitsukuri Rinshō, Issue Seven, May 1874, *MZ*, pp. 91–3.
54. Sugi Kōji, *MZ*, pp. 34–7 and pp. 49–50, respectively.
55. Sugi Kōji, *MZ*, pp. 62–4 and pp. 93–4.
56. Sugi Kōji, "Speculators", Issue Eight, May 1874, *MZ*, pp. 108–9; "On Reforming Trade", Issue Twenty-four, 16 December 1874, *MZ*, pp. 301–6; and "Conjectures on an Imaginary Closed Country", Issue Thirty-four, April 1875, *MZ*, pp. 413–7.
57. Sugi Kōji, "Human Social Intercourse" Part 2, Issue Eighteen, October 1874, *MZ*, pp. 228–30 and "On Reforming Trade", Issue Twenty-four, 16 December 1874, *MZ*, pp. 301–6. Also the final instalment of "Human Social Intercourse", Issue Twenty-one, November 1874, *MZ*, pp. 267–9.
58. Kanda Kōhei, "Reform of the National Finances", Issue Eighteen, September 1874, *MZ*, pp. 213–8.
59. Kanda Kōhei, "The Time for a Popularly Elected Assembly is Not Yet", Issue Nineteen, October 1874, *MZ*, pp. 240–1.
60. Kanda Kōhei, "Misgivings on the Outcome of Paper Currency: The Third of Four Essays on Currency", Issue Twenty-six, January 1875, *MZ*, pp. 327–9.
61. Kanda Kōhei, "Notes on Curing the Currency Disease", Issue Thirty-three, March 1875, *MZ*, pp. 408–11.
62. Nishimura Shigeki, *MZ*, pp. 356–8.
63. Huish, *op. cit.*, pp. 495–514.
64. Sakatani Shiroshi, "Should We Not First Determine the Political Structure Before Introducing a Popularly Elected Assembly?", Issue Thirteen, June 1874, *MZ*, pp. 169–75.
65. Sakatani Shiroshi, Issue Twenty-two, December 1874, *MZ*, pp. 279–81 and Issue Twenty-five, December 1874, *MZ*, pp. 311–15.
66. Huish, *op. cit.*, p. 498.
67. Sakatani Shiroshi, "On Concubines", Issue Thirty-two, March 1875, *MZ*, pp. 392–9 and "Descending from heaven", Issue Thirty-six, May 1875, *MZ*, pp. 439–42.

68. Nakamura Masanao, *MZ*, pp. 207–8.
69. Nishimura Shigeki, *Ōjiroku* in *Nishimura Shigeki Zenshū*, vol. 3, Shibunkaku, 1976, pp. 620–1.
70. A. Swale, *The Political Thought of Mori Arinori: A Study in Meiji Conservatism*, Japan Library, 2000, pp. 79–81. For the original text of Mori's speech, see Mori Arinori, *Mori Arinori Zenshū*, vol. 1, Seibundo, 1972, pp. 252–6.
71. See especially Maruyama's 1971 Misuzu address which discusses "Risshinron", an article that Fukuzawa had published in the *Jiji Shinpo* in 1885 under the pen name of "Uchūsei", *op. cit.*, 1996, vol. XV, pp. 275–321.
72. Meiji Bunka Kenkyukai (eds), *Zasshi-hen*, *Meiji Bunka Zenshū*, Nihon Hyoronsha, 1993, pp. 269–321. Fukuzawa is easily the stand-out contributor whereas the other articles seem to make up numbers.
73. Fukuzawa Yukichi, *MZ*, pp. 319–24.
74. Fukuzawa Yukichi, *MZ*, p. 263.
75. See Yamamuro Shinichi and Nakanome Tōru (eds), *op. cit.*, p. 86 and Earl Kinmonth, "Fukuzawa Reconsidered; Gakumon no susume and its audience", *Journal of Asian Studies*, vol. 37:4, pp. 687–8.
76. Fukuzawa Yukichi, "The Equal Numbers of Men and Women", Issue Thirty-one, March 1875, *MZ*, pp. 385–6.
77. Ōkubo Toshiaki, *Meiji no Shisō to Bunka*, Yoshikawa Kobunkan, 1988, p. 181.
78. Ōkubo Toshiaki (ed.), *op. cit.*, 1997, p. 86.
79. Mitsukuri Shūhei, "On Education", Issue Eight, May 1874, *MZ*, pp. 106–8.
80. Anzai Toshimitsu, *Fukuzawa Yukichi to Seiyō Shisō*, Nagoya Daigaku Shuppankai, 1995, pp. 159–93.
81. For more recent commentaries that will provide a broader overview of Fukuzawa's career beyond the *Meirokusha* association, refer to Tamaki Norio, *Yukichi Fukuzawa, 1835–1901: the Spirit of Enterprise in Modern Japan*, Palgrave Macmillan, 2001.
82. Okitsu Kaname, *Meiji Shimbun hajime: "Bunmei Kaika" no Janarizumu*, Daishukan Shoten, 1997, pp. 107–39.
83. Huish, *op. cit.*, pp. 506–8.

5   "The More Thorough Fulfillment of the Restoration"

1. Suzuki Jun, *Ishin no Kōsō to Tenkai*, Kodansha, 2002, pp. 270–1.
2. Regarding Kido Takayoshi, see Sakamoto Takao, *Meiji Kokka no Kensetsu*, Chuo Koronsha, 1999, pp. 184–99. Regarding Okubo and Saigo Takamori, see Suzuki, *ibid.*, pp. 188–92, and the same re Okubo's assassination, pp. 198–9, and the reconfiguration of the military after the Seinan War, pp. 217–28.
3. Suzuki, *ibid.*, pp. 199–200.
4. For one of the more recent overviews of this period that also provides well-nuanced commentary, see Banno Junji, *Meiji Demokurashii*, Iwanami Shinsho, 2005, pp. 54–62.
5. Banno, *ibid.*, pp. 62–78.
6. This is a contentious issue that I have dealt with at some length in "1890: The Meiji Constitution as Miscalculation" in B. Edstrom (ed.), *Turning Points in Japanese History*, Routledge-Curzon, 2002, pp. 120–37. Both Itō Yukio (2006) and Asukai Masamichi (2002) qualify the degree to which the

"Prussian model" can be assumed in Ito's case. The matter is dealt with more directly in the ensuing chapter.

7. Suzuki, *op. cit.*, pp. 284–8. Takii Kazuhiro, *Bunmeishi no Naka no Meiji Kenpō*, Kodansha, 2003, pp. 82–7.
8. Itō Yukio, *Rikken Kokka no Kakuritsu to Itō Hirobumi: Naisei to Gaikō 1889–1898*, Yoshikawa Kobunkan, 1999, pp. 264–7.
9. Swale, *op. cit.*, p. 120–37.
10. Y. M. Kim, *East Asia's Turbulent Century*, Appleton Century Crofts, 1966, pp. 26–8.
11. Inuzuka Takaaki, *Nippon Seishun Gaikōkan*, Nippon Hoso Shuppan Kyokai, 2006, pp. 123–9.
12. Kim, *op. cit.*, p. 29–31.
13. Inuzuka, *op. cit.*, p. 129–37.
14. Banno, *op. cit.*, pp. 55–62 and pp. 81–90. Sakamoto Takao, *Meiji Kokka no Kensetsu: 1871–1890*, Chuo Koronsha, 1999, pp. 324–40.
15. James A. Huffman, *Creating a Public: People and Press in Meiji Japan*, Hawaii University Press, 1997, pp. 114–5.
16. Kitaoka Shin'ichi, "The Army as a Bureaucracy: Japanese Militarism Revisited" in *The Journal of Military History*, vol. 57, no. 5, The Institute for Advanced Studies, Princeton, New Jersey. (October 1993), pp. 67–86.
17. Itō Yukio, *Meiji Tennō: Murakumo wo Fuku Akikaze ni Haresomete*, Minerva Shobo, 2006, pp. 232–7.
18. Kitaoka, *op. cit.*, pp. 71–3.
19. Yukihiko Motoyama, "The Confucian Ideal of Rule by Virtue and the Creation of National Politics" in *Proliferating Talent: Essays on Politics, Thought and Education in the Meiji Era*, J. S. A. Elisona and R. Rubinger (eds), University of Hawaii Press, 1997, pp. 195–237.
20. Motoyama, *ibid.*, pp. 211–31.
21. Banno, *ibid.*, pp. 86–94. Motoyama, *idem.*
22. To obtain Tani's own outline of the *Chūsei* principles, see Hirao Michio, *Kōshaku Tani Tateki Den*, Shozansha, 1981, pp. 498–510. Obinata Sumio, "1881-nen no Seihen wo Meguru Chūseiha no Kiseki", in *Nihonshi Kenkyū*, no. 205, September 1979, Japanese Society of Historical Studies, pp. 1–27.
23. Manabe Masayuki, "Torio Koyata ni okeru Seifu Hihan no Keisei" in *Nihon Rekishi*, no. 657, February 2003, Nihon Rekishi Gakkai, pp. 64–7.
24. Manabe, *ibid.*, pp. 67–8.
25. Manabe, *ibid.*, pp. 69–71.
26. Manabe, *ibid.*, pp. 71–3.
27. Manabe, *ibid.*, pp. 73–5.
28. Itō, *op. cit.*, 2006, 341–3.
29. Kitaoka, *op. cit.*, 72–3.
30. Itō, *op. cit.* (2006), pp. 186–93.
31. Itō, *ibid.*, pp. 221–3.
32. Obinata, *op. cit.*, pp. 1–27.
33. Itō, *op. cit.*, 2006, pp. 223–37.
34. Numata Satoshi, *Motoda Eifu to Meiji Kokka: Meiji Hoshushugi to Jukyōteki Risōshugi*, Yoshikawa Kobunkan, 2005, pp. 267–9.
35. Numata, *ibid.*, pp. 269–73.

36. Asukai Masamichi, *Nihon Kindai Seishishi no Kenkyū*, Kyoto University Press, 2002, pp. 335–9.
37. See Fujimoto Akinobu's commentary in *Nishimura Shigeki Zenshū*, vol. 1, Nihon Kodokai (ed.), Shibunkaku, 2004, pp. 734–44. Also Takahashi Masao, *Nishimura Shigeki*, Yoshikawa Kobunkan, 1987, pp. 88–100.
38. Takii Kazuhiro, *Bunmeishi no Naka no Meiji Kempō*, 2003, pp. 88–91 and Sakamoto, *op. cit.*, pp. 338–40.
39. Takii, *ibid.*, pp. 108–16.
40. Takii, *ibid.*, pp. 134–5.
41. Sakamoto, *op. cit.*, pp. 329–43.
42. Sakamoto, *ibid.*, p. 335.
43. Itō, *op. cit.*, 2006, 257–62.
44. Asukai, *op. cit.*, 2002, pp. 334–45.
45. Ōkubo, *op. cit.*, 1988, pp. 231–4.
46. Ōkubo, *ibid.*, pp. 263–4.
47. Nishimura Shigeki, *Ōjiroku*, in *Nishimura Shigeki Zenshū*, vol. 3, Shibunkaku, 1976, pp. 631–2.
48. Ōkubo, *op. cit.*, 1988, pp. 265–71.
49. Ōkubo, *ibid.*, pp. 257–60.
50. Banno, *op. cit.*, pp. 74–6.
51. Swale, *op. cit.*, 2000, p. 103.
52. Banno, *op. cit.*, pp. 78–83.

6   The Imperial Household, the Popular Press and the Contestation of Public Space

1. Yamashita Shigekazu, *Spensaa to Nihon Kindai*, Ochanomizu Shobo, 1983, pp. 104–18.
2. Nakanome Tōru, *Seikyōsha no Kenkyū*, Shibunkaku, 1993, pp. 3–6.
3. Yamashita, *op. cit.*, pp. 121–40; Nakanome, *ibid.*, p. 160.
4. Satō Yoshimaru, *Meiji Nashonarizumu no Kenkyū: Seikyōsha no Seiritsu to sono Shūhen*, 1998, pp. 267–72.
5. Satō, *ibid.*, pp. 273–7.
6. Satō, *ibid.*, pp. 273–7.
7. Okazaki Masamichi, *Itanshi to Hangyakusha no Shisōshi: Kindai Nihon ni okeru Kakumei to Ishin*, Perikansha, 1999, pp. 12–30.
8. Kurogi Yukichi, *Komura Jūtarō*, Kodansha, 1968, pp. 9–19.
9. Kurogi, *ibid.*, pp. 72–4.
10. Nakanome, *op. cit.*, pp. 146–71.
11. Nakanome, *ibid.*, pp. 146–9.
12. Nakanome, *ibid.*, p. 168.
13. Nakanome, *ibid.*, p. 171.
14. S. Saaler and V. Koschmann (eds), *Pan-Asianism in Modern Japanese History: Colonialism, Regionalism and Borders*, Routledge, 2006.
15. Sakamoto Takao, *Meiji Kokka no Kensetsu*, Chuo Koronsha, 1999, pp. 314–16.
16. Yomiuri Shimbun, 2 November–29 December 1886, as per CD-Rom Database (Meiji), Yomiuri Shimbunsha, 1999.

17. Inoue Kaoru, missive to Itō Hirobumi dated 19 November 1986 in Itō Hirobumi Kankei Monjō Kenkyukai (eds), *Itō Hirobumi Kankei Monjō*, vol. 1, Koshobo, 1973, p. 210.
18. For the song, see *Nihon no Uta*, vol. 1 Meiji-Taishō, Nobarasha, 1998, p. 43; for the caricature, see Isao Shimizu (ed.) *Bigō Sobyōshū, Iwanami Bunkō*, Tokyo: Iwanami Shoten, 2003.
19. See R. Payne, "Early Meiji Kabuki Censorship" in *Japan Forum*, vol. 19, issue 3, November 2007, pp. 317–39.
20. See, for example, Utagawa Kunimasa IV, "Norumanton-gō chinbotsu jiken" held by the Waseda University Library, Request Number: Chi5 4163, November 1886.
21. Nakanome, *op. cit.*, pp. 165–7.
22. Nakanome, *ibid.*, pp. 178–9.
23. The memorandum is reproduced in its entirety in *Itō Hirobumi Den*, Shunpo Kotsui Shokai (ed.), Toseisha, 1942, pp. 558–65.
24. Itō Yukio, *Meiji Tennō: Murakumo wo Fuku Akikaze ni Haresomete*, Minerva Shobo, 2006, pp. 261–2.
25. A. Swale, *The Political Thought of Mori Arinori: A Study in Meiji Conservatism*, Japan Library, 2000, pp. 113–42.
26. *Sūmitsuin Kaigi Gijiroku*, Tokyo Daigaku Shuppankai, 1984–90, pp. 226–8.
27. *Sūmitsuin Kaigi Gijiroku*, p. 175.
28. *Sūmitsuin Kaigi Gijiroku*, pp. 217–19.
29. *Sūmitsuin Kaigi Gijiroku*, pp. 220–1.
30. Swale, *op. cit.*, pp. 132–40.
31. M. John, *Politics and the Law in Late Nineteenth Century Germany*, Clarendon Press, 1989, pp. 58–72 and pp. 99–104.
32. Itō, *op. cit.*, pp. 271–3.
33. Swale, *op. cit.*, pp. 172–4.
34. Nakanome, *op. cit.*, pp. 178–9.
35. Nakanome, *ibid.*, p. 178.
36. Nakanome, *ibid.*, pp. 178–80.
37. Kobayashi Kazuyuki, *Meiji Rikken Seiji to Kizokuin*, Yoshikawa Kobunkan, 2002.
38. Swale, *op. cit.*, pp. 143–74.
39. Takahashi Masao, *Nishimura Shigeki*, Yoshikawa Kobunkan, 1987, pp. 161–70.
40. Numata Satoshi, *Motoda Eifu to Meiji Kokka: Meiji Hoshushugi to Jukyōteki Risōshugi*, Yoshikawa Kobunkan, 2005, pp. 365–74.
41. Numata, *ibid.*, pp. 375–7.
42. Numata, *ibid.*, pp. 276–80.
43. Numata, *ibid.*, pp. 287–301.
44. Takii Kazuhiro, *Bunmeishi no Naka no Meiji Kempō*, 2003, pp. 157–62.
45. Winston Davis, "The Civil Theology of Inoue Tetsujirō", in *The Japanese Journal of Religious Studies*, 3/1, March 1976, pp. 7–8.
46. Davis, *ibid.*, pp. 9–10.
47. K. M. Staggs, *Monumenta Nipponica*, vol. 38, no. 3., Autumn, 1983, pp. 251–81. Nakanome, *op. cit.*, pp. 113–15.
48. Nakanome, *ibid.*, pp. 172–3.
49. J. S. Brownlee, *Japanese Historians and the National Myths, 1600–1945*, UBC Press, 1997, pp. 77–80.

50. Ōkubo Toshiaki, *Nihon Kindai Shigaku no Seiritsu*, in *Ōkubo Toshiaki Rekishi Chosakushū*, vol. 7, Yoshikawa Kobunkan, 1988, pp. 138–40.
51. Ōkubo, *ibid.*, pp. 142–8; Brownlee, *op. cit.*, p. 101.

7   Conclusion: Conservatism, Traditionalism and Restoration

1. Ernest Gellner, *Nations and Nationalism*, Basil Blackwell, 1983, pp. 110–36.
2. M. Asukai, *Nihon Kindai Seishinshi no Kenkyū*, Kyoto University Press, 2002, pp. 380–1.

Select Bibliography

Anzai Toshimitsu, *Fukuzawa Yukichi to Seiō Shisō*, Nagoya University Press, 1995.

Art Directors' Club of Tokyo (eds), *Nihon no Kōkoku Bijutsu—Meiji, Taishō, Shōwa*, vol. III, *Pakkeeji*, Bijutsu Shuppansha, 1968.

Asukai Masamichi. *Bunmei Kaika*, Iwanami Shoten, 1985.

—— *Nihon Kindai Seishinshi no Kenkyū*, Kyoto University Press, 2002.

Banno Junji, *Meiji Demokurashii*, Iwanami Shinsho, 2005.

Beasley, William G., *The Rise of Modern Japan: Economic, Political and Social Change Since 1850*, St Martin's Press, 1995.

—— *Japan Encounters the Barbarian: Japanese Travellers in America and Europe*, Yale University Press, 1995.

Bird, Isabella, *Unbeaten Tracks in Japan*, John Murray, 1880.

Black, John, *Young Japan: Yokohama and Yedo, 1858–1879*, Oxford University Press, 1868.

Braisted, William, *Meiroku Zasshi: Journal of the Japanese Enlightenment*, University of Tokyo Press, 1976.

Brownlee, John S., *Japanese Historians and the National Myths, 1600–1945*, UBC Press, 1997.

Collingwood, Robin, *The Idea of History*, Clarendon Press, 1946.

Cortazzi, Hugh, *Mitford's Japan: Memories and Recollections 1866–1906*, Japan Library, 2002.

Edstrom, Bert, (ed.), *Turning Points in Japanese History*, RoutledgeCurzon, 2002.

Fukuchi Shigetaka, *Shizoku to Shizoku Ishiki*, Shunshusha, 1956.

Fukuzawa Yukichi, *Fukuō Jiden*, Jiji Shinpo Sha, 1899.

Gellner, Ernest, *Nations and Nationalism*, Basil Blackwell, 1983.

Gluck, Carol, *Japan's Modern Myths: Ideology in the Late Meiji Period*, Princeton University Press, 1985.

Gordon, Andrew, *A Modern History of Japan: From Tokugawa Times to the Present*, Oxford University Press, 2002.

Hall, Ivan P., *Mori Arinori*, Harvard University Press, 1973.

Hardacre, Helen, *Shintō and the State, 1868–1988*, Princeton University Press, 1989.

Havens, Thomas R.T., *Nishi Amane and Modern Japanese Thought*, Princeton University Press, 1970.

Hayashi Takeji, *Mori Arinori: Higeki e no Josō*, Chikuma Shobo, 1986.

Hirao Michio, *Kōshaku Tani Tateki Den*, Shozansha, 1981.

Holt, Edgar, *The Opium Wars in China*, Putnam, 1964.

Howland, Douglas, *Translating the West*, University of Hawaii Press, 2002.

Hoya Tōru (ed.), *Bakumatsu Ishin to Jōhō*, Yoshikawa Kobunkan, 2001.

Huber, T M., *The Revolutionary Origins of Modern Japan*, Stanford UP, 1981.

Huffman, James A., *Creating a Public: People and Press in Meiji Japan*, Hawaii University Press, 1997.

Inuzuka Takaaki, *Nippon Seishun Gaikōkan*, Nippon Hoso Shuppan Kyokai, 2006.

Ishii Kendō, *Meiji Jibutsu Jigen*, Kyonando, 1908.

Ishizuki Minoru, *Kindai Nihon no Kaigai Ryūgakushi*, Minerva Shobo, 1972.

Itō Hirobumi Kankei Monjō Kenkyūkai (eds), *Itō Hirobumi Kankei Monjō*, Koshobo, 1973.

Itō Yukio, *Rikken Kokka no Kakuritsu to Itō Hirobumi: Naisei to Gaikō 1889–1898*, Yoshikawa Kobunkan, 1999.

—— *Meiji Tennō: Murakumo wo Fuku Akikaze ni Haresomete*, Minerva Shobo, 2006.

Iwashita Tetsunori, *Bakumatsu Nihon no Jōhō Katsudō*, Yusankaku, 2008.

Iwata Masakazu, *Ōkubo Toshimichi: The Bismarck of Japan*, University of California Press, 1964.

Jansen, Marius, and Rozman, Gilbert, (eds), *Japan in Transition: from Tokugawa to Meiji*, Princeton University Press, 1986.

Jansen, Marius, *The Emergence of Meiji Japan*, Cambridge University Press, 1995.

—— *The Making of Modern Japan*, Harvard University Press, 2000.

John, Michael, *Politics and the Law in Late Nineteenth Century Germany*, Clarendon Press, 1989.

Kasahara Hidehiko, *Ōkubo Toshimichi, Meiji Ishin no Kosei*, Yoshikawa Kobunkan, 2005.

Keene, Donald, *The Japanese Discovery of Europe, 1720–1830*, Stanford University Press, 1969.

Kim, Young M., *East Asia's Turbulent Century*, Appleton Century Crofts, 1966.

Kobayashi Kazuyuki, *Meiji Rikken Seiji to Kizokuin*, Yoshikawa Kobunkan, 2002.

Koizumi Takashi, *Nishi Amane to Ōbei Shisō to no Deai*, Sanrei Shobo, 1989.

Kojima Tsuyoshi, *Kindai Nihon no Yōmeigaku*, Kodansha, 2006.

Kōsaka Masaaki, *Kōsaka Masaaki Chosaku Shū*, Risosha, 1969.

Kume Kunitake, *The Iwakura Embassy, 1871–73: A True Account of the Ambassador Extraordinary & Plenipotentiary's Journey of Observation Through the United States of America and Europe*, (Editors-in-chief, Graham Healey and Chushichi Tsuzuki), Japan Documents, 2003.

Kurogi Yukichi, *Komura Jutarō*, Kodansha, 1968.

Kutsuzawa Nobutaka (ed.), *Yōgakuji Hajime*, Bunka Shobo Hyakubunsha, 1993.

Mannheim, Karl, *Conservatism: A Contribution to the Sociology of Knowledge*, Kettler et al. (eds), Routledge and Kegan Paul, 1986.

Maruyama Masao, *"Bunmeiron no Gairyaku" wo Yomu*, Iwanami Shoten, 1986.

—— *Maruyama Masao Shū*, Iwanami Shoten, 1995.

—— (Matsuzawa Hiroaki, ed.), *Fukuzawa Yukichi no Tetsugaku: Hoka Rokuhen*, Iwanami Shoten, 2001.

Matsumoto Kenichi, *Kaikoku· Ishin 1853–1871*, Chuo Koronsha, 1998.

Matsumoto Sannosuke in *Nihon Seiji Shisōshi Gairon*, Keiso Shobo, 1982.

Matsumoto Sannosuke and Yamamuro Shinichi (eds), *Genron to Media*, Iwanami Shoten, 1990.

Matsumura Masaie, *Bakumatsu Shisetsudan no Igirisu Ōkanki—Vikutorian Inpakuto*, Kashiwa Shobo, 2008.

Matsuo Masato (ed.), *Meiji Ishin to Bunmei Kaika*, Yoshikawa Kobunkan, 2004.

Meiji Bunka Kenkyūkai (ed.), *Meiji Bunka Zenshū*, Nihon Hyoronsha, 1992–1993.

Miyanaga Takashi, *Bakumatsu Ken'ō Shisetsudan*, Kodansha, 2006.

Momose Hibiki, *Bunmei Kaika: Ushinawareta Fūzoku*, Yoshikawa Kobunkan, 2008.

Moore, Barrington, *The Social Origins of Dictatorship and Democracy: Lord and Peasant in the Making of the Modern World*, Beacon Press, 1966.

Mori Arinori, *Mori Arinori Zenshū*, Seibundo, 1972.
Motoyama Yukihiko, *Proliferating Talent: Essays on Politics, Thought and Education in the Meiji Era* (J. S. A. Elisona and R. Rubinger, eds), University of Hawaii Press, 1997.
Nagai Michio and Miguel Urrutia, *Meiji Ishin: Restoration and Revolution*, United Nations University, 1985.
Nakanome Tōru, *Seikyōsha no Kenkyū*, Shibunkaku, 1993.
Nish, Ian, *The Iwakura Mission in America and Europe: A New Assessment*, Japan Library, 1998.
Nishi Amane (Ōkubo Toshiaki, ed.), *Nishi Amane Zenshū*, Nihon Hyoron Sha, 1945.
Nishimura Shigeki, *Nishimura Shigeki Zenshū*, Shibunkaku, 1976.
Nishiyama Matsunosuke, *Edo Culture: Daily Life and Diversions in Urban Japan*, University of Hawaii Press, 1997.
Nosco, Peter, (ed.), *Confucianism and Tokugawa Culture*, Princeton University Press, 1984.
Numata Jirō et al. (eds), *Yōgaku Kenbun Shū*, Iwanami Shoten, 1974.
Numata Satoshi, *Motoda Eifu to Meiji Kokka: Meiji Hoshushugi to Jukyōteki Risōshugi*, Yoshikawa Kobunkan, 2005.
Oda Yasunori, *Ishin Kaika to Toshi Ōsaka*, Seibundo, 2001.
Okazaki Masamichi, *Itanshi to Hangyakusha no Shisōshi: Kindai Nihon ni okeru Kakumei to Ishin*, Perikansha, 1999.
Okitsu Kaname, *Meiji Shimbun hajime: "Bunmei Kaika" no Janarizumu*, Daishukan Shoten, 1997.
Ōkubo Toshiaki, *Ōkubo Toshiaki Rekishi Chosakushu*, Yoshikawa Kobunkan, 1988.
—— (ed.), *Tsuda Mamichi; Kenkyū to Denki*, Misuzu Shobo, 1997.
Ōkubo Toshimichi, *Ōkubo Toshimichi Nikki*, Nihon Shiseki Kyokai, 1927.
Ōnishi Hajime, *Ōnishi Hakase Zenshū*, Keiseisha Shoten, 1907.
Porter, Roy, *Enlightenment: Britain and the Creation of the Modern World*, Macmillan, 2000.
Saaler, Sven, and Koschmann, Victor, (eds), *Pan-Asianism in Modern Japanese History: Colonialism, Regionalism and Borders*, Routledge, 2006.
Sakamoto Koremaru, *Meiji Ishin to Kokugakusha*, Daimeido, 1993.
Sakamoto Takao, *Meiji Kokka no Kensetsu*, Chuo Koronsha, 1999.
Sasaki Takashi, *Media to Kenryoku*, Chuo Koronsha, 1999.
Satō Yoshimaru, *Meiji Nashonarizumu no Kenkyū: Seikyōsha no Seiritsu to sono Shūhen*, 1998.
Shunpō Kōtsui Shōkai (ed.), *Itō Hirobumi Den*, Toseisha, 1942.
Sims, Richard, *Japanese Political History Since the Meiji Renovation, 1868–2000*, Hurst, 2000.
Smith, Thomas C., *The Agrarian Origins of Modern Japan*, Stanford University Press, 1959.
Smitka, Michael, *Japanese Economic History 1600–1960*. The volume of most relevance here is *Japanese Economy in the Tokugawa Era, 1600–1868*, Garland Publishing, 1998.
Stegewerns, Dick (ed.), *Nationalism and Internationalism in Imperial Japan: Autonomy, Asian Brotherhood or World Citizenship?* RoutledgeCurzon, 2003.
Suzuki Jun, *Ishin no Kōsō to Tenkai*, Kodansha, 2002.
Swale, Alistair, *The Political Thought of Mori Arinori; A Study in Meiji Conservatism*, Japan Library, 2000.

Takahashi Masao, *Nishimura Shigeki*, Yoshikawa Kobunkan, 1987.
Takii Kazuhiro, *Doitsu Kokkagaku to Meiji Kokusei, Shutain Kokkagaku no Kiseki*, Minerva Shobo, 1999.
Tamaki Norio, *Yukichi Fukuzawa, 1835–1901: The Spirit of Enterprise in Modern Japan*, Palgrave Macmillan, 2001.
Tanaka Akira (ed.), *Kaikoku*, Chikuma Shobo, 1991.
Tokutomi Sohō, *Tokutomi Sohō Shū*, Chikuma Shobo, 1974.
Tōkyō Daigaku Shiryō Hensankyoku, *Meiji Ishinshi Shiryō Senshū*, vol. 1–2, Tokyo University Press, 1970–2.
Totman, Conrad, *Early Modern Japan*, University of California Press, 1993.
Wakabayahi, Bob, (ed.), *Opium Regimes: China, Britain, and Japan, 1839–1952*, University of California Press, 2000.
Wilson, George M., *Patriots and Redeemers in Japan: Motives in the Meiji Restoration*, University of Chicago Press, 1992.
Wong, John Y., *Deadly Dreams: Opium, Imperialism and the Arrow War (1856–1860) in China*, Cambridge University Press, 1998.
Yokoi Shōnan, *Shōnan Kikō*, Minyusha, 1898.
Yamamoto Taketoshi, *Kindai Nihon no Shinbun Dokushasō*, Hosei University Press, 2006.
Yamamuro Shinichi, *Hōsei Kanryō no Jidai: Kokka no Seikei to Chi no Rekitei*, Bokutakusha, 1988.
Yamamuro Shinichi and Nakanome Tōru (eds), *Meiroku Zasshi*, Iwanami Shoten, 1999.
Yamashita Shigekazu, *Supensaa to Nihon Kindai*, Ochanomizu Shobo, 1983.
Yoshino Sakuzō, *Yoshino Sakuzō Senshū*, Iwanami Shoten, 1995.

Index